Lecture Notes in Computer Scie

T0250693

Commenced Publication in 1973
Founding and Former Series Editors:
Gerhard Goos, Juris Hartmanis, and Jan van Leeuwen

Ita Richardson   Per Runeson
Richard Messnarz (Eds.)

Software Process Improvement

13th European Conference, EuroSPI 2006
Joensuu, Finland, October 11-13, 2006
Proceedings

 Springer

Volume Editors

Ita Richardson
University of Limerick
National Technological Park
Castletroy, Limerick, Ireland
E-mail: Ita.Richardson@ul.ie

Per Runeson
Lund University
Department of Communication Systems
Box 118, 221 00 Lund, Sweden
E-mail: per.runeson@telecom.lth.se

Richard Messnarz
ISCN
Florence House, 1 Florence Villas, Bray, Co. Wicklow, Ireland
E-mail: rmess@iscn.com

Library of Congress Control Number: 2006934304

CR Subject Classification (1998): D.2, K.6, K.4.2

LNCS Sublibrary: SL 2 – Programming and Software Engineering

ISSN   0302-9743
ISBN-10   3-540-47695-4 Springer Berlin Heidelberg New York
ISBN-13   978-3-540-47695-5 Springer Berlin Heidelberg New York

Springer is a part of Springer Science+Business Media

springer.com

© Springer-Verlag Berlin Heidelberg 2006
Printed in Germany

Typesetting: Camera-ready by author, data conversion by Scientific Publishing Services, Chennai, India
Printed on acid-free paper   SPIN: 11908562   06/3142   5 4 3 2 1 0

Preface

This textbook is intended for use by SPI (Software Process Improvement) managers and researchers, quality managers, and experienced project and research managers. The papers constitute the research proceedings of the 13th EuroSPI (European Software Process Improvement, www.eurospi.net) conference, held in Joensuu, Finland, 11-13 October 2006. The conference was held in 1994 in Dublin (Ireland), 1995 in Vienna (Austria), 1997 in Budapest (Hungary), 1998 in Gothenburg (Sweden), 1999 in Pori (Finland), 2000 in Copenhagen (Denmark), 2001 in Limerick (Ireland), 2002 in Nuremberg (Germany), 2003 in Graz (Austria), 2004 in Trondheim (Norway), and 2005 in Budapest (Hungary). EuroSPI has established an experience library (library.eurospi.net) which will be continuously extended over the next years and will be made available to all attendees. EuroSPI has also initiated a European Qualification Network in which different SPINs and national initiatives join mutually beneficial collaborations (EQN -- EU Leonardo da Vinci network project).

With a founding conference on 5.12.2006 through EuroSPI partners and networks, in collaboration with the European Union (supported by the EU Leonardo da Vinci Programme), a European certification association will be created for the IT and services sector to offer SPI knowledge and certificates to industry, establishing close knowledge transfer links between research and industry. The biggest value of EuroSPI lies in its function as a European knowledge and experience exchange mechanism for SPI know-how between research institutions and industry.

September 2006

Richard Messnarz
www.eurospi.net

Organization

Organization Committee

EuroSPI 2006 is organized by the EuroSPI partnership (www.eurospi.net), internationally coordinated by ISCN, and locally supported by the University of Joensuu.

Program Committee

Conference Chair:	Richard Messnarz (ISCN, IRL)
Scientific Program Chair:	Ita Richardson (University of Limerick, Ireland)
Scientific Program Chair:	Per Runeson (University of Lund, Sweden)
Industrial Program Chair:	Jorn Johansen (DELTA, Denmark)
Industrial Program Chair:	Mads Christiansen (DELTA, Denmark)
Industrial Program Chair:	Nils Brede Moe (SINTEF, Norway)
Industrial Program Chair:	Risto Nevalainen (STTF,Finland)
Tutorial Chair:	Richard Messnarz (ISCN, Ireland)
Exhibition Chair:	Stephan Goericke (ISQI, Germany)
Organizing Chair:	Markku Tukiainen(University of Joensuu, Finland)
Organizing Chair:	Adrienne Clarke (ISCN, Ireland)

Local Committee

Local Organizer:	University of Joensuu, www.joensuu.fi

Additional Scientific Reviewers

Abrahamsson, Pekka (VTT Electronics, Finland)
Ambriola, Vincenzo (Università di Pisa, Italy)
Aurum, Aybüke (University of New South Wales, Australia)
Baddoo, Nathan (University of Hertfordshire, UK)
Biffl, Stefan (Technische Universität Wien, Austria)
Biro, Miklos (Corvinus University of Budapest, Hungary)
Bunse, Christian (Fraunhofer IESE, Germany)
Cater-Steel, Aileen (The University of Southern Queensland, Australia)
Ciolkowski, Marcus (TU Kaiserslautern, Germany)
Coleman, Gerry (Dundalk Institute of Technology, Ireland)
Dalcher, Darren (School of Computing Science, UK)

Table of Contents

Introduction

Software Process Improvement – EuroSPI 2006 Conference   1
Richard Messnarz, Ita Richardson, Per Runeson

SPI and Processes

Developing Software with Scrum in a Small Cross-Organizational
Project   5
*Torgeir Dingsøyr, Geir Kjetil Hanssen, Tore Dybå, Geir Anker,
Jens Olav Nygaard*

Implementing an ISO 9001 Certified Process 16
Tor Stålhane

Software Process in Practice: A Grounded Theory of the Irish Software
Industry 28
Gerry Coleman, Rory O'Connor

SPI and Problem/Risk Management

Improving the Software Problem Management Process: A Case Study . . . 40
Marko Jäntti, Kari Kinnunen

A Framework for Overcoming Supplier Related Threats in Global
Projects 50
Darja Šmite, Juris Borzovs

Three Case-Studies on Common Software Process Problems in Software
Company Acquisitions 62
Jarmo J. Ahonen, Anne-Maria Aho, Hanna-Miina Sihvonen

SPI Measurement

Simple Indicators for Tracking Software Process Improvement
Progress 74
Anna Börjesson

Investigating Suitability of Software Process and Metrics for Statistical
Process Control 88
    Ayça Tarhan, Onur Demirörs

Current Practices of Measuring Quality in Finnish Software
Engineering Industry 100
    Jari Soini, Vesa Tenhunen, Markku Tukiainen

SPI and Process Modelling

An Industry-Based Evaluation of Process Modeling Techniques 111
    Brent Cahill, David Carrington, Brian Song, Paul Strooper

Process Model Difference Analysis for Supporting Process Evolution 123
    Martín Soto, Jürgen Münch

Changing Role of SPI – Opportunities and Challenges of Process
Modeling 135
    Antero Järvi, Tuomas Mäkilä, Harri Hakonen

SPI and Human Success Factors

Mentality Patterns: Capturing and Dealing Explicitly with Recurring
Turns of Mind in Software Development 147
    Georgios Koutsoukos

Improving by Involving: A Case Study in a Small Software Company 159
    Nils Brede Moe, Tore Dybå

Trust Facilitating Good Software Outsourcing Relationships 171
    Kerstin V. Siakas, Dimitri Maoutsidis, Errikos Siakas

SPI Implementation

Assessing Software Replacement Success: An Industrial Case Study
Applying Four Approaches 183
    Jussi Koskinen, Henna Sivula, Tero Tilus, Irja Kankaanpää,
    Jarmo J. Ahonen, Päivi Juutilainen

Leveraging Feedback on Processes in SOA Projects 195
    Daniel Lübke, Kurt Schneider

Taba Workstation: Supporting Software Process Improvement
Initiatives Based on Software Standards and Maturity Models 207
Analia Irigoyen Ferreiro Ferreira, Gleison Santos,
Roberta Cerqueira, Mariano Montoni, Ahilton Barreto,
Ana Regina Rocha, Sávio Figueiredo, Andrea Barreto,
Reinaldo C. Silva Filho, Peter Lupo, Cristina Cerdeiral

Author Index 219

Software Process Improvement – EuroSPI 2006 Conference

R. Messnarz[1], I. Richardson[2], and P. Runeson[3]

[1] EuroSPI , c/o ISCN LTD, Bray, Co. Wicklow, Ireland
http://www.eurospi.net
[2] Department of Computer Science & Information Systems and ISERC,
University of Limerick, Limerick, Ireland
[3] Lund University, Dept. of Communication Systems, SE-221 00 LUND, Sweden

Abstract. This book constitutes the refereed research proceeding of the 13th European Software Process Improvement Conference, EuroSPI 2006, held in Joensuu, Finland in October 2006. The 18 revised full papers presented were carefully reviewed and selected from 62 submissions. The papers are organized in topical sections on SPI (Software Process Improvement) processes, SPI and risk management, measurement, process modelling, human factors, and implementation of SPI.

1 EuroSPI

EuroSPI's mission is to develop an experience and knowledge exchange platform for Europe where SPI practices can be discussed and exchanged and knowledge can be gathered and shared. This mission is implemented by three major action lines:

1. An annual EuroSPI conference supported by Software Process Improvement Networks from different EU countries.
2. Establishing an Internet based knowledge library, newsletters, and a set of proceedings and recommended books.
3. Establishing an effective team of national representatives (in future from each EU country) growing step by step into more countries of Europe.

EuroSPI represents a European experience forum collaborating with nearly all SPINs in Europe. EuroSPI offers experiences which can be re-used creating benefits in your own organization.

EuroSPI is a successful initiative since 1994. Annual conferences were held 1994 in Dublin (Ireland), 1995 in Vienna (Austria), 1996 in Brighton (UK), 1997 in Budapest (Hungary), 1998 in Gothenburg (Sweden), 1999 in Pori (Finland), 2000 in Copenhagen (Denmark), 2001 in Limerick (Ireland), 2002 in Nuremberg (Germany), 2003 in Graz (Austria), and 2004 in Trondheim (Norway), 2005 in Budapest (Hungary), 2006 in Joensuu (Finland), and is scheduled /planned 2007 in Berlin (Germany).

1.1 Board Members

EuroSPI is managed by a partnership of large Scandinavian research companies and experience networks (SINTEF, DELTA, STTF), the ASQF as a large German quality

I. Richardson, P. Runeson, and R. Messnarz (Eds.): EuroSPI 2006, LNCS 4257, pp. 1–4, 2006.
© Springer-Verlag Berlin Heidelberg 2006

association, the American Society for Quality, and ISCN as the co-ordinating partner. EuroSPI collaborates with a large number of SPINs (Software Process Improvement Network) in Europe.

ASQ, http://www.asq.org
ASQF, http://www.asqf.de
DELTA, http://www.delta.dk
FiSMA, http://www.fisma.fi
ISCN, http://www.iscn.com
SINTEF, http://www.sintef.no

1.2 EuroSPI Scientific Program Committee

EuroSPI applies strict quality management procedures and each paper is reviewed by three independent reviewers. The research program committee for EuroSPI 2006 comprises 35 reviewers from 17 different countries.

ABRAHAMSSON Pekka, VTT Electronics, FINLAND
AMBRIOLA Vincenzo, Universita di Pisa, ITALY
AURUM Aybüke, University of New South Wales, AUSTRALIA
BADDOO Nathan, University of Hertfordshire, UK
BIFFL Stefan, Technische Universität Wien, AUSTRIA
BIRO Miklos, Corvinus University of Budapest, Hungary
BUNSE Christian, Fraunhofer IESE, GERMANY
CATER-STEEL Aileen, The University of Southern Queensland, AUSTRALIA
CIOLKOWSKI Marcus, TU Kaiserslautern, GERMANY
COLEMAN Gerry, Dundalk Institute of Technology, IRELAND
DALCHER Darren, School of Computing Science, UK
DAUGHTREY Taz H., James Madison University, USA
DESOUZA Kevin C., University of Illinois at Chicago, USA
DINGSOYR Torgeir, SINTEF IKT, NORWAY
DUNCAN Howard, Dublin City University, IRELAND
DYBA Tore, SINTEF Telecom and Informatics, NORWAY
GORSCHEK Tony, Blekinge Institute of Technology, SWEDEN
GRESSE VON WANGENHEIM Christiane, Universidade do Vale do Itajai,
    BRAZIL
HEIJSTEK Andre, SEI-Europe, GERMANY
JORGENSEN Magne, Simula Research Laboratory, NORWAY
LANDES Dieter, Fachhochschule Coburg, GERMANY
MCQUAID Patricia, California Polytechnic State University, USA
MUELLER Matthias, Universitaet Karlsruhe, GERMANY
MUENCH Juergen, Fraunhofer IESE, GERMANY
OIVO Markku, University of Oulu, FINLAND
OSTOLAZA Elixabete, European Software Institute, SPAIN
PRIES-HEJE Jan, IT University of Copenhagen, DENMARK
RUHE Guenther, University of Calgary, CANADA
SCHNEIDER Kurt, Universitaet Hannover, GERMANY
SHEPPERD Martin, Bournemouth University, UK

SIAKAS Kerstin, Technological Educational Institute of Thessaloniki, GREECE
SILLITTI Alberto, Free University of Bolzano-Bozen, ITALY
STALHANE Tor, Norwegian University of Science and Technology, NORWAY
TUKIAINEN Markku, University of Joensuu, FINLAND

1.3 EuroSPI Scientific Chairs

The EuroSPI general chair is responsible for the entire conference, including the research and the industry tracks. The EuroSPI Scientific Program Committee Chairs represent acknowledged scientific experts in the SPI field who coordinate the reviews of papers in collaboration with the members of the scientific program committee.

Dr Richard Messnarz
General Chair of EuroSPI
ISCN, Ireland and Austria
rmess@iscn.com

Dr Ita Richardson
EuroSPI Scientific Programme Committee Chair
University of Limerick , Ireland
Ita.Richardson@ul.ie

Prof. Dr Per Runeson
EuroSPI Scientific Programme Committee Chair
Lund University, Sweden
per.runeson@telecom.lth.se

2 European Certification Association

The EuroSPI group with partners joined a consortium and received EU funding (EU Leonardo da Vinci Network EQN – European Quality Network, 2005 - 2007) to establish a European qualification strategy for job roles, such as SPI manager, project manager, scope manager, innovation manager, etc.) Key job roles are being identified, and all job roles need to fulfil certain European quality criteria to become accredited.

An EU-Certificates association will be founded in December 2006 as an accreditation association, seated in Vienna, managed by EuroSPI partners. All partners of EQN become founding members, plus those who will be invited to the founding conference. Project partners from participating EU projects and programs will join as members as well. Every 2 years a director is elected from all members who will be heading the management team (those managing the EU certificates and the test portal systems).

The services are

- Accreditation of training institutions who offer specific job roles and publishing the list of accredited training institutions
- Accreditation of trainers who offer specific job roles and publishing the list of accredited trainers
- Certification of students and publishing the list of certified students (list of all innovation managers who are certified...etc.)
- Access to the online knowledge library through a flat fee per year

The core group contains 17 organisations, plus approx. 50 European training organisations who will be invited to the founding conference in December 2006.

3   How to Read the Proceedings

Since its beginning in 1994 in Dublin, the EuroSPI initiative outlines that there is not a single silver bullet to solve SPI issues but you need to understand a combination of different SPI methods and approaches to achieve concrete benefits. Therefore each proceeding covers a variety of different topics and at the conference we discuss potential synergies and combined use of such methods and approaches. This proceeding contains selected research papers for 6 topics:

SPI and Processes (3 papers)
SPI and Problem / Risk Management (3 papers)
SPI and Measurement (3 papers)
SPI and Process Modelling (3 papers)
SPI and Human Success Factors (3 papers)
SPI Implementation (3 papers).

3.1   Recommended Further Reading

In [1] we integrated the proceedings of 3 EuroSPI conferences into one book which was edited by 30 experts in Europe. In [2] you find the EuroSPI research proceeding published by Springer and based on EuroSPI 2004. In [3] you find the most recent EuroSPI research proceeding published by Springer and based on EuroSPI 2005.

References

1. Messnarz R., Tully C. (eds.), Better Software Practice for Business Benefit - Principles and Experience, IEEE Computer Society Press, ISBN: 0-7695-0049-8, paperback, 409 pages, Wiley-IEEE Computer Society Press, September 1999
2. Dingsøyr, T. (Ed.) , Software Process Improvement 11th European Conference, EuroSPI 2004, Trondheim, Norway, November 10-12, 2004. Proceedings, 2004, X, 207 p., Softcover, ISBN: 3-540-23725-9, in: Lecture Notes in Computer Science, Vol. 3281 , Springer Verlag, November 2004
3. Richardson I., Abrahamsson P, Messnarz R., (Ed.) , Software Process Improvement 12th European Conference, EuroSPI 2005, Budapest, Hungary, November 9-11, 2005. Proceedings, 2005, X, 213 p., Softcover, ISBN: 3-540-30286-7, in: Lecture Notes in Computer Science, Vol. 3792, Springer Verlag, November 2005

Developing Software with Scrum in a Small Cross-Organizational Project

Torgeir Dingsøyr[1,2], Geir Kjetil Hanssen[1], Tore Dybå[1]
Geir Anker[3], and Jens Olav Nygaard[3]

[1] SINTEF Information and Communication Technology,
NO-7465 Trondheim, Norway
[2] Dept. of Computer and Information Science,
Norwegian University of Science and Technology,
NO-7491 Trondheim, Norway
[3] SINTEF Information and Communication Technology,
N-0314 Oslo, Norway

Abstract. In an action research study, we describe the application of the scrum software development process in a small cross-organizational development project. The stakeholders in the project report many of the benefits we have found in previous studies, such as increased overview of the project, flexibility and motivation. In addition, we have found that estimation can be challenging in cross-organizational projects due to the customer-provider relationship between the participating organizations.

1 Introduction

Agile development has recently attracted much interest because of claims of many improvements on areas such as work performance, quality and work environment. This paper discusses experience with the introduction of Scrum to improve certain aspects of the software development process for a department in a research institute working with mathematical and geographical software. The context is a joint project for, and in cooperation with, a public limited company to develop a digital map application.

The purpose of this paper is to add to the scant literature on empirical studies of software development with Scrum, specifically in a small-team setting comprising developers from two organizations, in this case a public limited company (customer) and a research institute.

The rest of the paper is organized as follows: First we set the theoretical context for the study, summarize previous empirical studies of Scrum, and discuss our research question. Further, we discuss action research, which is the research method applied in this study. We have organized the findings according to the phases of action research: we describe how we diagnosed the development processes at the research institute, how we planned to introduce Scrum, what actually happened when introducing Scrum to a pilot project, and how we evaluate this with respect to the business goal and research goal. Finally, we specify the contributions of this study in relation to the existing empirical knowledge base of Scrum.

R. Messnarz (Ed.): EuroSPI 2006, LNCS 4257, pp. 5–15, 2006.

2 Theoretical Context

Rising and Janoff [8] described Scrum as a development process for small teams, which includes a series of short development phases, "sprints", which typically lasts from one to four weeks. The team captures identified tasks in a backlog, which is reprioritized and updated in the beginning of each sprint. This also includes estimating the effort required to complete each task. The customer participates in the sprint meetings, but is not allowed to influence the team in between the meetings. During a sprint, the team holds short daily Scrum meetings to discuss progress, plans and potential problems. Scrum is thoroughly described by Schwaber and Beedle [11] and Schwaber [10].

2.1 The Theory of Scrum

The cornerstone argument for the suitability of Scrum is that software development is a complex process where many factors influence the final result. It is therefore difficult or even impossible to plan ahead such as described in traditional waterfall-like development processes. Scrum extends incremental software development to what is called "empirical process control"; where feedback loops is the core element. Scrum is inspired by a range of fields like complexity theory [4], system dynamics [12] and Nonaka and Takeuchi's theory of knowledge creation [7, 15], adapted to a setting of software development.

2.2 Studies on Scrum

There are few studies of Scrum in the research literature. Most of the studies are reports with little scientific backing of claims. We have found three lessons-learned reports from companies taking up Scrum and one case study examining overtime amongst developers and customer satisfaction in Scrum. We briefly summarize these four studies:

AG Communication systems have tried using Scrum in several development projects [8], and reported improved teamwork, more efficient problem-solving and increased motivation in development projects.

Primavera, a company that develops project management solutions, reported a 30% decrease of software defects the first nine months after release [9]. They also claimed that Scrum improved the time to market, and improved the work environment for the development team. It made the teams more aware of the importance and the business value of the features they were implementing. Another effect observed was that the stakeholders got closer to the work through seeing the product evolve during monthly sprint reviews.

Easel Corporation applied Scrum in developing an object-oriented analysis and design tool in 1993 [14]. Lessons learned from this case were that the company delivered software on time and with more functionality than expected. Customer satisfaction was also high. The study does not give details as it is reported more than 10 years after the project ended.

Mann and Maurer reported on Scrum's impact on overtime and customer satisfaction. In a case study in a small company that developed software for the oil and gas industry [6], PetroSleuth, overtime data for a period over two years showed that there was a significant drop after introducing Scrum, from a mean percentage of 19 to 7. Customers were interviewed about the software delivered before and after Scrum was introduced, and they state that they were more satisfied with the software after Scrum was introduced. One customer said "I believe there have been far greater consistency, transparency and coordination since the implementation of Scrum". Also, developers themselves were more satisfied with their products after introducing Scrum.

2.3 Study Aim and Research Question

This study is made in a research institute with a department developing mathematical software ("Applied Mathematics") and a department focusing on software process improvement. The goal of the applied mathematics department was to improve their software development processes, particularly improving change management, knowledge management, estimation and risk management.

The research goal of this study is to add to the literature of empirical studies of Scrum by providing an action research study of the introduction of Scrum in a small cross-organizational development team. We hope this research can contribute to building theory on which situations and contexts Scrum is a suitable development method. Our research question is:

What characterizes the use of Scrum in small-team cross-organizational development projects?

Do we still see the benefits reported in other Scrum-studies like team motivation, increased productivity, and higher customer satisfaction in cross-organizational projects? And what might be new problems arising in this context? How would, for example, the management of the project be seen by the participants in such a model?

3 Research Method

To investigate our research question and to achieve the improvement goals of the department, we used the participative research method *action research* [1, 5]. We have organized the research according to the five principles suggested by Davison et al. [2].

As for the first principle of researcher-client agreement, this research is done in a project on agile software development, where one department of a research institute is participating as well as one of their customers: a public limited company: Avinor. We have agreed on an improvement and research plan, which gives an overview of what data was to be collected during the study, which included semi-structured interviews (interview guide given in the appendix) with three of the four participants in a pilot project, minutes of sprint reviews, versions of backlogs and other documents.

We followed the cyclical process model (principle two) proposed by Susman and Evered [14] in discussing the situation of the company, planning action, taking action,

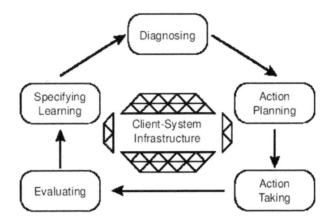

Fig. 1. The cyclical model of action research (taken from Susman and Evered)

evaluating action, and finally specifying what we think others can learn from our study. The third principle, of theory, is satisfied in our research question, although our study is not intended to validate theory, but to add a descriptive study of practice in a particular setting. We analyzed the qualitative interview material using principles from grounded theory [13]. The fourth principle ("change through action") is satisfied through the actions taken in our cycle, when introducing Scrum into the project.

Table 1. The five principles of canonical action research, suggested by Davison et al

Principles of canonical action research
1. The principle of the researcher-client agreement.
2. The principle of the cyclical process model.
3. The principle of theory.
4. The principle of change through action.
5. The principle of learning through reflection.

The fifth principle of action research deals with learning through reflection. This was ensured in the project through arenas where researchers and case participants discussed actions that were taken, and the following analysis by the all participants from the research institute. This included phone discussions, a workshop, a postmortem review [3] and interviews.

The participants in this study include three parties, the Applied Mathematics (SAM) and Software Process Improvement departments at SINTEF ICT as well as a public limited company, Avinor, which is a customer of SAM.

SAM delivers mathematical software, mainly to the Norwegian market, and has about 20 employees. The business of SAM is organized in projects, which may range from a few man-months to more than 15 man-years in size. This is usually spread out so that between one and five employees work on a project at a given time. The customers range from institutions such as the Research Council of Norway to smaller private technology-oriented startups. This makes for an interesting mix of projects with composition of research and development ranging pure research to development projects.

SAM's "equity" consists largely of its intellectual property, and it is traditionally "encoded" in the form of computer software and libraries. This is also the main deliverable in projects with companies and many other institutions as customers. Thus, much time in SAM is spent developing, maintaining and extending software. The ideas behind agile development present an interesting approach both with respect to the problems of handling changes during development and estimation of time and costs.

The process improvement group conducts empirical studies of software process improvement, and has lately been particularly interested in agile methods like Scrum. Avinor has a long customer relation to SAM.

4 Action Research Study

We present the action research study through the phases suggested by Susman and Evered [13]: Diagnosing, action planning, action taking, evaluating and specifying for learning.

4.1 Diagnosing

We started the diagnosing phase by conducting a postmortem review [3] at SAM in order to identify strong and weak aspects with their software development processes. Four developers and project managers from the department participated in a half-day workshop. We found that the main strong aspects were:

- Good products – customers get value for money through efficient software developed by ambitious developers.
- Research-oriented environment – the environment is creative and develops good product ideas, through informal self-organization.
- Customer relations – good dialogue and cooperation with customers.

We found some points that could be improved, where the most important ones were:

- Software development process – few common methods and standards, poor estimation, change and risk management, sharing of competence and reuse.
- Software development method – poor documentation from projects, projects often continues after the product is "good enough", some "dirty hacks".

Other problems identified, were related to the management of software projects and the fact that many projects involve only one person.

4.2 Action Planning

Based on the postmortem review, we discussed what could be the right tasks in order to improve the situation and still keep what the department held as their strong aspects. The researchers from the process improvement group were interested in trying out principles from agile software development, which we also thought was a suitable choice given the size and type of organization. Research-based software solutions require development processes that give sufficient room for creativity, which is found in the agile development methods. During the discussions, we found that improving project management and change management would help with many of the problems that were aired. We decided to run a pilot project with an agile software development method focusing on these two aspects. The choice was then to try Scrum, because this method focuses mainly on project management and also has solutions for change management. We selected a pilot project which was run by Avinor to develop a digital map application. The project involved one developer and one project manager from SAM and two developers from the public limited company (the customer), where one also was the general project manager. The pilot study covered the first phase of the project, which started with a kick-off on the 28th of April 2005 and continued throughout that year. The project is planned to end by the summer of 2006 and has a total budget of approximately 100,000€. The contractor and the customer were not co-located, although the developer from SAM stayed at the customer's site for shorter periods. To handle the practicalities, the developers worked on separate tasks and had little cooperation at the development-level. As the solution involved advanced graphics functionality for maps, new browser technology and various other state-of-the-art components, it was technically challenging although the developers made use of pre-existing components.

4.3 Action Taking

The first task was to discuss with the customer if they would be interested in using Scrum as a development process in the project. Because of good prior relations to the department, they agreed to participate, even though there was a contract written with a requirement specification and a fixed price in the traditional way. We organized a kick-off where all project members participated. In addition some observers from other projects at SAM, who considered using Scrum in their own projects, attended the beginning of the workshop. The workshop started with a researcher from the process improvement group introducing Scrum, followed by a discussion to determine if the project was appropriate for trying this out. The project decided favorably, and discussed the consequences of this change, and proceeded to generate an initial backlog in the form of an excel-sheet. This was mainly based on the original requirement specification and planned the first sprint. The project manager said: *We defined each task on an A4 sheet, and discussed what needed to be done first.* The first phase of the project was set to contain six sprints. The backlog contained 46 tasks, of which five were included in the first sprint. The sprints lasted approximately ten work-days, but would always take more calendar time as all people involved were working on other projects in parallel. The sprint durations were adjusted slightly to optimize placement of holidays and meetings in other projects.

4.4 Evaluating

We evaluated the project after interviewing three of the four participants in the project after sprint five, and after gathering backlog data from the first five sprints.

We present the evaluation in three parts, first we let the participants describe how they experienced the main elements in Scrum, present what the participants view as positive aspects of the development method, and then discussed challenges in this particular project.

Main Scrum Principles Followed

In the project, the sprint meetings were organized after approximately ten full work-days. The project manager said: *The agenda was very simple: we divided the sprint meeting in two, where the first part was the sprint review and the next sprint planning. And then we opened the product backlog to check out completed tasks and record time spent, and discussed the tasks in the sprint. Then, we made a new sprint out of the remaining requirements. I think that worked well.* Scrum meetings were organized at regular intervals, but the participants decided to organize them separately as they worked on different parts and thus was not synchronized. Also, for much of the time the SAM part and the customer's developers were not located together. The Scrum master from SAM said: *We did not do daily Scrums, we found that to be overkill. Here, we had a Scrum meeting every third day in the beginning, and I think it got a bit more seldom after a while.* The short meetings were seen as valuable by both participants. The Scrum master said: *It was very useful in the beginning, when I asked what are the problems, what happened since the last time and so on. I think just wording those questions is beneficial.* The developer from SAM said: *Yes it makes you conscious of things, but also makes sure that the Scrum master is in control, that there will not be any bombs under way.*

The concept of having working software which increases customer value after each sprint seems to have been successful. The people from SAM said: *We have tried to have a working system as a result of each sprint, it has not only been a demo ... I think it worked really well, because the software has in fact been working after every release.* This was also appreciated by the customer, the project manager said: *I remember the first delivery, which we got on a CD, and it was like: 'here is the delivery'.*

Perceived Benefits of Scrum

In total, both the SAM department and the customer were satisfied with the process followed. The Scrum master from SAM said: *I think it has worked very well... It would have worked perfectly if we had started working at the same time and if we had filled more of the backlog at the beginning of the project.* The developer from SAM said: *I feel this is the way to go in future projects. I see clear benefits by working in this way compared to the traditional way. And I have the impression that this is also what the customer is thinking.* The project manager said: *I am very satisfied with the way we have worked. You get an early overview of what has been done. It is easier to know what remains. We are very happy with Scrum, we just wish we had been able to use it more ... A dream situation would be that everyone could be in one place, in the same room.* The project manager described the flexibility of Scrum as an advantage: *Maybe we have been a bit more flexible. ... we have not reverted totally from what was written in the requirement specification, but new tasks have appeared.*

The developer from SAM was satisfied with working at the customer site during some sprints of the project: *There you have everything... People that know something about how the back-end systems your software talks to works, it is a lot easier to get answers to things you wonder about.*

Challenges with Scrum in Cross-Organizational Projects

The project manager described effort estimation as the main problem with the project so far: *...we have not at all been good at... effort estimation. ... There were many tasks that took twice as much time as estimated.* The developer from SAM said: *I really have a hard time making effort estimates. It is R&D we are doing, there is a lot of new technology which is pushed to the extreme in this project. But the benefit of Scrum is that you do the estimates at a low level, and have more control with the mistakes you do when you have broken it down to task level.* But the people from SAM thought that they themselves had become better and more realistic at doing estimation during the project, because of the frequent feedback. The Scrum master said: *after all, I feel that we have much better control.* However, the backlog grew during the project, which was a problem because the contract for the project was fixed on functionality. The developer agreed that he would like to continue working in this manner. If we look at the planned and actual effort given in Table 2, we see that the largest deviation was in sprint number two, which could indicate that the project participants got better at estimating as the project proceeded. The deviation in sprint one was low as the tasks were initial preparations and basic setup that was more or less straight forward and thus easy to estimate more precise.

Table 2. Total effort estimate and actual use for the first five Sprints in number of hours

Sprint #	1	2	3	4	5
Planned effort (h)	76	48	56	136	112
Actual effort (h)	80	84	52	180	132
Deviation (%)	5	75	-7	32	18

The project participants from SAM expressed that it was difficult to estimate the effort when Avinor participated in the development team as well as being the customer of SAM's part. The Scrum master said: *We have a customer-supplier relationship, even though we participated in the same project, and I think we lowered the estimates more for us than we would if the customer was to do the tasks themselves [maybe unconsciously].* This could have been easier if both parties had experienced problems with estimates at the same time: *If they had worked more in the beginning, I think they would have experienced that the estimates were too low, and they would not implicitly lower the estimates. If they said "hmm... two days?" for a task, then after maybe five seconds, we suggested "maybe we can do it in one and a half".* SAM was working alone for the first two sprints, and the customer started working as well from sprint three. The project manager said: *The reason for that was that we had a lot of other matters to take care of, which forced us to wait, and also that SAM were working on the basic maps and issues on the server-side, which had to be completed before we could start our tasks.*

The problem with estimation would not have been of the same magnitude if Scrum was followed fully, but in this project there was a signed contract which specified what SAM was to do, and it was a problem for them when they spent a lot of time in the initial phase of the project. The overall work was to be divided equally between the parties, but there was not a clear model on how this should be done. For the lower level tasks, it was clear who was to do what, but as these were only precisely defined as work progressed, this problem of workload splitting could arise.

4.5 Specifying Learning

What were the main learning points from using Scrum in the way described in the digital map project? The goal of SAM Applied Mathematics was to improve their development process, in particular change management and project management, and with a focus on small projects. It is of course necessary also in smaller projects to be able to estimate resources precisely. One problem with such projects is that management easily grows to an inappropriate fraction of the whole project. Hence, a goal for SAM was to figure out a way to manage projects with an "agility scaled to the size of the project", if at all possible.

Some key experiences can be singled out:

- Resource (especially development time) estimation is hard. Furthermore, it is not obvious that it helps breaking tasks down. Instead of missing the total with a large amount, SAM felt that they missed a lot of smaller tasks with smaller amounts (but maybe equal percentage wise) at the cost of having to add more of these smaller tasks. One big advantage is of course the possibility of discovering such issues at a much earlier time.
- Continuous monitoring of the state of progress came inexpensively with this development process. The agile process worked well both for the SAM developer and project manager. The latter could concentrate on the actual development work, and did not have to spend much time on management. The mix of combined sprint reviews and sprint starts together with the short scrum meetings appears to have given a very good "real work to management" ratio.
- One improvement to SAM's process could be to spend some more time inititally trying to complete the backlog. This would make it even easier to detect a budget overflow at early stages. For projects of a more research-oriented nature than the current one, this would maybe not be so important, or even possible or desirable.

The research question for this study was to examine what characterizes the use of Scrum in small-team cross-organizational development projects. We have found many of the benefits expressed in previous lessons learned-reports, like increased overview of the project, more flexibility and motivation.

However, we also found that resource estimation became problematic for SAM as the customer was participating in discussing the estimates. SAM thinks this implicitly lowered the estimates because it happened at a point where the customer had not yet worked enough in the project to encounter estimation-errors themselves. It can seem that the nature of a relationship where a customer and contractor participates in development can lower the learning effect of frequent feedback, when one party is carrying more workload than the other in a period. Another problem for SAM is the duality of working in a flexible manner with Scrum on a project with fixed price and functionality.

5   Conclusions and Further Work

In an action research project, we have tried out and evaluated the use of Scrum in a cross-organizational project to develop a digital map application. Scrum is found to offer a good development process for smaller R&D projects at SAM. The project currently described has encouraged SAM to consider this model also for other projects. However, effort estimation was found to be challenging due to the customer-provider relationship in the project.

We will continue to follow the digital map application project in 2006, mainly focusing on the learning effects of Scrum.

Acknowledgement

We are grateful to Anette Johnsrud at Avinor for participating in this study, and for commenting on this article.

References

1. David Avison, Francis Lau, Michael Myers, and Peter Axel Nielsen, "Action Research," *Communications of the ACM*, no. 1, vol. 42, pp. 94-97, 1999.
2. Robert M. Davison, Maris G. Martinsons, and Ned Kock, "Principles of canonical action research," *Information Systems Journal*, no. 1, vol. 14, pp. 65 - 86, 2004.
3. Torgeir Dingsøyr, "Postmortem reviews: Purpose and Approaches in Software Engineering," *Information and Software Technology*, no. 5, vol. 47, pp. 293-303, 2005.
4. Kevin Kelly, *Out of Control*. Reading, Massachusets: Addison-Wesley, 1994,
5. Ned Kock, "The three threats of action research: a discussion of methodological antidotes in the context of an information systems study," *Decision Support Systems*, no. 2, vol. 37, pp. 265 - 286, 2003.
6. Chris Mann and Frank Maurer, "A case study on the Impact of Scrum on Overtime and Customer Satisfaction," in *Proceedings of Agile 2005*. Denver: IEEE Press, 2005.
7. Ikujiro Nonaka and Hirotaka Takeuchi, *The Knowledge-Creating Company*: Oxford University Press, 1995, ISBN 0-18.509269-4.
8. L. Rising and N. S. Janoff, "The Scrum software development process for small teams," *Ieee Software*, no. 4, vol. 17, pp. 26-+, 2000.
9. Bob Schatz and Ibrahim Abdelshafi, "Primavera gets agile: A successfull transition to agile development," *IEEE Software*, no. May/June, pp. 36 - 42, 2005.
10. Ken Schwaber, *Agile Project Management with Scrum*. Redmond: Microsoft Press, 2004,
11. Ken Schwaber and Mike Beedle, *Agile Software Development with Scrum*. Upper Saddle River: Prentice Hall, 2001,
12. Peter M. Senge, *The Fifth Discipline: The Art & Practise of The Learning Organisation*: Century Business, 1990, ISBN 0-7126-56871.
13. Anselm Strauss and Juliet Corbin, *Basics of Qualitative Research: Second edition*: Sage Publications, 1998, ISBN 0-8039-5939-7.
14. G Susman and R Evered, "An assessment of the scientific merits of action research," *Administrative Science Quarterly*, no. 4, vol. 23, pp. 582-603, 1978.
15. Hirotaka Takeuchi and Ikujiro Nonaka, "The new product development game," *Harvard Business Review*, no. January, pp. 137 - 146, 1986.

Appendix: Interview Guide

1.   How has the previous relationship between <the customer> and <the software provider> been?
2.   How did you organize the work in the project?
3.   How has the work been in this project compared to previous projects?
4.   What changes were done during the project?
5.   How were sprint meetings carried out?
6.   How were changes from the customer handled?
7.   How were contracts and formalism handled?
8.   What did collocation lead to?
9.   How were daily scrum meetings organized?
10. What was the effect of these meetings?
11. Were there ad-hoc meetings after the scrum meetings? How did they work out?
12. Are you satisfied with the scrum model in this project?
13. What would you do differently if you were to start again?

Implementing an ISO 9001 Certified Process

Tor Stålhane

Norwegian University of Science and Technology - NTNU
stalhane@idi.ntnu.no

Abstract. This paper presents a case study of how a Norwegian company introduced an ISO certified process. By identifying the company's strong and weak sides plus the expectations and fears of the developers, we managed to introduce process changes in an efficient manner. By reusing the existing processes and procedures used in the company, the additions needed in order to be ISO 9001confromant was surprisingly small – only 37 pages. The way we worked to achieve our goal can serve as a starting point to other companies that are in the same situation as our company – a company with lots of good processes and procedures but without the framework needed to make it ISO 9001 conform.

1 Introduction

How difficult is it to develop an ISO 9001 certifiable process? Since ISO 9001 focuses on what to do and not on how to do it, it is flexible and should thus be simple to implement, at least for small companies. Some companies have, however, claimed that the large implementation costs and the large amount of documents needed are major obstacles to ISO 9001 [7]. We believe that ISO 9001 is just common sense and that it thus should be easy to implement. The SPIKE project provided us with an opportunity to show that we were right.

Our company wanted to implement an ISO 9001 certified development process, not because they thought that they needed it but because the market increasingly demanded it. They already had their own documented development process which was quite satisfactory and hoped that this would give them a flying start to ISO certification. The work was done by two NTNU researchers – both with extensive consultancy experience – in cooperation with the company's developers and managers.

ISO does not give any guidelines on how to introduce an ISO 9001 conformant process. We thus started the work by setting down some principles – reuse as much of the current processes as possible, control risk and opportunities, involve all stakeholders, and introduce the process in a stepwise manner. In our opinion, these principles contributed significantly to our success.

Our company is a small Norwegian company with seven developers plus a managing director and a chief analyst. Everybody working in the company have a long experience, with an average software development experience of ca. five years. The company mainly develops software for the public and financial sectors and most of the development is done in-house. Most of their systems are web-based and in many cases the company is also responsible for maintaining the system and the server where the system runs.

R. Messnarz (Ed.): EuroSPI 2006, LNCS 4257, pp. 16 – 27, 2006.

The rest of this paper is organized as follows: first we describe some related work in the field of ISO certification. Then we describe how we arrived at our questionnaire and how this was used to identify risks and opportunities. We then discuss how we advanced in order to be able to reuse as much as possible of exiting processes before describing what we produced and the results of the first audit. At last, we describe the lessons learned and what we think can be extracted as general results from this case study and discuss our plans for future work in this area.

2 Related Work

The papers that are published focus on the effect of introducing an ISO 9001 certified process into a software development company [1, 2] or the comparison of ISO 9001 to other quality models, e.g. CMM [3]. Norris et al sums up a lot of important experiences in [4] but the paper is mainly related to assessment of development processes. There are, however, also published important papers on the experience of introducing the ISO 9001 or other quality assurance standards. Two of them [5, 6] will be summed up below and related to our own experiences.

Some studies have also been performed on the key question for all process changes – does it pay? The results reported in [1] shows that companies that are ISO 9001 certified and are heavy users of the introduced processes outperform non-certified companies and companies that are certified but are not heavy users of the processes. The difference in ROA – Return On Assets - is significant at the 5% level. FitzGibbon reports similar results in [7]. His survey shows that ISO certified companies had a larger profit margin – 5.4% versus 1.9% for the non-certified companies – and a larger ROA.

FitzGibbon [7] also reports a survey on the problems related to an ISO 9001 certified process. The top three problems reported were "Time to write the manual" – reported by 31% of the respondents, "High volume of the paper work" – 27% of the respondents and "The high cost of implementation" – 25% of the respondents.

Since we later will present what we think are the main reason for a successful implementation of an ISO 9001 conformant process, it is interesting to see what success factors others have identified. In [5], based on the experiences from 12 change processes, the following success factors are identified as the most important ones:

- A consistent perception of change objectives. In successful companies, all interviewees identified the same goals and described them with the same level of detail.
- Managing resistance. In successful companies possible conflicts were anticipated and taken into account during the change process.
- Collective decision process. In successful companies, all decisions on whether and how to implement changes were based on agreement.
- Involvement of affected staff members. In the successful companies, there was a considerable effort to include those employees who would later be affected by the changes of the work process.

In a survey of 56 software companies [6], the following success factors are identified as the most important ones:

- Management commitment and support. Process change requires investing time, money and effort – all of which are controlled by management.
- Staff involvement. If staff members do not buy into the proposed changes, the change initiative is useless.
- Providing enhanced understanding. Process change can only be successful if mangers and staff have a thorough understanding of how the process contributes to the company's mission.
- Tailoring improvement initiatives. Many problems of process improvement may seem like details. However, to quote Humphrey [8]: "It is such details that make the difference between an annoying and inconvenient process and a comfortable and efficient one".

What is common for these papers is their focus on involving all stake holders – staff and management – and on a collective decision process. The latter is important in order to handle possible resistance. As should be expected, these factors are also found to be important success factors for software process improvement [12].

If we look at the goals – what the companies want to achieve – the most comprehensive research results are again reported by FitzGibbon [7]. Based on a survey of 647 representatives from British software organisations he found that 69% of all asked answered that they want better procedural efficiency while 55% wanted to reduce their error rates. Customer satisfaction came third with 49%.

A paper from 1995 is also important because the authors did a large UK survey to obtain answers to three important questions – what are the most frequent non-conformities discovered during an audit, what is difficult to implement and what is perceived as most useful [11]. The survey gave the following results:

- The three most common non-conformity areas were design control, management responsibility and contract review.
- The three areas that were considered to be most difficult to implement were corrective and preventive action (SPI), purchasing control and design control / statistical techniques.
- The three areas that the organisations considered most useful were corrective and preventive actions (SPI), contract review and internal quality audits / management responsibility.

It is surprising to note that e.g. contract review is in the top three both for non-conformity and usefulness. SPI is in the top three both for usefulness and for difficult to implement. The paper's conclusion in this area is interesting [11]: "A general problem is the lack of adequate analysis of non-conformances. Few companies perform regular analysis of processes and roles in order to remove sources of non-conformances". They never learn, do they?

3 Risks and Opportunities

The first things to consider when we want to change a people intensive process are:

- What do the people involved fear? These are the risks - things that we must prevent.
- What do people hope for? These are the opportunities – things that we must strive to obtain.

In order to better understand risks and opportunities, we used a two-step approach. We started by interviewing two developers and one manager. The interviews were semi-structured in that we had a set of questions that we needed answers to but in addition, we used follow-up questions to gain a better understanding of the answers to the predefined questions. The focus of the interview was on what they expected would happen if the company implemented an ISO 9001 certified process. Two typical examples of what came out of the interviews are shown below – one from a developer and one from a manger.

Manager: Implementing ISO 9001 will cost quite a lot. At the same time, the company will get a better overview of its competence, its experience and its document templates. ISO certification is an investment. We are, however, unsure of how long we have to wait before we can reap the benefits.

Developer: Some of the developers may have a negative attitude towards ISO certification because they are afraid it will hurt creativity. This is not only true for ISO standards but holds also for coding standards and other rules and regulations. Rules and standards can take away all the fun from the job. In many ways this is the same attitude as we saw when we started to reuse components – many developers were afraid that they would not be allowed to develop things but just had to use "toy bricks".

After the interviews we extracted all opinions, ideas, fears and hopes. Based on this, we constructed a questionnaire. The full questionnaire is included as appendix A. Everybody in the company – both mangers and developers - filled in the questionnaire. The items in the questionnaire that got an average score of 5.0 or more were considered for risk and opportunity analysis. This gave us the following items:

- When we get ISO certified, we will have to generate more documents for each development project. This is consistent with FitzGibbon's observations in [7].
- It is important that all employees participate actively in the introduction of new processes, standards and procedures. This is consistent with e.g. Trittmann et al's observation in [5].
- Active management participation is important in order to make the introduction of an ISO certified process a success. This, and the next point is consistent with e.g. the observations of Stelzer et al in [6].
- Active management support is important in order to make the introduction of ISO certification a success.
- An ISO certified process will lead to better working practices in the company in general. This is consistent with FitzGibbon's findings in [7].

Based on our findings, we identified the following risks that needed to be controlled throughout the implementation of the ISO 9001 certified process:

Risk 1: The introduction of new documents or additions to existing documents. We decided that we should not make new documents except if absolutely needed.

Risk 2: Developer participation. The developers must be included at all steps in the process. Their experiences and advices are important input to the new processes and procedures.

Risk 3: Management participation and support. Management must show their commitment by allocating money and time to the ISO implementation activities.

Opportunity 1: Better working practices. The changes in the development process must be considered to be improvements by the developers.

Management and developers are in agreement in the sense that everything the developers found important also was ranked high by management. There were, however, some cases where the two groups disagreed strongly - average score difference greater than 2.0. In all cases, management ranked these items higher than the developers. The points are:

- Introducing an ISO certified process will cost a lot but will be a good investment – developers 3.3 vs. mangers 6.0
- Introducing an ISO certified process will give the company a better control over the order situation – developers 3.0 vs. mangers 6.0
- Introducing an ISO certified process will give us more satisfied customers already after one year – developers 3.2 vs. mangers 6.0

Management is more optimistic than the developers when it comes to business related issues such as order situation and customer satisfaction.

4 What We Had and What We Needed

By reusing as much as possible of existing standards and procedures we hoped to obtain two things: keep the number of new documents down to an absolute minimum and reduce the need for unlearning old processes before learning the new ones. This leads us to make up status as to what we had and what we needed, which was done early in the change process. We took ISO 9001 [9] – the quality assurance standard - and ISO 90003 [10] – a set of guidelines to ISO 9001 for software development and maintenance – as our starting points. In order to get a good overview we created a table as shown below.

Table 1. What we had, what ISO 9001 requires and what ISO 90003 recommends

Company ref.	ISO 9001 ref.	ISO 9001 activity description	ISO 90003 comments
Status and document ref.	Paragraph number	What the standard requires	Explanations and comments

The contents of the three rightmost columns are taken from the appropriate ISO documents. The leftmost column was filled in while going through all available company standards, documents and procedures. The status for each ISO 9001 item was found to be one of the following:

- OK – no further action is needed. In addition, no new training is needed.
- Partly OK – some additions are needed. We also need to include some training on these points.
- Missing – we need to develop new procedures and processes. The personnel must learn new ways of working.

The final version of the table showed what was needed. In this way we made sure that we did not miss any of the ISO 9001 requirements. The list of missing or incomplete procedures and processes also served as a basis for cost estimation for the rest of the work. It turned out that we needed additional or new processes in all sections of the standard. The section that needed most attention was section 7 which contains processes related to product realization – in our case software development.

Our total estimate was 20 person days for writing new material plus training for seven persons. The total costs later turned out to be 61 person days over two years. This should be compared to the total company turn-over which is 1400 person days per year. The costs were thus ca. 2% per year.

Even though the company did not plan to introduce any SPI processes, this was included since it is part and parcel of ISO 9001. This did not create much fuss in the company – it just seemed like a practical thing to do. There are clear requirements in the standard that the company shall identify:

- The sources of all non-conformities and remove or reduce them – reactive improvement
- Processes, procedures or activities that can lead to non-conformities and change them – proactive improvement.

The big challenge when introducing the new processes is ISO 9001's requirements concerning process traceability – "evidence of conformity". The reason for this is that these evidences are not needed by anybody in the company – only by the auditors. It is thus something we do only because the ISO 9001 standard requires us to do so. The standard uses three forms of conformity, namely conformity to:

- The quality system – "Records shall be established and maintained to provide evidence of conformity to requirements and of the effective operation of the quality management system" – ISO 9001, 4.2.4.
- Product requirements –"The organization shall determine the monitoring and measurement to be undertaken and the monitoring and measurement devices needed to provide evidence of conformity of product to determine requirements" – ISO 9001, 7.6.
- The acceptance criteria – "Evidence of conformity with the acceptance criteria shall be maintained. Records shall indicate the person(s) authorizing release of product" – ISO 9001, 8.2.4

In principle, almost anything can be used for evidence - emails, notes, meeting agendas, logs etc. Our company already had a document driven development process and thus found it natural to build on this also for evidences. In this way, we did not change any process but added the requirement that the resulting documents must be placed in the project archive and that they should be easy to retrieve.

5   Implementing an ISO 9001 Conformant Process

5.1 Our Starting Point

Development of new processes and procedures used the current company processes as a basis. We knew what we needed to write from scratch and what we needed to enhance. Where the company already had processes in place, the relevant section just contains a reference to the existing document. All other sections are written according to the following template:

1.   Title and reference to the part of ISO 9001 that is covered in this section.
2.   Description of all compulsory and optional documents that are used as input to this process.
3.   The role that is responsible and how the process should be performed.
4.   The results of this process: one part that describes the documents generated and one part that describes the decisions made based on the process' results - for instance to start another process. The output documents are important for other processes and are also used as evidence that the process has been performed.

Defining a template simplified the job of writing the new processes and helped us to focus on the important points, like what is the necessary input and what should be the result of this process.

The following table shows the results of applying our method to the implementation of ISO 9001, section.2.3.

Table 2. The project evaluation process

Title: Project Evaluation
Input: • Planned and real project duration, measured in weeks. This can be found in the project plan document, chapter 4.2   • Planned and real costs - measured in NOK. Real cost is defined as all costs registered to the project. Planned cost includes all variation orders and other contract extensions and can be found in the project status report.
Process: We will assess deviations from planned cost and durations as follows: If the real duration or cost is more than 20 % larger than the planned one, we shall initiate the process "Corrective actions"- see section 5.2.1 - for the project under consideration.
Output: The result of this process is a report with one of the following contents: • The situation is normal. All measurements are within acceptable limits.   • One or more problem areas that should be improved, together with the decided corrective actions.

5.2 The New Standards

The new standard contains templates for 16 documents normally produced in a development project. Some of the templates existed before we started to implement an ISO 9001 certified process but all are collected in the new standard for ease of reference. The templates consist of four parts with the following contents:

- The purpose of the document – why we need this document.
- The file id for the document on the format <report name>< version number>.doc. This makes it easy to find the latest version of each document in the project archive.
- The table of contents. This is used to describe what we expect to find inside this document.
- Miscellaneous. This part contains references to the processes where this document is produced or used, who is responsible for the quality of this document and to who shall it be distributed.

Both the documents and the process descriptions are simple. Beside the general principle that things always should be made as simple as possible, there are some specific reasons for our choices:

- First and foremost the simplicity is a result of a tug-of-war between the researchers – who wanted an advanced process with lots of metrics and statistical analysis – and the company representatives – who wanted a minimum of changers and extra work and documents.
- Simple processes and document templates make the start-up phase easy. This will increase the speed of take-up in the organization.
- By choosing simple processes – e.g. just a few project metrics – it is easier for the developers and management to see that the metrics are useful.
- In most cases, a simple solution will suffice. If there are processes or templates that need to be extended, we can extend them later, as we get more experience as to what is needed. The rest can be kept simple.

Considering all that the ISO 9001 standard requires and that our company had never before been ISO 9001 certified, the size of the new document is rather surprising – 37 pages all in all in addition to the 50 pages already used to describe the existing development processes. This includes all new document templates and forms for such things as checking customer satisfaction. Thus, no new large documents were needed on the company's intranet. In our opinion, there is no reason why an ISO 9001 conformant process should be any larger for a larger company. The amount of procedures needed will, however, most likely increase.

This confirms our observation that ISO 9001 is a practical document for practical people and not an excuse for defining an enormous amount of new processes and documents. The knowledge that a large amount of new documents would make the ISO certification a sure fiasco had a moderating effect on any attempts to go beyond the bare necessities when it comes to defining new documents.

The main reason for the small volume of the new processes is ISO 9001's focus on what shall be done – not on how it should be done. This enabled us to tailor the process to this specific company's needs and it also gave us the opportunity for considerable reuse of processes and templates.

5.3 Implementing the New Processes

We decided to introduce the new processes stepwise and only in one project in order to gain practical experience. In this way we could limit any counterproductive effect. At the same time both we and the developers had the chance to learn more about the new processes. It was furthermore decided to hold an internal quality audit when this first project was well under way in order to see if the process worked as intended and whether it was followed by developers and project manager. The first internal quality audit identified five non-conformities – three of medium severity and two of low severity. In addition, there were seven observations – items that were not in complete agreement with the standard but not important enough to be considered deviations. All deviations were fixed in the next release of the quality manual.

The three non-conformities of medium severity were:

- There was no review of the offers that were sent from the company to a prospective customer. This review should be linked to the project risk analysis.
- The system's test log did not contain references to the relevant system requirements. Such references are needed in order to ensure traceability.
- The system's documents do not follow the relevant document templates.

A follow-up audit - the last before final certification – was held during the beginning of March 2006 and the company was certified in May 2006.

6 Lessons Learnt

First and foremost, our belief that ISO 9001 is just common sense and thus is easy to implement has been confirmed.

The results reported come from one single case study. Based on the many similarities between our case study and the results reported from related studies and surveys, we see that the goals, risks and problems - see for instance [6, 7 and 11] – are the same as are found elsewhere.

Based on our experiences from the case study, we have extracted some lessons that we believe to be generally applicable, not only for implementing an ISO 9001 certified process but for process change in general.

- Perform a survey or set of interviews in order to identify risks and opportunities that are relevant for the planned changes. After having analysed the results we must include in our plan actions that help us to avoid the identified risks and help us to reap the benefits from identified opportunities. Thus "We cannot introduce X because it leads to too much of B" is a dead end and an example of defensive thinking. Instead, we should think "We want to introduce X. How can we control the risk of getting too much of B?"
- Reuse as much as possible of existing processes, procedures, templates and activities. This will reduce the need for new documents and the need for

training. Thus, we will get a much steeper learning curve and large parts of the new process will be useful already for the next project.

- Any new process should start out as simple as possible and be introduced in a stepwise fashion. Extra details and process steps should only be added after we have identified a specific need. There is also an element of strategic considerations here – the auditing company expects to see improvements in the quality system from one audit to the next. Starting out simple give us more opportunities to show improvements over time.

- Both developers, management and change agents must participate in all activities. The resulting tug-of-war gives a process that is adapted to the company and has just enough formalities. If we cannot reach an agreement, the developers and management should, however, have the final say.

7 Further Work

When the company is certified we plan to do follow-up interviews and surveys in order to see if – and how - the developers' attitudes towards ISO 9001 certification change. At the present we plan to do this every six months, at least the first two years after certification. We will use a questionnaire that is an adapted versions of the one we used before certification, e.g. instead of "When we get ISO certified, we will have to generate more documents for each development project" we will use the statement "After we got ISO certified, we have to generate more documents for each development project" and so on.

The most important things that we want to check out are:

- Have we been able to implement a quality standard that does not flood the developers with extra paper work?
- Did the developers feel that they participated in the work and contributed to the company's quality standard?
- Have the working practices in the company improved after ISO 9001?
- Has the customers' satisfaction improved?

As pointed out, for instance by [1, 7], the ISO certificate is not the end of an improvement initiative – it is the beginning. We believe that the customer surveys introduced into our company will serve as a catalyst for greater focus on customer needs and process improvement. Only a follow-up survey, however, can show if this will really be the case.

References

1. E. Naveh and A. Marcus: Achieving competitive advantage through implementing a replicable management standard: Installing and using ISO 9000. Journal of Operations Management, vol. 24, issue 1, December 2005.
2. D. Stelzer, W. Mellis and G. Herzwurm: Software Process Improvement via ISO 9000. Results of two surveys among European Software Houses. IEEE 1996.

3. I. Rozman, R. Vajde and J. Gyrøkøs: United view on ISO 9001 model and SEI CMM. IEEE, 1994.
4. M. Norris, P. Rigby and S. Stockman: Life After ISO 9001: British Telecom's Approach to Software Quality. IEEE Communications Magazine, October 1994.
5. R. Trittmann et al.: Changing software development: A case study at SAP AG. Proceedings of the 7th European Conference on Information Systems - Copenhagen, Denmark 23 – 25 June, 1999, vol. 2.
6. D. Stelzer, W. Mellis: Success Factors of Organizational Change in Software Process Improvement. Software process Improvement and Practice, vol. 4, issue 4, 1999.
7. C. FitzGibbon: Are Companies Earning Return on Investment in ISO 9000 Registration? A Review of the Empirical Evidence. 2000
8. W.S. Humphrey: A discipline of software engineering, Addison-Wesley, Reading, MA, 1995.
9. ISO: ISO 9001 International Standard – Quality management systems – Requirements. Reference number ISO 9001:2000(E).
10. ISO: ISO 90003 International Standard – Software Engineering – Guidelines for the application of ISO 9001:2000 to computer software. Reference number ISO 90003:2000(E).
11. C.B. Løken and T. Skramstad: ISO 9000 Certification – Experience from Europe. World Congress for Software Quality, June 20 – 22, 1995, San Francisco, CA.
12. T. Elisberg, G. Hansen and N.G. Hansen: Success in SPI – the stakeholders' point of view. In "On the road to improvement" (in Danish). A Talent@IT report. Edited by O. Vinter and J. Pries-Heje. Delta, Copenhagen, December 2004.

Appendix A

The following answer alternatives were available: 1 - Totally disagree, 2 - Partly disagree, 3- Disagree somewhat, 4 - Agree somewhat, 5 - Partly agree, 6 - Totally agree

Statement	Score		
	Dev.	Mng.	All
When we get ISO certified, we will have to generate more documents for each development project	5.0	6.0	5.1
An ISO certified process will make us less creative but only in the short term perspective	4.0	3.0	3.9
An ISO certified process will make us less creative, also in the long term perspective	3.3	3.0	3.3
We will be less flexible in our customer relationship but only in the short time perspective	3.3	4.0	3.4
We will be less flexible in our customer relationship also in the long time perspective	2.7	4.0	2.9
Processes, standards and procedures must be introduced gradually	4.8	5.0	4.9
It is important that all employees participate actively in the introduction of new processes, standards and procedures	5.2	5.0	5.1
An ISO certified process will lead to better working practices in the company in general	4.8	6.0	5.0
An ISO certified process will lead to better project management in the company	4.5	6.0	4.7

The customers will fear that an ISO certified process will lead to extra costs without adding value but only in the short time perspective	4.0	5.0	4.1
The customers will fear that an ISO certified process will lead to extra costs without adding value also in the long time perspective	3.0	4.0	3.1
Also those who work as consultants in an other companies will benefit from an ISO certified process	4.2	5.0	4.3
Introducing an ISO certified process will create enthusiasm in the company	3.0	3.0	3.0
The attitude towards an ISO certified process is generally positive in our company	4.2	4.0	4.1
If we introduce an ISO certified process I will continuously be watch to check that I do everything "by the book"	3.5	4.0	3.6
Introducing an ISO certified process will cost a lot but will be a good investment	3.3	6.0	3.7
Introducing an ISO certified process will cost a lot. This is a waste of money	2.8	1.0	2.6
Introducing an ISO certified process will give the company a better control over the order situation	3.0	6.0	3.4
The developers that follow the new procedures and processes will do a better job but only in the short time perspective	3.2	5.0	3.4
The developers that follow the new procedures and processes will do a better job also in the long time perspective	4.5	5.0	4.6
Introducing an ISO certified process will give us more satisfied customers already after one year.	3.2	6.0	3.6
Introducing an ISO certified process will give us more satisfied customers but only in the long term perspective	3.5	5.0	3.7
Active management participation is important in order to make the introduction of ISO certification a success	5.3	6.0	5.4
Active management support is important in order to make the introduction of ISO certification a success	5.8	6.0	5.9

Software Process in Practice:
A Grounded Theory of the Irish Software Industry

Gerry Coleman[1] and Rory O'Connor[2]

[1] Department of Computing, Dundalk Institute of Technology, Dundalk, Ireland
gerry.coleman@dkit.ie
[2] School of Computing, Dublin City University, Dublin 9, Ireland
roconnor@computing.dcu.ie

Abstract. This paper presents the results of a Grounded Theory study of how software process and software process improvement (SPI) is applied in the practice of software development. This study described in this paper focused on what is actually happening in practice in the software industry. Using the indigenous Irish software product industry as a test-bed, we examine the approaches used to develop software by companies at various stages of growth. The study used the grounded theory methodology and the results produce a picture of software process usage, with the outcome being a theory, grounded in the field data, that explains how software processes are formed and evolve, and when and why SPI is undertaken. The grounded theory is based on two conceptual themes, Process Formation and Process Evolution, and one core theoretical category, Cost of Process. Our research found that SPI programmes are implemented reactively and that many software managers reject SPI because of the associated implementation and maintenance costs and are reluctant to implement SPI models such as ISO 9000 and CMMI.

1 Introduction

A software process defines what steps a development organisation should take at each stage of production and provides assistance in making estimates, developing plans, and measuring quality. There is a widely held belief that a better software process results in a better software product. SPI models, such as Capability Maturity Model Integration (CMMI) and ISO 15504, claim to represent best practice. However, although these models have been highly publicised and marketed, they are not being widely adopted.

The motivation for our research originates in the premise that, in practice software companies are not following 'best practice' process improvement models. On this basis, we initially set out to explore two primary questions: *Why are software companies not using 'best practice' SPI models?*, and *What software processes are software companies using?*

In order to answer these questions it was first necessary to define both a context and scope for the study. To ensure the participation of software development professionals who would be familiar with the considerations involved in using both

R. Messnarz (Ed.): EuroSPI 2006, LNCS 4257, pp. 28 – 39, 2006.

software process and process improvement models, it was decided to limit the scope to software product companies whose primary business is software development. In addition, given the geographical location of the researchers, it was decided to confine the study to Irish software product companies, which has the added advantage of restricting the study to within the same economic and regulatory regime. Finally as the Irish software industry is populated by both indigenous and multinational software companies, a decision was made to limit the scope of the study to indigenous Irish software product companies, as they could provide the historical information required to understand process foundation and evolution. To support the capture and analysis of this information, we chose grounded theory as the methodology most suited to our research.

2 Research Methodology

The two research paradigms that have received most attention in the literature can be broadly labelled as positivist and phenomenological [21] or positivist and interpretivist [3]. The most commonly used terms to differentiate these paradigms with respect to their associated methods and techniques, are quantitative and qualitative respectively, with quantitative methods being based on the positivist paradigm while qualitative methods are built on a phenomenological world view [7, 8]. Quantitative methods are used to establish general laws or principles [4] and its scientific approach can provide answers which have a provable base. However, if one wants to study human behaviour and the social and cultural contexts in which it functions, then the limitations of quantitative research become apparent [17] and direct the researcher towards qualitative techniques. Advocates of qualitative methods in software engineering research propose that a principal advantage of their usage is that they force the researcher to delve into the complexity of the problem rather than abstract away from it and therefore the results are richer and more informative [25].

Researching in software engineering is more appropriately placed in the domain of Information Systems (IS). IS research is the formal study of information systems within an organisation, which differs from the field of software engineering in that takes social and organisational aspects into account. Lee and Liebenau [15] believe that qualitative research is required in IS because, 'while there has been great success in applying natural science and engineering models to research into computer technology, they have been inadequate and inappropriate in explaining the human, group, organisational and societal matters which surround the use of information systems'. Bertelsen [2] also supports the use of qualitative research in IS stating that as software development is socio-cultural in nature any research conducted cannot be based exclusively on natural science approaches but must include provision for interpreting social, psychological and cultural issues.

2.1 The Study Methodology

There are a number of basic study methodologies, including phenomenology, ethnography, case studies and action research, which are used within qualitative research.

However, this study chose another approach, grounded theory, as the method of enquiry for the following reasons:

- Given the lack of an integrated theory in the literature as to why software companies are avoiding SPI models, an inductive approach, which allowed theory to emerge based on the experiential accounts of software development managers themselves, offered the greatest potential.
- It has established guidelines for conducting inductive, theory-generating research.
- It is renowned for its application to human behaviour. Software development is a labour intensive activity and software process relies heavily on human compliance for its deployment.
- It is an established and credible methodology in sociological and health disciplines (e.g. nursing studies, psychology), and a burgeoning one in the IT arena. This study provided an opportunity to apply a legitimate and suitable methodology to the software field.

A number of researchers have used grounded theory to look at a diverse range of socio-cultural activities in IS. [1] used a novel combination of action research and grounded theory to produce a grounded action research methodology for studying how IT is practiced. Others have used the methodology to examine, the use of 'systems thinking' practices [11], software inspections [6, 24], process modelling [5], requirements documentation [19] and virtual team development [32, 20]. [14] used grounded theory to study the use of development practices in a Danish software company and concluded that it was a methodology well suited for use in the IS sector.

3 Grounded Theory

Grounded Theory was first established by Glaser and Strauss [10]. As the objective with the methodology is to uncover theory rather than have it pre-conceived, grounded theory incorporates a number of steps to ensure good theory development. Its main components are:

- **Theoretical Sampling -** Theoretical sampling refers to the process of collecting, coding and analysing data whilst simultaneously generating theory. The researcher engages in 'constant comparison' between the analysed data and the emerging theory and this process continues until 'theoretical saturation' has been reached, i.e. where additional data being collected is providing no new knowledge about the categories.
- **Open Coding and Analysis -** From the interview transcripts the researcher analyses the data line-by-line and allocates codes to the text. The codes represent concepts that will later become part of the theory. From the initial interviews, a list of codes emerges and this list is then used to code subsequent interviews. At the end of the sampling process a large number of codes should have emerged.
- **Axial Coding -** Axial coding is the process of relating categories to their subcategories (and) termed axial because coding occurs around the axis of a category linking categories to subcategories at the level of properties and dimensions. This involves documenting category properties and dimensions from the open coding

phase; identifying the conditions, actions and interactions associated with a phenomenon and relating categories to subcategories.

- **Selective Coding -** Selective coding is the process of integrating and refining the theory. Because categories are merely descriptions of the data they must be further developed to form the theory. The first step is to identify the central, or 'core' category around which the theory will be built. As the core category acts as the hub for all other identified categories, it must be central in that all other categories must relate to it and it must appear frequently in the data.

- **Memoing -** Memoing is 'the ongoing process of making notes and ideas and questions that occur to the analyst during the process of data collection and analysis' [23]. Typically, ideas which are recorded during the coding process, memos assist in fleshing out the theory as it emerges and are written constantly during a grounded theory study. Memos may take the form of statements, hypotheses or questions. In the latter part of the study, following extensive coding and analysis, memos become increasingly theoretical and act as the building blocks for the final report.

Since the initial launch of grounded theory, the Glaser and Strauss alliance gradually separated until each was developing a different version of the methodology. Though acknowledging and recognising the spirit of Glaser's original version of the methodology, this study employed the Strauss and Corbin approach [26] as:

- They believe that the researcher's personal or professional experience, is supportive of theory building and contributes to 'theoretical sensitivity', the ability to understand the data's important elements and how they contribute to theory. The researchers have operated as software process consultants and professional software engineers for a number of years.

- They favour setting the research question in advance of commencing a grounded theory study, as was done in this case.

- This study aimed to generate hypotheses, testable within the study, an approach supported by Strauss and Corbin.

4 The SPI Case Study

Despite the research questions being clearly defined, the theoretical sampling approach of grounded theory means it is unclear in advance exactly the types of practitioners and companies that need to be interviewed during a study to meet the research objectives. Because of this, a preliminary study phase involving 4 interviews, was embarked upon to generate more detailed information on how the sampling process should progress.

To support the semi-structured interviewing process, an interview guide, based on the researchers' experience as 'cultural insiders' and their prior familiarity with the literature, was created for use with the first two interviews. The first interview was taped and then transcribed and printed. The interview was then coded, by hand, in accordance with the open coding procedure of grounded theory. Memos were written as and when they occurred to the researcher during the coding. The second interview was coded in the same way as the first one, with the second being compared to the first and coded where possible according to the list of codes generated from the first interview. The initial interviews highlighted several drawbacks with the interview guide, and these limitations drove the development of a second interview guide which was then used on interview 3. Then, and in each successive instance, the interviews and the line of questioning concentrated more on the memos and codes from the prior interview coding and analysis rather than on the formalised question set.

The conclusion of interview 4 heralded the end of the preliminary study stage, which was primarily used to drive the theoretical sampling process. The stage highlighted two issues in particular which would steer the immediately subsequent sampling activity. Firstly, analysis of the software companies' target market indicated that the intended list of companies, in the full study, should incorporate as many sectors as possible. Secondly, a specialist qualitative analysis tool, which supported the grounded theory approach, was essential.

4.1 Software Support for Grounded Theory

Having investigated the range of tools which are used for data management in qualitative research, Atlas TI [16], a tool designed specifically for use with grounded theory was selected. Atlas allows for the linking, searching and sorting of data. It enables the researcher to keep track of interview transcripts, manage a list of codes and related memos, generate families of related codes and create graphical support for codes, concepts and categories. It also supports the axial and selective coding process as proposed by Strauss and Corbin [26], which is used in this study. A sample list of codes from this stage is contained in Table 1.

Table 1. Sample codes as assigned using Atlas TI

Absence of process	Automated documentation	Background of CEO
Acceptance test process	Automated testing	Background of CTO
Actual Vs 'official' process	Background drives SPI	Beginnings of formality

4.2 Conducting the Full Study - Stages 1 and 2

Study Stage 1 involved interviews with an additional 11 companies. Closely following the tenets of grounded theory meant that, following the initial open coding, the interviews were then re-analysed and coded axially across the higher-level categories that had emerged from earlier interviews. Any memos, or propositions, that emerged through the coding process were recorded for further analysis and inclusion as questions in subsequent interviews. A consequence of this was that the interview guide was constantly updated. In conjunction with the theoretical sampling process, the constant comparative method was also used. This involved comparing interview-to-interview and searching for any themes or patterns in the data. Though a number of theoretical concepts emerged during the early fieldwork, the researchers decided to re-evaluate the study progress following the interview with Company 14. This suggested that the range of companies interviewed should be diversified. This approach is in accordance with both Strauss and Corbin [26] and Goulding [13], who advocate diversity in the data gathering and 'staying in the field' until no new evidence emerges.

The researchers believed that to conclude the sampling process at this point would constitute premature closure, a mistake often associated with grounded theory [9].

To progress the study, the data, memos and propositions created during the constant comparative process were further analysed by the researchers and a number of provisional hypotheses formulated (Table 2). These hypotheses had the potential to explain how the concepts and categories emerging from the study were linked. Hypothesis testing can also be used within grounded theory to validate the theory that is emerging [26]. The analysis of the results from 14 companies and the subsequent hypothesis creation, constituted the end of Stage 1. Stage 2 would be used to test these hypotheses and ensure the emergent theory was properly grounded.

Table 2. Study Stage 1 Provisional Hypothesises

H1	The initial software process used by Irish software product companies is based on the prior experience of the software development manager.
H2	The initial software development process used by Irish software product companies is tailored to suit the requirements of the target product market.
H3	Within Irish software product companies, SPI occurs as a result of positive and negative 'trigger' events
H4	The recruitment of external management expertise is used by Irish software product companies to solve positive and negative 'trigger' events
H5	The use of minimum process in Irish software product companies does not diminish the company's ability to satisfy its business objectives
H6	Within Irish software product companies, restrictions are imposed on team sizes to achieve minimum process requirements
H7	The use of XP practices satisfy an Irish software product company's minimum process requirement better than ISO 9000 or CMM/CMMI
H8	Development managers in Irish software product companies believe that by using XP practices they get more developer buy-in to process, than if using ISO 9000 or CMM/CMMI
H9	Non-ISO 9000/CMM/CMMI-certified Irish software product companies generate only minimum documentation
H10	Within Irish software product companies, adoption of ISO 9000 and CMM/CMMI is limited because of their emphasis on what development managers perceive as non-essential process elements
H11	XP is perceived by development managers in Irish software product companies to be more cost effective than ISO 9000 and CMM/CMMI
H12	The costs associated with achieving and adhering to ISO 9000 and CMM/CMMI prevent their adoption in Irish software product companies

Stage 2 involved the participation of 7 new companies. Three of the Stage 2 interviews involved re-interviewing Stage 1 participants a technique available to grounded theory studies and supported by [12]. Building on the need for diversity within the data, the companies in Stage 2 came from different business sectors than those in Stage 1. During the Stage 2 fieldwork, the semi-structured interview questions were primarily derived from the Stage 1 hypotheses. This meant that less time was spent exploring issues which did not directly relate to the hypotheses thus allowing more time to ensure the categories and subcategories were fully 'saturated'. During Stage 2, full category saturation was reached after an additional 9 interviews as, in line with Goulding's [13] assertion, similar incidences within the data were now occurring repeatedly.

4.3 The Emergent Categories

Where axial coding's role is to identify the categories into which the discovered codes and concepts can be placed, selective coding is used to identify a key category or theme that can be used as the fulcrum of the study results [26]. In this instance, the analysis showed that there was one central category to support and link the two theoretical themes. Furthermore, as the relationships were developed and populated, new categories emerged that were not explicitly covered by the hypotheses generated in Stage 1.

Table 3. Themes, Core Categories and Main Categories

Theme	Category
Process Formation[1]	*Background of Software Development Manager*
	Background of Founder
	Management Style
	Process Tailoring
	Market Requirements
Theme	**Category**
Process Evolution	*Process Erosion*
	Minimum Process
	Business Event
	SPI Trigger
	Employee Buy-in to Process
	Hiring Expertise
	Process Inertia
Core Category	**Category**
Cost of Process	*Bureaucracy*
	Documentation
	Communication
	Tacit Knowledge
	Creativity Flexibility

The final list of themes, the core category and the main categories identified by the study are shown in Table 3. Each category and code can be linked to quotations within the interviews and these are used to provide support and rich explanation for the results. The 'saturated' categories and the various relationships were then combined to form the theoretical framework.

---

[1] From heron, the themes, categories and core category are denoted in italics.

5   Evaluation

5.1   Verification of the Theory

The issue of verification of a grounded theory study is one which distinguishes the positions of its founders Glaser and Strauss. To Glaser [9], grounded theory merely produces hypotheses and nothing more and these need not be verified or validated because that is the responsibility of verificational studies which are carried out using a different methodology. Strauss and Corbin's argue that theories are conceived, elaborated on, and checked out, in that order and this is facilitated through the concurrent processes of induction, deduction, and verification [26]. As the Strauss and Corbin version of grounded theory, was used in this research, the study has been verified through a systematic approach of data collection, sampling and analysis which then allowed the emerging concepts, memos and propositions to lead the subsequent sampling effort. Then, from the field data, a series of provisional hypotheses were derived and these were tested as the study developed.

On the issue of theory generalisability, differences arise between the two founders of grounded theory. Whereas Glaser believes generalisability is related to verificational studies and not to grounded theory, Strauss and Corbin contend that the use of a theory-building methodology is to build theory and, therefore, in grounded theory studies, the researcher is talking more about explanatory power than generalisability [26]. Context is always relevant to any grounded theory study whereas generalisability describes a situation that is essentially context-free. The findings from this research are context-dependent and this is reflected in the categories. Therefore it is not proposed that the findings are generalisable beyond the defined study boundaries.

5.2   Adequacy of the Research Process

In judging the quality of any research study designed to generate theory, reviewers must be provided with information to allow them to assess its adequacy. This information relates to how the original sample was selected, how the categories and core category emerged and subsequently drove the sampling process and how were any hypotheses were treated during the analysis activity.

Category development continued throughout the research. The hypotheses that were formulated during the study were validated according to the procedures described above. Whilst all of the hypotheses were 'tested' and verified in Stage 2 of the study, one hypothesis (H6) – *Within Irish software product companies, restrictions are imposed on team sizes to achieve minimum process requirements* – failed to develop further during that stage. Despite not fully supporting hypothesis H6, the findings in Stage 2 did support the remaining hypotheses and these in turn were incorporated into the theoretical categories and attributes. However, a number of categories emerged in Stage 2 which were not directly included in the Hypotheses list in Stage 1. The field data from the diversity of companies used for Stage 2 helped these categories to emerge.

The selection of the core category, *Cost of Process*, was made during Stage 2 of the study, though attributes of it had been apparent in Stage 1. In selecting the core category, the researcher closely followed the steps recommended by Strauss and

Corbin [26], including the fact that all other categories must relate to it and that it appears frequently in the data. Whilst many others were contenders as core categories in their own right, it was the additional analysis from Stage 2 that created the core category. The fact, therefore, that it did not crystallise until Stage 2 provided reassurance to the researchers that the correct category had been identified.

5.3 Grounding the Findings

Strauss and Corbin [26] also provide a list of criteria to assist in determining how well the findings are grounded. The foundations of any theory are a set of concepts grounded in the data. Table 1 shows an example of some of the codes produced from the coding processes and includes both terms used by the practitioners, and conceptual codes assigned by the researcher. Through the use of network diagrams we established the linkages and relationships between concepts, which categories act as predecessors and successors within the theory, and how the categories link to the core category and research themes.

Strauss and Corbin suggest that variation is important because it signifies that a concept has been examined under a range of different conditions and dimensions. Though this research is concerned with indigenous Irish software product companies, we have endeavoured to incorporate the views of as wide a range of practitioners as possible. Furthermore, Stage 2 of the study expanded the range of interview participants to achieve coverage of a greater range of markets, and thus reduced the prospects of phenomena relating only to specific market domains, or company size.

5.4 Study Findings

On the primary question of *what software processes are software companies using*, the study has found that all of the companies are *Tailoring* standard software processes to their own particular operating context such as the size of the company, the target market, and project and system type.

One of the key theoretical themes addressed by the research was *Process Formation*. The findings show that this depends on several factors including the *Background of the Software Development Manager*, essentially the expertise that manager has accumulated over their working and educational lives, the demands of the market in which the company operates, the founder's *Management Style*, and the organisational culture.

The second key theoretical theme of the study is *Process Evolution*. There, evidence from the study data suggests that managers instigate SPI as a reaction to *Trigger* events, essentially business occurrences which the current process does not adequately cater for. The *Triggers* for process change can be either positive or negative. The field data shows that many of the companies feel they don't have the capability to deal with the change from within their own resources and, therefore, hire an individual externally who has the necessary expertise to deal with the *Business Event*. However, companies experience difficulty in institutionalising any SPI gains and subsequent retrenchment reflects a clear *Erosion* from the process in place immediately following the SPI initiative. This *Erosion* eventually resolves to a *Minimum Process* which is 'barely sufficient' to satisfy the organisation's business objectives.

The periods between SPI initiatives witness *Process Inertia*, wherein the existing process is capable of satisfying all of the business demands that arise. The SPI cycle only restarts when the appropriate *Business Event* triggers the necessity for change.

The second primary research question addressed in the study, *why are software companies not using 'best practice' SPI models* produced the study's core category *Cost of Process*. Implementing and maintaining any SPI initiative incurs significant cost. Participant companies perceive *Documentation* as the greatest process-related cost-inducing element. There was also a clear link between the amount of *Documentation* carried out and the size and growth stage of the company; the smaller the company the greater the hostility towards *Documentation*. However, even in the larger organisations, *Documentation* was regarded as a 'necessary evil'. Many companies substituted verbal *Communication* for *Documentation*, and co-located their development teams in an effort to reduce process cost. A benefit of doing this was an increase in the sharing of *Tacit Knowledge*.

From the commercial SPI perspective, the study was dominated by two particular models CMMI and ISO 9001, and the development methodology XP. Respondents did not differentiate between processes and methodologies and categorised XP as a process. As a result, XP, albeit tailored to various degrees, was by far the most popular commercial 'process' model used by organisations across all size sectors. XP was perceived to have the least associated *Cost of Process* and its low level of *Documentation* was deemed to be attractive. Where managers were familiar with CMMI or ISO 9000 they were against introducing it to their new organisations. Overall, respondents felt that the resources required to implement the commercial models far exceeded the benefits that may accrue.

6 Discussion

This section will briefly discuss two issues central to this paper: The suitability of Grounded Theory as a research methodology for the SPI researcher and the implications of the research study findings.

Software engineering is a highly social activity. In attempting to study human behaviour and the social contexts in which it functions, the researcher is directed towards qualitative techniques. In seeking an appropriate methodology to investigate the software process aspects of software engineering we have selected grounded theory as being a suitable candidate and describe the successful implementation of grounded theory in a study of SPI. The grounded theory approach is inductive, pragmatic and provides a highly concrete methodology [18]. Using grounded theory in the software engineering context, the researcher's task is to generate theory from holistic data gathered through naturalistic inquiry, to understand the interaction between software engineers and their environment and the impacts, consequences and outcomes of these interactions. Researchers can use grounded theory to 'reality test' their own theories of action and the relationships between action and effects can serve to take researchers into the empirical world so that they can discover whether what they think to be the nature of the empirical world is really the case. It is our contention that grounded theory is both an appropriate and valuable methodology for the software engineering researcher, specifically for exploring and understanding the action and interaction between practitioners and their environment, in relation to software process and SPI.

The findings presented in this paper are potentially significant to software entrepreneurs who will need to make decisions about process and process change within their organisations as they grow. The theory presented here represents a form of 'experience road map' illustrating some of the potential pitfalls an Irish software product company could face and how others have avoided or resolved them. With respect to the rejection of CMM/CMMI and ISO 9000 by Irish software product companies, it is the associated *Bureaucracy* which needs to be addressed to help increase acceptance. Both models rely heavily on documentary evidence in respect of certification. However, the study practitioners believe that *Documentation* is no proof of capability. Perhaps therefore, if the models had an increased emphasis on non-documentary evidence, in relation to the development practices followed, they would have greater appeal to practitioners. Furthermore, CMM/CMMI is firmly wedded to the belief that better processes mean better products. But many of the small Irish software product companies are merely concerned about getting a product released to the market as quickly as possible. As noted in [1] *Quality* is not the most important thing in this environment, rather time to market and innovation are key. It is development models such as those in the agile family, rather than CMM/CMMI, which support these objectives. Until models are adapted to take account of this reality, they will remain largely ignored by a great portion of the software development community.

References

[1] Baskerville, R. and Pries-Heje, J., 1999, 'Grounded Action research: A Method for Understanding IT in Practice', Accounting, Management & Information Technologies, No. 9, pp. 1-23.

[2] Bertelsen, O.W., 1997, 'Towards a Unified Field of SE Research and Practice', in IEEE Software, November/December, pp. 87-88.

[3] Bryman, A., 2001, 'Social research methods', Oxford University Press.

[4] Burns, R. B., 2000, Introduction to Research Methods, 4th Edition, Sage Publications.

[5] Carvalho, L., Scott, L. and Jeffery, R., 2005, 'An Exploratory Study into the Use of Qualitative Research Methods in Descriptive Process Modelling', in Information and Software Technology, No. 47, pp. 113-127.

[6] Carver, J. and Basili, V., 2003, 'Identifying Implicit Process Variables to Support Future Empirical Work', in Journal of the Brazilian Computer Society, October-December.

[7] Creswell, J. W., 2003, 'Research design: Qualitative, quantitative, and mixed methods approaches' (2nd ed), Sage.

[8] Firestone, W. A., 1987, 'Meaning in method: The rhetoric of quantitative and qualitative research', Educational Researcher 16(7), 16-21.

[9] Glaser, B., 1992, Basics of Grounded Theory Analysis: Emergence Vs Forcing, Mill Valley, CA, Sociology Press.

[10] Glaser, B. and Strauss, A., 1967, The Discovery of Grounded Theory: Strategies for Qualitative Research, Chicago, Aldine.

[11] Goede, R. and De Villiers, C., 2003, 'The Applicability of Grounded Theory as Research Methodology in Studies on the use of Methodologies in IS Practices', in Proceedings of SAICSIT, pp. 208-217.

[12] Goulding, C., 1999, 'Grounded Theory: Some Reflections on Paradigm, Procedures and Misconceptions', Technical Working Paper, University of Wolverhampton, UK.

[13] Goulding, C., 2002, Grounded Theory: A Practical Guide for Management, Business and Market Researchers, Sage Publications.

[14] Hansen, B. and Kautz, K, 2005, 'Grounded Theory Applied – Studying Information Systems Development Methodologies in Practice', in Proceedings of 38th Annual Hawaiian International Conference on Systems Sciences, Big Island, HI.

[15] Lee, A.S. and Liebenau, J., 1997, 'Information Systems and Qualitative Research', in Proceedings of Information Systems and Qualitative Research, eds. A. Lee, J Liebenau and J.I. DeGross, Kluwer Academic, Boston, MA.

[16] Muhr, T., 1997, Atlas TI User's Manual, Scientific Software Development, Berlin.

[17] Myers, M.D., 1997, 'Qualitative Research in Information Systems', in Management Information Systems Quarterly, Vol. 21, No. 2, June, pp. 241-242.

[18] Patton Quinn, M., 1987, 'How to use Qualitative Methods in Evaluation', Sage.

[19] Power, N., 2002, 'A Grounded Theory of Requirements Documentation in the Practice of Software Development', PhD Thesis, Dublin City University, Ireland.

[20] Qureshi, S., Liu, M. and Vogel, D., 2005, 'A Grounded Theory Analysis of e-Collaboration Effects for Distributed Project Management', in Proceedings of 38th Annual Hawaiian International Conference on Systems Sciences, Big Island, HI.

[21] Reichardt, C. S., & Cook, T. D. (1979). Beyond qualitative versus quantitative methods. In T. D. Cook & C. S. Reichardt (Eds.), Qualitative and quantitative methods in evaluation research (pp. 7-32). Beverly Hills: Sage.

[22] Sarker, S., Lau, F. and Sahay, S., 2001, 'Using an Adapted Grounded Theory Approach for Inductive Theory Building About Virtual Team Development', in The Data Base for Advances in Information Systems, Vol. 32, No. 1, pp. 38-56.

[23] Schreiber, R.S., 2001, 'The 'How To' of Grounded Theory: Avoiding the Pitfalls', in 'Using Grounded Theory in Nursing', Schreiber, R.S. and Noerager Stern, P. (Eds.), Springer.

[24] Seaman, C. and Basili, V., 1997, 'An Empirical Study of Communication in Code Inspections', in Proceedings of the 19th International Conference on Software Engineering.

[25] Seaman, C., 1999, 'Qualitative Methods in Empirical Studies of Software Engineering', IEEE Transactions on Software Engineering, Vol. 25, No. 4.

[26] Strauss, A. and Corbin, J.M., 1998, Basics of Qualitative Research: Techniques and Procedures for Developing Grounded Theory, 2nd Edition, Sage Publications.

Improving the Software Problem Management Process: A Case Study

Marko Jäntti[1] and Kari Kinnunen[2]

[1] University of Kuopio, Department of Computer Science,
P.O Box 1627, 70211, Kuopio, Finland
mjantti@cs.uku.fi
[2] TietoEnator Forest&Energy Oy, Microkatu 1,
P.O Box 1199, 70211, Kuopio, Finland
kari.kinnunen@tietoenator.com

Abstract. This paper describes the results of a case study focusing on improving the software problem management process in TietoEnator Oyj. The research question is what kind of challenges are related to the software problem management process. As main findings, we show a list of challenges identified during the study. Those challenges include the increasing number of open and duplicate problems in the problem database, difficulties in combining existing problem management concepts with ITIL-based concepts, a lack of performance metrics such as incident turnaround times, and a lack of knowledge base. The main contribution of this study is to help IT organizations to identify the challenges and problems that are related to ITIL-based problem management.

1 Introduction

One of the most important goals of software process improvement (SPI) is identifying challenges and problems with current processes. In this paper, we focus on software problem management process that is categorized into support and maintenance processes in the ISO/IEC standard [1]. Implementing a systematic problem management process is an effective way to improve customer satisfaction. Many IT organizations have started to adopt a problem management model described by the IT Infrastructure Library (ITIL) because of the following reasons: firstly, ITIL is a most widely accepted de facto standard for IT service management [2]. Hence, organizations have started to update their current processes to the ITIL-compliant processes because their customers require it. Secondly, IT organizations see ITIL as a way to decrease operational costs and increase the quality of services and customer satisfaction.

Problem management has two different dimensions: 1) proactive and 2) reactive problem management. The purpose of the proactive problem management is to prevent incidents and problems before they occur. An incident can be defined as "any event which is not part of the standard operation of a service and which may cause a reduction in the quality of that service" [2]. Reactive problem control focuses on identifying the underlying cause of reported incidents.

I. Richardson, P. Runeson, and R. Messnarz (Eds.): EuroSPI 2006, LNCS 4257, pp. 40–49, 2006.

Proactive problem management methods include problem analysis based on the incident/problem history recorded in the knowledge base. *Knowledge base* is a repository that contains information on known errors and their solutions [3]. Customers and end users have usually a restricted access to the knowledge base that is maintained by the service desk and problem management teams [4].

The functions of software problem management partly overlap with those of software defect management. Many studies have explored software defect management activities such as defect causal analysis method [5], implementation of the defect management process [6], defect measurement checklists [7], and creating defect profiles for application modules [8]. Similarly, previous studies have emphasized the role of the causal analysis in identifying the root cause of the defects and problems [9], [10]. Many organizations use the Capability Maturity Model (CMM) to improve software processes. The level 5 of CMM includes defect management as a key process area [11]. While software defect management methods are more often used by software developers and testers, software problem management is performed by the service desk, maintenance and support teams.

However, few studies have dealt with software problem management. Sandusky and Gasser have focused on a distributed software problem management process and its phases [12]. Kajko-Mattsson et al. combine software problem management with corrective maintenance [13], [14] and state that service level agreements are useful for monitoring service quality issues between IT providers and customers [15]. Further research is needed to gather information on field experiences with software problem management.

This study continues the previous work where we examined the use of a UML-based test model in identifying software problems [16], [17]. More recently we proposed a conceptual model of IT service problem management. In this paper, the results of the validation of the problem management model in a case organization are presented. Several challenges were identified during the model validation. As main findings of this paper we present a list of the challenges regarding the ITIL-based problem management. Identified challenges include, for example, dealing with duplicate incidents, mapping ITIL concepts and existing business concepts, a lack of performance metrics, unnecessary datafields in problem records, and availability problems of the online support site.

The rest of the paper is organized as follows. In Section 2 we describe the research method of this study. In Section 3 findings of the case study are presented. Section 4 is the analysis of findings. The discussion and the conclusions are given in Section 5.

2   Research Methods

This case study is a part of the work of the research project SOSE (Service Oriented Software Engineering) at the University of Kuopio, Finland. SOSE is funded by the National Technology Agency TEKES, the European Regional Development Fund (ERDF), and four partner companies. The study was carried out during SOSE problem management pilot project (January - March 2006), which focused on improving problem management methods in TietoEnator Oyj, Forest&Energy.

The research question in this paper is what kind of challenges are related to the improving the software problem management process. Figure 1 shows the general research plan for developing the problem management model. In phases 1 and 2, we examined how different organizations perform defect management and problem management activities and identified bottlenecks regarding those activities. In the third phase, we presented an improved problem management model based on the ITIL. The main purpose of this study is to describe the challenges that we identified during the validation of our software problem management model.

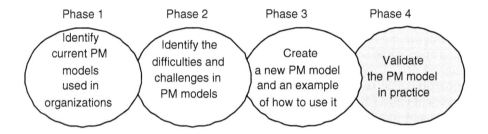

PM = Problem Management

Fig. 1. The research plan for developing the problem management model

A case study research method was used because it is well suited for the study of information systems in organizations. A case study is "an empirical inquiry that investigates a contemporary phenomenon within its real-life context [18].

2.1   A Case Organization and Data Collection Methods

TietoEnator is one of the largest IT service companies in Scandinavia with over 15 000 employees. It supplies information systems to various industries, such as banking and insurance, energy, telecom and media, and healthcare.

The methods used to examine the improvement of software problem management have included 1) direct observation (participation in support team meetings, the support tool training provided by the tool supplier and ITIL training), 2) open discussions with a problem manager, a customer support manager and service desk workers, 3) participative observation (meetings related to improvement of the knowledge base with a service desk worker and a research assistant), 4) access to the incident/problem management tool (participating in configuring the user interface of the knowledge base during the problem management study). Support team meetings included persons who held different roles within the organization (configuration management, service desk, problem management). During personal discussions participants were encouraged to identify problems that decrease their productivity.

2.2 Data Analysis Methods

A within-case analysis technique was used in this study to analyze data from the case organization [19]. In the data analysis, we created first a list of challenges and bottlenecks in the case organization's problem management process. For each challenge, we defined the source who reported the issue within the case organization. For some challenges, there were several sources. Then, the vision state was defined, and tasks or activities required to solve the challenge were determined. Additionally, we analyzed why it is important to solve these challenges or problem areas. Finally, we analyzed how the organization could improve its support processes in general level. The process improvement was based on the process framework of ITIL [6] that consists of the following questions:

1. Where are we now? What are the difficulties or bottlenecks in the current problem management process?
2. Where do we want to be? What is the vision state and business objectives?
3. How do we get where we want to be? What are practical means to reach the vision state?
4. How do we know we have arrived? What metrics can be used to measure the process?

We use the first three steps in Section 3.2. First, the process bottleneck (problem) is defined. Then, we propose how the process should work and present business benefits for the process change. Finally, we present a practical solution to eliminate the problem.

3 Empirical Findings

This section presents our main findings from the case organization. In this study, we explored the strengths and challenges regarding the problem management process of the case organization. After challenges and bottlenecks were identified, we analyzed how we can solve them and defined the rationale (benefits) why it is important to resolve challenges.

3.1 The Strengths of the Problem Management Process

Besides challenges, several positive observations were made regarding the problem management process of the case organization. The first strength was that the roles and responsibilities of problem management, incident management, and change management were clearly documented in the organization's business framework called WayToExcellence (W2E). The second strength was that the case organization provides already customers with online support site where customers are able to browse FAQs and reported cases. The third strength was that the organization had started to train both management and workers effectively for process changes. Several managers of the business unit had participated in ITIL practitioner and foundation courses. ITIL awareness training was organized for ordinary workers. Finally, we found that the support tool used by the organization is easy to configurate for various business needs without programming.

3.2   The Challenges in the Problem Management Process

The following challenges were identified regarding the case organization's problem management process. Abbreviations after the issues refer to the source of the reported issue: AU=Author, SD=Service Desk, PM=Problem Manager, SM=Service Support manager, CU=Customer (an energy company), SA=System Analyst (product delivery unit). The source of the issue was documented in order to clarify roles of different actors in identifying challenges.

1. Combining ITIL concepts to the existing business concepts is difficult. ITIL-based concepts such as known errors and knowledge base articles are not included in the current problem management process. Additionally, there is no knowledge base available for the service desk or customers at the moment (AU).
2. There is an increasing number of duplicate or open incidents and problems in the database (AU, SD, PM, SM).
3. Problem management and Service Level Management have no connection (SM, AU, PM). There is no Service Level Manager or templates for Service Level Agreements.
4. There is no category for errors in third party products in the incident/problem record (AU).
5. Incident/problem records include some datafields that are never used (SD, PM, SA, SM, AU).
6. The connection between testing and problem management is unclear in the current process (PM, AU).
7. Incidents and problems can not be linked to hardware configuration items (AU).
8. Several customers have complained about problems with the availability of the web-based support service site (CU, SD).
9. The information required by the support and maintenance teams is stored on separate locations but is not linked to the support tool (SA, AU).
10. Service desk workers have difficulties in assigning certain cases to other teams (a lack of guidelines how to use different types of actions in the support tool)(SD).

1) The first challenge is related to the lack of a known error concept. Problems should have a known error status after the work around/solution has been found. There are two solutions to the first challenge: first, adding a new case type (Known Error) and second, designing and implementing a knowledge base. The benefit of solving the first challenge is that resolved problems and errors with resolution data are stored in the knowledge base that is available for both the service desk and customers. Thus, it is possible to conduct a more powerful search for known errors, problems, and solutions. The knowledge base helps the organization to learn from the experiences [20] and transfer the knowledge quickly to the organization [21].

2) The second challenge is the increasing number of similar incidents and problems recorded in the datastore. Similar incidents and problems should be

combined or merged by the service desk using the support tool. The solution to this challenge is to train support staff to use Merge Cases and Relate Cases functions. Hence, it is possible to close several incidents by resolving one problem.

3) The third challenge is the disconnection between problem management and service level management. Service level requirements should be defined for problem management such as target resolution times for incidents and problems. We recommend as a solution that the case organization appoints a professional service level manager that is responsible for creating SLA templates and defining the monitoring system for SLAs. Somebody must be trained to configure the SLA module of the support tool and SLA rules related to SLA templates. As a result, it is possible to negotiate SLAs with customers and monitor whether SLAs are met or breached.

4) The fourth challenge relates to the missing category for errors in third-party products and services. The problems and errors caused by third party products should be recorded by the service desk of the case organization. A simple solution to this problem is to create new category "Error in third party product". The benefit is that problem management is able to monitor errors in third party products more effectively and collect information to support decision making whether service providers meet the required quality standards.

5) The fifth challenge addresses the issue that incident/problem records inlude too many datafields that reduce the productivity. Problem records should include only the fields that are really important. The recommended solution is to organize the meeting with important stakeholders to identify which data fields are really needed. As a benefit, recording incidents and problems will be faster and more effective.

6) The sixth challenge is the unclear connection between testing and problem management. Problem records, error records and change records should include references to test cases, for example, a test case id to maintain the traceability chain. The simplest solution is to add a new datafield *test case id* that is a link to the test case record. Another way is to insert the whole description of the test case(s) to the problem record. As a benefit, customers can easily see that changes and errors have been tested.

7) The seventh challenge relates to the monitoring problems in hardware configuration items. Organization needs a problem or error category that includes errors in application components, hardware components, and third party products. The recommended solution is similar than in the challenge number 4: a new data field "category" is added to the incident and problem records. The benefit of a category field is that problems can be linked to the hardware components such as servers and third party components such as database components and service packs.

8) The eighth challenge needs very careful investigation. The customers of the case organization have complained a couple of times that the online support service site is not working. The root cause of the problem is the internal server that is maintained by another business unit within the case organization. The

solution to the challenge is to create an operational level agreement (OLA) between business units defining reliability and availability requirements for the support site service. The benefit is the decreased number of service outages concerning the support site and the increased level of customer satisfaction.

9) The ninth challenge is also very important issue addressing that the information required by problem solving: bug fixes, quick deliveries, release notes, user instructions are stored in separate locations and are not linked to the support tool. The recommended solution is to use a knowledge base module (see Figure 2) of the support tool as a common datastore for known errors, user instructions, delivery notes, and release notes. The benefit is that the service desk is able to find solutions to problems more rapidly from the knowledge base than by browsing a large number of folders.

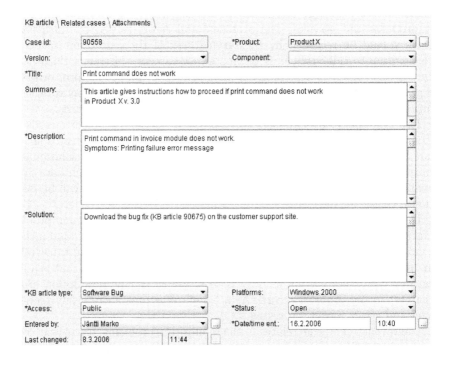

Fig. 2. A knowledge base record

10) The last challenge emphasizes the importance of clear instructions for service desk and product support teams such as how to handle a simple service request or one that requires information from a specialist, how to manage change orders, development ideas and other incidents, who is responsible for closing incidents, and how to relate incidents and problems. The benefit is that service desk and product support are able to classify incidents rapidly and assign them to specialist teams. Hence, the number of open incidents should decrease.

4   Lessons Learned

Implementing an ITIL-based problem management model seemed to be more difficult task than expected although the problem management process (roles, responsibilities, and activities) was well-described in the organization's business framework. Several challenges were identified during the study. The following list of lessons learned is based on our case study results. Firstly, a large part of challenges were somehow related to the support tool. Introduction of new tool features such as a knowledge base module and service level agreement module requires both time and patience. Some of the process bottlenecks (adding new and deleting unnecessary datafields) can be easily solved by making simple tool configurations. The tool might require a lot of configuration work before it can be used to measure the quality of service (e.g. incident turnaround times, cases per period metrics).

Secondly, the service desk and problem management teams need clear instructions how to manage different incident scenarios such as what are the rules for handling different types of service requests. Additionally, it is important to define who are responsible for recording data on incidents, problems, and known errors, how to change a status of the incident, or how to classify and categorize incidents and problems.

Thirdly, managers have to allocate sufficient resources to proactive problem management to prevent incidents and problems before they occur. Focusing on proactive problem management is more useful than perform only reactive actions (correcting a large number of repetitive incidents, problems, and errors).

Fourthly, the case organization needs a service level manager to design and implement a service level management process including methods of service level monitoring. It might be hard to create SLA rules based on the priority levels of incident and problems because customers and end users tend to consider each incident as a critical incident.

Fiftly, organizations can use the knowhow of external stakeholders (e.g. university researchers and consults) to enhance process improvement. However, it takes several months to learn how processes work, how business concepts are related to each other and how challenges and problems regarding processes could be solved. Finally, the cooperation with international business partners creates challenges to business and to problem management. Solving and reporting problems with foreign business units requires more efforts than one with domestic units.

5   Discussion and Conclusions

This paper described the results of a case study focusing on improving the problem management process in TietoEnator Oyj, Forest&Energy. Our findings show that improving a problem management process based on ITIL principles requires a lot of efforts and might cause several tool-related and process-related challenges. However, tool-related challenges can often be solved by making simple configurations such as changes to the user interface of the support tool. It is more difficult to solve process-related challenges such as to create a common datastore for the support and maintenance or implement an effective service level monitoring system. Clear instructions for handling problems play also an important role in process improvement. The challenge is how to produce guidelines that cover various scenarios of incident and problem handling.

As with all case studies, there are threats to the validity of this study. First, construct validity is problematic in case study research. We tried to avoid problems with construct validity by collecting data using several sources of evidence: by investigating the problem management tool, participating in support team work, and collecting information based on informal discussions. Second, we have taken into consideration the threat to external validity (the generalizability of the results). In future work we are going to examine whether the results of this study are generalizable to other organizations such as small-sized IT service providers.

The main contribution of this study is to help IT companies to identify difficulties in implementing ITIL-based problem management model. In future studies we intend to improve our research framework by examining proactive problem management methods such as how to build an effective knowledge base for known errors.

Acknowledgment

This paper is based on research in the SOSE project (2004-2006), funded by the National Technology Agency TEKES, European Regional Development Fund (ERDF), TietoEnator Corp., Savon Voima Oyj, Softera Solutions Oy, and DNA Finland Oy.

References

1. ISO/IEC 12207: Information Technology Software Life-Cycle Processes. ISO/IEC Copyright Office (1995)
2. Office of Government Commerce: ITIL Service Delivery. The Stationary Office, UK (2002)
3. Jackson, A.L., Lyon, G., Eaton, J.: Documentation meets a knowledge base: blurring the distinction between writing and consulting (a case study). In: SIGDOC '98: Proceedings of the 16th annual international conference on Computer documentation, New York, NY, USA, ACM Press (1998) 5–13
4. Saunders, A.: Online solutions: looking to the future of knowledgebase management. In: SIGUCCS '04: Proceedings of the 32nd annual ACM SIGUCCS conference on User services, New York, NY, USA, ACM Press (2004) 194–197
5. Mays, R.G., Jones, C.L., Holloway, G.J., Studinski, D.P.: Experiences with defect prevention. IBM Syst. J. **29**(1) (1990) 4–32
6. Office of Government Commerce: ITIL Service Support. The Stationary Office, UK (2002)

7. Florac, W.: Software quality measurement a framework for counting problems and defects. Technical Report CMU/SEI-92-TR-22 (1992)
8. Hirmanpour, I., Schofield, J.: Defect management through the personal software process. Crosstalk, The Journal of Defense Software Engineering (2003)
9. Leszak, M., Perry, D.E., Stoll, D.: A case study in root cause defect analysis. In: ICSE '00: Proceedings of the 22nd international conference on Software engineering, New York, NY, USA, ACM Press (2000) 428–437
10. Zhen, J.: It needs help finding root causes. Computerworld **39**(33) (2005) 26 ID: EBSCO Academic Search Elite.
11. Jalote, P.: CMM in Practice, Processes for Executing Software Projects at Infosys. Addison-Wesley (2000)
12. Sandusky, R.J., Gasser, L.: Negotiation and the coordination of information and activity in distributed software problem management. In: GROUP '05: Proceedings of the 2005 international ACM SIGGROUP conference on Supporting group work, New York, NY, USA, ACM Press (2005) 187–196
13. Kajko-Mattsson, M.: Problem management maturity within corrective maintenance. Journal of Software Maintenance and Evolution - research and practise **14**(3) (2002) 197–227 Article; English; ID: Web of Science (ISI).
14. Kajko-Mattsson, M., Forssander, S., Olsson, U.: Corrective maintenance maturity model (cm3): maintainer's education and training. In: ICSE '01: Proceedings of the 23rd International Conference on Software Engineering, Washington, DC, USA, IEEE Computer Society (2001) 610–619
15. Kajko-Mattsson, M., Ahnlund, C., Lundberg, E.: Cm3: Service level agreement. In: ICSM '04: Proceedings of the 20th IEEE International Conference on Software Maintenance, Washington, DC, USA, IEEE Computer Society (2004) 432–436
16. Jäntti, M., Toroi, T.: Uml-based testing: A case study. In: Proceedings of NWUML'2004. 2nd Nordic Workshop on the Unified Modeling Language, Turku: Turku Centre for Computer Science (2004) 33–44
17. Kruchten, P.: The Rational Unified Process: An Introduction. Addison-Wesley (2001)
18. Yin, R.: Case Study Research : Design and Methods. Beverly Hills, CA: Sage Publishing (1994)
19. Eisenhardt, K.: Building theories from case study research. Academy of Management Review **14** (1989) 532–550
20. Garvin D.A: Building a learning organization. Harward Business Review (1993) 78–91
21. Gasston, J., Halloran, P.: Continuous software process improvement requires organisational learning: An australian case study. Software Quality Control **8**(1) (1999) 37–51

A Framework for Overcoming Supplier Related Threats in Global Projects

Darja Šmite and Juris Borzovs

Riga Information Technology Institute
Kuldigas 45b, LV-1083, Riga, Latvia
{Darja.Smite, Juris.Borzovs}@riti.lv

Abstract. The process of globalization expands with each year along with the growing complexity of software development. Outsourcing transforms a common way of producing software to distributed software life cycle activities among teams separated by various boundaries, such as contextual, organizational, cultural, temporal, geographical, and political. Risks associated with these boundaries make managers struggle with pressures unique to this type of environment. In this paper we describe a research that aims to investigate the nature of global risks and build a comprehensive and easy to use framework for risk management. We emphasize the necessity of awareness about global factors and threats that distinguish distributed projects and require adequate attention throughout the project.

1 Introduction

1.1 Global Software Development

While the process of globalization expands with each year, complexity of software development grows. The concept of global software development (GSD) addresses distribution of common software life cycle activities among teams separated by various boundaries, such as contextual, organizational, cultural, temporal, geographical, and political. Risks associated with these boundaries make managers struggle with pressures unique to this type of environment [9, 13].

Although global work is not a new phenomenon, distributed software development is relatively new. Global Software Work (GSW) described by Sundeep Sahay et al. [13] is recognized as still an unexplored form of work and is enabled through organizational forms quite distinctive from traditional global arrangements as typified by large multinational corporations. It extends the concept of traditional outsourcing (the practice of subcontracting manufacturing work to outside [11]) through involving complex interdependencies between the teams involved in a joint software development life cycle. Virtual product development is recognized as considerably more complex, than even the most complex project managed entirely in house [9].

The importance of timely risk management in the extremely dynamic and diverse environment of global software development grows. Global risks are recognized as just the part of everyday existence that cannot be avoided, that must be confronted on a continuous basis [13]. On the other hand, lacking expertise and experience precludes effective risk identification.

R. Messnarz (Ed.): EuroSPI 2006, LNCS 4257, pp. 50–61, 2006.
© Springer-Verlag Berlin Heidelberg 2006

This paper describes research results on global software development project threats and provides an introduction to a framework that addresses risk management practices for global risk elimination.

1.2 Research Context and Motivation

Most of research in the area of global software development was conducted mainly from the customer's perspective because the objective of outsourcing was to self-maximize their internal resources without taking into account the service provider's situation [7]. Subsequently, there is still a lack of research on how achieve effective performance in distributed environment [10]. Motivated by its industrial background and market demand, the research described in this paper focuses on outsourcing service supplier related risks.

The research takes place in one of the largest software houses in Latvia that is involved in global collaboration (custom and product software development as either a direct supplier for foreign customers, as an associate contractor or as a subcontractor for a related prime contractor). The research is motivated by a necessity of global software development projects performance improvement. The nature of projects and their success is not stable. The projects suffer from lack of common practices addressing global risks and unpredictable performance. In addition, a single study conducted within the company uncovered problems with knowledge and awareness transfer [17]. As a result, it becomes difficult to introduce a new inexperienced project manager to the corporate culture of managing distributed projects.

1.3 Concepts of Risk Management

As the terminology in the area of risk management is inconsistent and does not allow a precise vision of project risk [3, 5], we first define the concepts being used.

Risk management activities are directed to systematically identifying, analyzing, and responding to risks throughout the project life cycle before they turn into problems. The term "risk" and related concepts "risk factor" and "risk exposure" are exploited by various authors differently. In this paper we use the term "risk" to describe an uncertain future event that has a potential for negative effect on a project objective. Although some authors and frameworks, including Project Management Body of Knowledge (PMBOK) [12], combine the ideas of risks and opportunities, it argues with the well-established concepts used by practitioners. Therefore, we use the term "event" meaning an occurrence of a threat and its negative consequences on project objectives.

Threats can be defined as items or activities that have potential for negative consequences. Consequences include but are not limited to unexpected management costs, customer cost escalation, budget overrun, late product delivery, time delays, customer dissatisfaction, undermined morale, disputes and litigations.

For risk prioritization we calculate risk exposure as a probability of risk occurrence multiplied by its magnitude (assessment of negative effects of a risk):

$$\textbf{Risk exposure} = \text{probability (risk)} \times \text{magnitude (risk)}$$

To illustrate these definitions, let's consider an example.

- -

Poor communication, that has potential to endanger the project schedule, is a threat for a project. It can lead to time delays and cause late product delivery. Time delays and late product delivery are consequences of poor communication. Accordingly we can say that the project has 2 risks:

- *Time delays due to poor communication;*

- *Late product delivery due to poor communication.*

In order to quantify risk exposure, we have to assume different values of the consequences, in other words, evaluate risk magnitude. This is necessary, because each of these risks (possible event) has potential to different significance of the time delays and size of the slip of product delivery, and has its own probability of occurrence.

- -

However, the nature of threats can be more complex. One threat can lead to another, which can lead to another … etc. This produces a hierarchy of threats. The threat that initiates the hierarchy is called a root threat.

- -

A good example to illustrate the risks hierarchy would be exploring the causes of poor communication. Poor communication can be caused e.g. by distance between the virtual teams, by language differences, and poor cultural fit.

- -

In this paper we discuss global threats as threats that endanger software projects in distributed environment, and their potential consequences. We highlight global factors as roots of global threats (e.g., geographical distribution being the root of various threats, such as dominant use of asynchronous communication and increased costs of holding face to face meetings). In the same way as in the threat hierarchy, a global factor can cause several global threats, and a global threat can be caused by several root threats or global factors. We emphasize global factors because they characterize the difference between in-house software development projects and global projects.

The paper is organized as follows. The next section provides insight in how the theory on global threats was built. Research results are described in section 3. Section 4 provides an overview of the proposed framework for global risk management. The paper ends with a discussion (section 5), conclusions and future work (section 6).

2 Research Overview

In this paper we describe an ongoing research project which aims to answer the following research questions:

- What is the nature of global software development?
- What are the GSD project threats?
- How to assist project managers in managing global threats?

2.1 Approach

The entire research is run as an action research [8] - "learning by doing" - which aims to improve global software development projects in the investigated company. In practice project managers involved in the research help to identify the problems faced by their projects, investigate possible solutions, test them in project environments and learn from experience. Researchers play the role of "coaches" supporting practitioners in risk management activities. Knowledge and experience is being accumulated for further utilization in a database that is developed according to the concepts referred to as Experience Factory [4].

In order to investigate the nature of global software development projects, an exploratory study has been performed aiming to derive the major global threats. Grounded theory building methodology developed by Glaser and Strauss [6] was chosen as the basis for the study. This methodology introduces a qualitative approach that generates theory from observation [14].

Theory-creating studies are very suitable for exploratory investigations, i.e., when there is no prior knowledge of a part of reality or a phenomenon [8]. Grounded theories, because they are drawn from data, are likely to offer insight, enhance understanding, and provide a meaningful guide to action [15].

The study started with the definition of the phenomenon under study – GSD project risk management. Thereafter a theory was evolved grounded by systematically gathered and analyzed data about the phenomenon. The data was gathered from a variety of sources, including interviews [16] and enhanced analysis of related literature. Data analysis was performed according to principles prescribed by a grounded theory through applying open, axial, and selective coding techniques [14], also called as theoretical sampling. A Lotus Notes-based database was used for data storage and further analysis facilitating in easy categorization.

Application of grounded theory in more detail is described in the next section.

2.2 Theory Building

Data sources. Various data sources were used for building the theory, including interviews with experienced project managers, research literature (journal articles, papers form conference proceedings), and books on global software development. The data was gathered from a variety of sources, including interviews and field observations [16] and enhanced analysis of related literature.

We have chosen to interview project managers from different business units in the organization, from projects with different destinations (customer countries). These project managers were advised by the business unit managers to be the most experienced in global projects, by this providing representative input for the research. The interviews were written down for further analysis.

Data analysis. To start analyzing the data we used open coding for data breaking down and examining, comparing, conceptualizing and categorizing. While examining data sources, items related to risk management in GSD projects were identified and labeled. These items and their context (total of 253 GSD related issues) were then stored into the database. Each issue at the beginning was represented by a single label.

Then we analyzed the existing labels in order to identify issues that are similar in meaning. They were then grouped under more general concepts called "categories".

- -

E.g., the categories "Cultural barriers", "Cultural distance", and "Poor cultural fit" were coded under a joint category "Poor cultural fit".

- -

This reduced the number of GSD related categories to 163.

By analyzing the existing categories we identified, that many issues are related between each other and form cause-effect interconnections. We have used axial coding for deriving connections between the existing categories and the risk management concepts, during which the identified GSD related issues from open coding were categorized into a hierarchy of sub-categories as follows:

- Global factors – root of global threats, that distinguish global projects;
- Global threats – items or activities that have potential for negative consequences and result from one or a combination of global factors (Customer related threats and Supplier related threats);
- Consequences – an outcome of a threat (Customer related consequences and Supplier related consequences);
- Practices – recommendations for risk treatment (Customer related practices and Supplier related practices).

Then selective coding was used for systematically validating relationships and filling in categories that need further refinement and development. During axial coding we discovered that some of the existing categories have to be reconsidered. For some categories identified during open coding this meant dividing into two or even more categories.

- -

E.g., the category "E-mail communication causes time delays and misunderstandings" was divided into "E-mail communication" – a threat, and "Time delays" and "Misunderstandings" – consequences. "E-mail communication" was then united with one of the more general existing categories – "Asynchronous communication". The relations between these three categories were then produced.

- -

Customer related issues were not analyzed in detail at this point. But we kept the data for a possibility to analyze it in future. In addition, we have chosen only those threats that appeared more than once, i.e. the threats that are strongly dependent on particular environment were omitted. New versions of records were processed, saving the history and notes reflecting the decisions within the database.

Results. Grounded theorizing resulted in 7 global factors, 32 supplier related threats, 7 supplier related major consequences and 32 supplier related practices.

As the theory was built, we concluded that the most valuable results refer to global factors and threats. In its turn consequences and relationships between the global factors, threats and consequences are weak and inconsistent. Therefore, further research steps aim to empirically validate these considerations and improve the theory.

3   Research Results

3.1   Global Factors

The following are global factors or root threats that have been derived:

- Geographic distribution - distance that separates the participating teams;
- Socio-cultural differences - diversity in social, ethnic, and cultural gospel;
- Time zone differences - temporal distance, level of working hours overlay;
- Language differences - linguistic diversity;
- Multisourcing - multiple team involvement in a single life cycle;
- Contextual differences - organizational differences, diversity in process maturity, inconsistency in work practices, goals and expectations;
- Cross border transaction - political and legislative diversity.

3.2   Global Threats Within Taxonomy

We highlight the importance of global threats. The identified issues can be used in GSD projects during risk management to identify threats for further evaluation. Aiming to facilitate risk management in global projects, we have chosen to use the taxonomy of software development risks, developed by Software Engineering Institute (SEI) [2]. We have applied a taxonomy-based approach for threat identification in a set of the company's projects earlier and received positive references.

The SEI developed taxonomy-based risk identification method facilitates the systematic and repeatable identification of threats associated with development of software dependent projects. Taxonomy organizes software development threats into 3 levels – class, element, and attribute. The major classes are: A. Product Engineering, B. Development Environment, and C. Program Constraints.

We used SEI proposed taxonomy to classify the uncovered global threats. SEI taxonomy is developed to support risk management in different kinds of software development projects, while our aim was to facilitate risk management in global projects. The Program Constraints class of the SEI taxonomy contains an element called Program Interfaces, which consists of attributes such as Customer, Associate Contractors, Subcontractors, Prime Contractor, and other. The nature of distributed projects, in fact, prescribes these attributes to be a part of the project work environment. However, we didn't want to produce one more version of an existing taxonomy. Thereby, we prescribe that the risks identified within the Work Environment element's attributes (such as Cooperation, Communication, and others) in global projects shall also focus on all related collaboration partners (Customer, Associate Contractors, Subcontractors, Prime Contractor).

While mapping the identified threats onto the SEI taxonomy components, we identified that some of the threats overlap with the taxonomy's elements or attributes; other can be sub-categorized under one or more taxonomy's attributes.

The following global threats caused by the previously discussed global factors have been identified and classified within the taxonomy (see Table 1).

The results show that most of the identified threats address Work Environment issues (14 threats) and Management Process and Methods issues (9 threats). This relates to the distinguishing nature of the distributed projects and indicates the areas of concern for global project management.

Table 1. Global Threats within the Taxonomy

A. Product Engineering	
1. Requirements	• Poorly defined or inconsistent SRSs
c. Clarity	• Terminology differences
2. Design	• Poorly defined / inconsistent design or architecture
B. Development Environment	
1. Development Process	
b. Suitability	• Poor/disadvantageous distribution of SW life cycle activities
c. Process Control	• Increased level of unstructured poorly-defined tasks • Relatedness with other suppliers
d. Familiarity	• Lack of experience with outsourcing projects
3. Management Process	• Increased level of complexity of project management
a. Planning	• Increased complexity of project/activ./resource planning • Relatedness with other suppliers
b. Project Organization	• Supplier's complex hierarchy / several escalation levels • Poor/disadvantageous distribution of SW life cycle activities
c. Management Experience	• Lack of experience with outsourcing projects
d. Program Interfaces	• Lack of clarity about responsibility share • Lack of joint risk management • Increased level of reporting on project progress to the contractor • Relatedness with other suppliers
4. Management Methods	• Increased level of complexity of project management
a. Monitoring	• Poor or complex project measurement
d. Configuration Management	• Poor artifact version control
5. Work Environment	
b. Cooperation	• Lack of trust and commitment • Lack of team spirit • Belief that the work cannot be done from a far location • Poor socio-cultural fit • Prime contractor employees' unwillingness to collaborate caused by threat of being fired due to switching to outsourcing mode

Table 1. (*continued*)

	• Lack of common goals • Lack of understanding of each other's context of decision making • Diversity in process maturity/inconsistency in work practices
c. Communication	• Lack of language skills of the supplier employees • Dominant use of asynchronous communication • Increased virtualness between the parties • Prime contractor's complex hierarchy / several escalation levels • Time zone difference
d. Morale	• Prime contractor employees' unwillingness to collaborate caused by threat of being fired due to switching to outsourcing mode • Lack of trust and commitment • Lack of team spirit
C. Program Constraints	
1. Resources	
a. Schedule	• Relatedness with other suppliers • Faulty effort estimates
b. Staff	• Lack of experience with outsourcing projects
c. Budget	• Faulty effort estimates • Incr. cost of logistics of holding face to face meetings
3. Program Interfaces	
a. Customer	• Poor/disadvantageous distribution of SW life cycle activities
b. Associate Contr.	
c. Subcontractors	• Lack of experience with outsourcing projects
d. Prime Contractor	

3.3 Consequences

We find consequences rather dependent on project environment. In our study we identified the following supplier related negative consequences in the project results that are used for threat magnitude evaluation: Unexpected management costs; Budget overrun; Customer costs escalation; Time delays; Late product delivery; Customer dissatisfaction; Undermined morale; Disputes and litigations. However, this list can be enlarged by other potential consequences for a given project to be evaluated.

3.4 Global Practices

We have gathered 32 different supplier related practices through this study to support project managers during the process of risk treatment. Most of the practices facilitate proactive project management at the beginning of distributed collaboration. Some practices help to avoid global threats, other mitigate the magnitude of their consequences or probability of occurrence.

4   Experience Factory and Risk Management

We have developed an Experience Factory based on a Lotus Notes tool to provide users with various functions, including global threat description and categorization according to various keywords; risk treatment experience generalization; new issue proposal; templates and checklists for risk management; discussions; notifications; wide searching opportunities.

However, Experience Factories are recognized as rarely used. Therefore, to motivate the reuse of existing practices accumulated in our database, we have integrated it into the process of risk management (see Fig. 1).

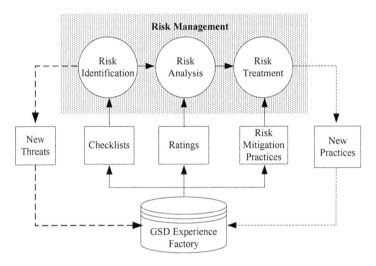

Fig. 1. Risk Management Scheme [16]

Recognized as a means for stimulating effective knowledge interchange, "coaching" is used to assist project managers in organizing risk management activities. It provides an opportunity for effective organizational learning by supporting knowledge dissemination from the Experience Factory along with continuous improvement of risk management processes within the organization.

The Experience Factory also helps to introduce new software development projects and project managers with earlier experiences.

5   Discussion

5.1   Global Factors and Threats

Global software development puts new demands on the software processes stressed by increased complexity of project coordination (through temporal and geographical distances), communication (lacking proximity and troubled by cultural diversity), cooperation (lacking trust and commitment), and infrastructure management (uniting heterogeneous contexts). Global factors, that have been derived, very precisely characterize the nature of distributed software development projects. These factors in fact form unavoidable elements that shall be analyzed throughout the project.

The identified global threats tend to be general. During the process of coding global issues, we aimed to avoid too detailed categorization of the threats to prevent the complexity of correlated threat hierarchy. We derived general concepts that are evaluated along with various consequences. This will also relieve the process of threat identification (too long checklists with odd issues are rarely used).

5.2 Future Project Management Within Globalization

The root of major global threats is hidden in the complex diversity of environmental elements of a global project, such as internal and external contexts, temporal and geographical distance, culture, and politics. Therefore, in order to eliminate the threats of a distributed environment, a strategy that addresses diversity minimization shall be implemented. A set of practices that helps to establish a common work environment for every team involved in the project shall form a shared domain for successful collaboration. This includes implementing adequate technological infrastructure (modern communication tools, fast connection channels, etc.) and achieving common understanding of goals, tasks, methods, cultural and moral expectations, etc. through organizing socialization workshops.

As globalization expands the "future software development workspace" will focus on supporting multiple distributed teams by minimization of distance and diversity between the virtual teams.

5.3 Threat Avoidance – Possible or Not?

It is worth to mention though that some of the threats cannot be eliminated.

- -

E.g. you can hardly exclude the cultural differences if they exist; however, being aware about them helps to preclude or eliminate misunderstandings and disputes. This is why experienced managers advise to train project personnel in soft skills.

- -

Subsequently, we emphasize the importance of being aware of global threats that endanger your project. Joint risk management involving every participating party in a distributed project is an essential practice for successful global project management.

6 Conclusion and Future Work

The nature of global software development brings forward new areas of concern that require careful attention from project managers. While practitioners lack standardized approaches to overcome these risks in global software development [16], various managers are experimenting and quickly adjusting their tactical approaches [12]. Threats caused by such unique factors as context diversity, geographical distribution, temporal and socio-cultural differences, cross-border transaction and multisourcing, not only make global projects different but can also lead to project failure if managed inadequately.

Marvin J. Carr describes [1] that as simple as it sounds, many organizations however are unable to manage risks effectively for any of the following three reasons:

- a risk-averse culture;
- an inadequate management infrastructure to support effective risk management;
- lacking systematic and repeatable method to identify, analyze, and plan risk mitigation.

The framework described in this paper provides all the necessary preconditions for successful risk management. In addition, the provided framework facilitates tacit knowledge accumulation and precludes loss of achieved experiences with the loss of human resources within the organization.

The current work within the research focuses on research results validation using global and in-house project surveys, however due to the limited length of this paper, we couldn't provide any detail on validation results.

This study is limited to focusing on global software development suppliers related risks and can be further enlarged by investigating the customer related risks.

Acknowledgements

The author appreciates valuable research input received from the project managers within the investigated software house.

This research is partly supported by European Social Fund and the Latvian Council of Science project Nr. 02.2002 "Latvian Informatics Production Unit Support Program in the Area of Engineering, Computer Networks and Signal Processing".

References

[1] Carr M.J., "Counterpoint: Risk Management May Not Be for Everyone", IEEE Software, Vol.30 No.5, 1997, pp. 21,24

[2] Carr M., Kondra S., Monarch I., Ulrich F., Walker C., "Taxonomy-Based Risk Identification", CMU/SEI-93-TR-6, ADA266992, SEI, Carnegie Mellon University, Pittsburgh, June 1993

[3] Dedolph F. M. "The neglected management activity: Software risk management". Bell Labs Technical Journal, Vol. 8, Issue 3, 2003, pp. 91-95

[4] Dingsøyr T., "An Evaluation of Research on Experience Factory", Workshop on Learning Software Organisations at the 6th Int. Conf. on Product Focused Software Process Improvement (PROFES), Oulu, Finland, pp. 55 – 66

[5] Émond C., "From Donald Rumsfeld to Little Gibus... "Revisited": Understanding and managing risks and other project uncertainties", Le Bulletin, PMI Monteral, Vol. 15, No 2., December 2005, pp.8-11

[6] Glaser B., Strauss A. "The discovery of grounded theory: Strategies of qualitative research", Wiedenfeld and Nicholson, London, 1967

[7] Jae-Nam Lee et al, "The Evolution of Outsourcing Research: What is the Next Issue?", In the Proc. of the 33rd Hawaii Int. Conf. on System Sciences, 2000

[8] Jarvinen P. "On research methods", Opinpajan Kirja, Tampere, 2001

[9] Karolak D.W., "Global Software Development: Managing Virtual Teams and Environments" , IEEE Computer Society, 1998

[10] Loh, L., Venkatraman, N. "An empirical study of information technology outsourcing: Benefits, risks, and performance implications". In Proc. of the 16th Int. Conf. on Information Systems, 1995, Amsterdam, the Netherlands, pp. 277-288

[11] Merriam-Webster Online Dictionary, www.m-w.com

[12] Project Management Institute, "A Guide to the Project Management Body of Knowledge: PMBOK guide. – 3rd Edition", ISBN 1-930699-45-X, 2004

[13] Sahay S., Nicholson B., Krishna S., "Global IT Outsourcing: Software Development across Borders". Cambridge University Press, 2003

[14] Strauss A., Corbin J. "Basics of qualitative research – Grounded theory procedures and techniques", Sage Publications, Newbury Park Ca, 1990

[15] Strauss, A., Corbin, J., "Basics of qualitative research: Techniques and procedures for developing grounded theory". Thousand Oaks, CA: Sage Publications, 1998

[16] Smite D., "A Case Study: Coordination Practices in Global Software Development", In Proc. of the 6th Int. Conf. on Product Focused Software Process Improvement (PROFES), Springer, Oulu, Finland, June 2005, pp. 234-244

[17] Smite D., Moe N.B. "An ISO 9001:2000 Certificate and Quality Awards from Outside – What's Inside? – A Case study" accepted for publication in proc. of the 7th Int. Conf. on Product Focused Software Process Improvement (PROFES), Amsterdam, the Netherlands, June 2006

Three Case-Studies on Common Software Process Problems in Software Company Acquisitions

Jarmo J. Ahonen[1], Anne-Maria Aho[2], and Hanna-Miina Sihvonen[1]

[1] Department of Computer Science
University of Kuopio
P.O. Box 1627
FI-70211 Kuopio, Finland
{jarmo.ahonen, hanna-miina.sihvonen}@uku.fi
[2] School of Information and Communication Technology
Seinäjoki University of Applied Sciences
Kampusranta 9 A
FI-60320 Seinäjoki, Finland
anne-maria.aho@seamk.fi

Abstract. In this article three cases of small or medium sized software companies acquiring companies of the same or smaller size are analyzed from the software process point of view. The analysis shows that the problems in those acquisitions are fairly common and the types of those problems are fairly similar in different cases. Although those acquisitions have the potential to satisfy their goals of complementing or improving the product portfolio or the customer base of the companies, the actual success of the acquisitions may not be as good as expected. The main reasons for the relative unsuccessfulness of the analyzed cases seem to be the lack of proper planning for the merger and communication problems which hinder effective and high-quality work in the new post-acquisition organization.

1 Introduction

It seems to be a law of the nature that bigger software companies buy smaller software companies. In some cases both the buyer and the bought are not very large companies and in some extreme cases a smaller company buys a larger one. The use of acquisitions as the way to grow may look very tempting in the current business environment in which the mad days of the dot-com mania are over and an annual growth of 20 % of the turnover is not a bad performance at all. Such acquisitions are not, however, as rosy for software companies as one might assume.

The acquisition of another company may be the means of growing the turnover of the purchasing company, or the means for getting the customer base of the acquired company, or the means for getting the product portfolio of the acquired company in order to make the purchaser's product portfolio more complete. In addition to the acquisition of a complete company it is possible to buy only certain parts of the other company. For buying just a part of another company the reasons for the purchase are the same as for buying a complete company. In the case that only a part of a company

R. Messnarz (Ed.): EuroSPI 2006, LNCS 4257, pp. 62–73, 2006.

is sold, the relative sizes of the purchasing company and the purchased business may be of almost any combination.

It is a well-known fact that most of the business acquisitions fail due to the uncompromising difficulties in merging the acquired company or business into the acquirer. Most of those studies are, however, of big companies purchasing each others. Only a few of those studies of mergers or acquisitions cover software engineering oriented businesses. The possibility of success is not much better in the case of software companies. An illustrative story of the possible problems and mistakes that can be made in merging software engineering businesses is outlined in [1]. The story illustrates the fact that in the case of software engineering organizations the nature of the software engineering work may make the merging even more difficult. That is at least partly due to the fact that software engineers are specialists who do creative work. The companies discussed in [1] are not, however, from the smallest size of companies that purchase each others. In this article the most interesting type of software companies are small or medium sized software engineering organizations that purchase each others.

Three separate cases of a small or medium sized software engineering organizations acquiring another software engineering organization of a smaller or a quite similar size are analyzed in this article. Turning the acquired business into a seamlessly incorporated part of the acquirer failed at least in some respects in every one of the analyzed cases, and the reasons for all of those failures were related to the difficulties of incorporating different software engineering processes and the mistakes made during the attempted incorporation. The problems were practically identical in every case and were caused by communication problems and misunderstandings.

In this paper the features of those failed incorporations are outlined, analyzed and discussed. The surprising similarity of the cases is pointed out and the common mistakes made in every case are outlined and analyzed. The structure of this article is as follows: Section 2 represents the settings of the studies, Section 3 outlines how the data on the cases was collected and briefly outlines the data, Section 4 consists of an analysis and Section 5 is the discussion.

2   Research Question and Background

The reason why the reported studies were performed was — in every case — the substandard quality of the software produced by the post-acquisition company. In every case the quality had dropped after the merger and the estimated benefits had not been achieved as expected. The aim of each of the individual studies was to find out the current state of the merger and to propose relevant corrective activities. Only one of the authors was involved in every case — although with a couple of other people who did not wish to participate in the article writing process.

The cases were analyzed independently and the companies that were involved did not know about each other. They were interested in finding practically usable solutions for their real problems, but they agreed to scientific reporting if their identities would not be revealed. The research situation was set up as individual consulting projects. The aims for those projects were to find out

1. What went wrong?
2. What are currently the most serious problems?
3. What steps should be taken in order to resolve the most serious problems?

Although the companies do not wish to be identified, some of the background of each of the cases must be presented in order to make the cases understandable. Those backgrounds are vague, but that vagueness is intentional and required in order to publish the results.

In every case the rationale of the acquisition decision had been based on a careful analysis of the market situation and the bought company. The rationales for the acquisitions are outlined in Table 1. From the table it should be noted that in all cases the role of the products acquired through the purchase was important but the role of the customer base was not considered relevant in one case. Although the authors of this article have got the impression that many of the similar purchases are made in order to get rid of existing competition, only one of the analyzed cases fell into that type of purchases.

In all cases the insufficient level of quality had not been an issue for some time, in every case the acquisition had been performed from two to three years ago and quality problems had crept in during that time. At least in one case the reason why no attention had been paid to the quality problems had been the previous management of the acquiring company. In other cases similar reasons could be guessed due to the fact that corrective or analytic actions had been decided to be taken only after at least some of the top-management people had changed in every company.

In Case A the merger had been successful in the sense of technology transfer. The technological leadership of the bought company had been successfully transferred to the acquiring company. That technology transfer was brilliantly done and had been the main reason for the current successfulness of the new combined company due to the fact that the strong but technologically out of date product portfolio of the acquiring company had been successfully updated to the same technological level as the products of the purchased company. The excellent quality of the products of the acquired company had, however, deteriorated after the merger. Therefore the management wanted to find out what had happened and what could be done.

In Case B corrective actions were sought after the owners of the company had changed. During the previous owners and the previous management such actions were not actively pursued. It is not known why that was, but it can be assumed that the personal relations of the management and the owners prohibited any critical analysis of the decisions made by the owners who were actively participating in running the company. After the ownership of the company changed the new management was much keener on getting software engineering activities up to the task.

In Case C the problems were a bit different. The quality of produced software had also deteriorated but the original products of the acquired company were to be phased out in a few years. The deteriorating software quality might not have been a major issue if its impact would have been mainly on the original products of the purchased company. The deteriorating software quality was considered a major issue because the lack of quality was especially evident in those products and projects that were performed by using the technology of the purchaser. In addition to that, even the customer base acquired through the purchase had started to fall apart.

Table 1. The rationale of the acquisition decision

Rationale	Case A	Case B	Case C
Strengthen the product portfolio.	Yes. The bought company was the technology leader.	Yes. The bought company had products that are necessary for the business and were lacking from the buyer's portfolio.	Yes, but not a major way.
The role of the bought company.	Technology leader.	The only independent provider of similar products.	Master of marketing in its niche.
The role of the customer base of the bought company.	Irrelevant because the customers of the bought company were already customers of the buyer.	A well-come bonus.	The most important factor.
The relation between the buyer and the bought before the deal.	Deepening cooperation.	Cooperation. The bought company sold its products as parts of larger systems provided by the buying company. Other providers of compatible products were scooped up by the competition of the buying company	Competition.
Improved presence in the international market.	Buyer already present in all important markets.	Buyer already present in all important markets.	Improved access to one important market.
The software engineering resources of the bought company.	Very valuable and necessary for keeping up the technology leadership. In addition to that, it was planned that the buying company would adopt the technology acquired through the deal and gradually stops using its own technological architecture.	Very valuable due to the fact that the buyer's staff had no knowledge of the internals of the products of the bought company.	Relevant, because the required domain knowledge is scarce. The products and the technology of the bought company were to be phased out over time and replaced by new products that would conform to the buyer's technological decisions.

In other words: none of the acquisitions had fulfilled its original promise. All mergers were plagued with quality problems. Two of the cases also showed some signs of problems with the customer relations and the size of the customer base. Therefore the managements of the companies in question were seriously concerned and the search for the reasons of the problems was a priority.

3   Research Method and Data Collection

The research method used in all cases was a combination of case-specific analysis and action research [2]. When the researcher's intention is not only to observe, interpret and understand a case, but also participate in the efforts of changing the situation of the case, the approach can be described an action case research. In all cases the studies were performed as consulting cases, not as academic research although the permission to publish academic results was obtained from every company involved.

In all process-improvement oriented approaches the first step is to get an overview of the actual situation. In order to get that overview a sufficiently detailed but relatively light-weight procedure was performed. The procedure consists of three steps that were:

1. The modeling of the actual information flows in the organization.
2. The modeling of the actual software engineering processes of the organization.
3. Interviews of several members of the staff of the organization.

The actual information flows were modeled by using the technique outlined in [3]. The technique was used in its original form and with some variations. The variations included the modeling of information flows between different roles and different geographical locations. The modeling technique was, however, similar to the original technique — the diagonal matrix technique was used in all cases.

The software engineering processes were modeled by using the light-weight technique described in [4]. The most important aspects of that approach are its light-weight nature and its informal nature. Due to those features that modeling technique has turned out to be very effective in revealing the real software engineering processes and their problems, see e.g. [5] and [6].

The modeling workshops were directed by the researchers in every case, although the researchers were working under a commercial agreement and were called consults. It is, however, worth to note that only one of the authors participated in every case and therefore there might be some slight variation in the flow of the events. In addition to that it must be noted that the author who participated in every modeling session did not act as the chairman in all modeling sessions.

During the information-flow modeling sessions the relative number of the software engineers and other relevant staff members who participated in the sessions were 70%, 91% and 83% for Case A, Case B, and Case C, respectively. That is, of course, possible only in fairly small software organizations. In the analyzed cases the total number of software engineers in the post-acquisition organizations was about 120, 50, and 70 for Case A, Case B and Case C, respectively. In Figure 1 a part of a wall-chart produced during a modeling session is shown. In order to get the permission to use the picture we had to paint over most of the texts. That is regrettable but understandable from the company's point of view.

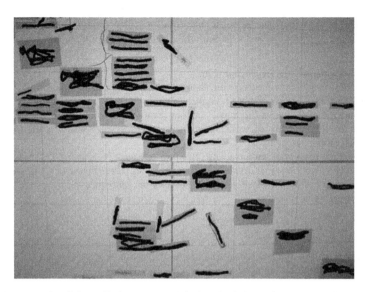

Fig. 1. An example of the wall-charts created during the information flow modeling sessions

The process-modeling sessions were also based on the use of wall-charts. The reason for the use of the technique was its familiarity to both the staff of the companies and the researchers. The problems with modeling processes with this technique are outlined in [4]. The most difficult issue with process modeling turned out to be the fact that in some cases the concept of a process was not familiar to everyone and there really were no standard ways to perform various activities. The lack of standard processes was manifested in quite illustrative discussions between the software engineers. It must be noted, however, that the "software engineers" who participated in the sessions included software engineers, project managers and involved members of the management. The percentages of the relevant staff that participated in the sessions were about the same as for the information flow modeling sessions.

After the information flow modeling sessions and the process modeling sessions the models were written into electronic forms and sent to the representatives of the company in question. The companies added missing knowledge to the models and changed them in some degree. In only one case the additions were substantial, namely in Case C. In other cases the additions were only cosmetic. The reason why there were so many additions required in Case C is not known to the authors. After the companies had corrected the models of information flows and processes a subset of the staff of the companies were interviewed. The subset was selected by the management of the company in question.

The interview questions were based on the results of the modeling sessions and were somewhat different to every company. The difference can, however, be thought only superficial because the questions were based on the problems and difficulties encountered or revealed in the modeling sessions, and those problems were surprisingly similar in all cases, as will be seen later on. The basic structure of the interviews was the one shown in Figure 2. The case-specific interviews were surprisingly similar despite the fact that the case specific information flow models and process models were used as background in order to tune the contents of the interviews.

1. How many people belong to your team?
2. How many products or projects your team manages in a six-month period?
3. Please describe your work during a typical month.
4. What are the main quality hindrances in your team and the company in general?
5. Which are the strengths of software engineering processes, issues or parts in your team and the company in general?
6. What are the tools your team is using? Are they adequate?
7. How is your working time divided between different tasks? Please describe the tasks and the time you use for each task. Please use at least the following tasks:
    – creating new products
    – maintaining old products
    – fixing bugs
    – testing
8. Do you think that the amount of training (tools, methodologies, domain training, or any other type training) is enough?
9. What kind of training would you like to get?
10.How should software quality be improved in your company?
11.How would you like to improve your working environment?
12.Do you have any personal concerns regarding your job?

Fig. 2. The basic structure of the interviews

After the information flow models and the process models were accepted by the representatives of the company in question and the interviews were analyzed the results were combined into company-specific reports in which the situation was analyzed and corrective steps proposed. In the following section the analysis and the steps are outlined on a level that has been accepted by the companies.

4   Analysis and Proposed Improvements

The analysis of the situations in each case was performed by using the collected information and additional material provided by the company. In this section the common features of the cases are analyzed and discussed. Case specific features are mentioned only in the case that they are especially interesting.

In every case the acquisition had been performed at least a couple of years ago. Despite that fact the structure of the companies had not been changed to reflect the new situation. The original situation in which the companies and the processes of the companies had been separate was present in every case. That separation was clearly illustrated in the information flow models. An illustration of the problem outlined by the models is shown in Figure 3.

The diagram in Figure 3 shows that the flow of information is directed through a central role, Role G (the diagram is not one of the real models, it has been created for clarifying the problem). Such a central role existed in Case A, Case B, and Case C. In the central role there was either a member of the previous management of the acquired company or a new manager appointed by the acquiring company. In every case

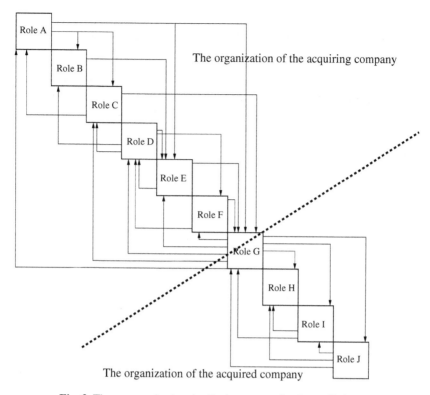

Fig. 3. The communication deadlock common for the studied cases

the manager had started to slow down the flow of information and hence his/her role had started to build up a deadlock which severely affected the smoothness of software engineering processes. It must, however, be noted that the deadlock was not a result of the manager's intentional activities. The problem was a natural result of the setting of the situation in which no specific attention had been paid to the integration of information flows.

The process modeling sessions in which the software process of both the acquirer and the acquired were modeled showed quite a similar situation. Although there was no deadlock in the same way as in the case of information flows, the software engineering processes were still surprisingly dissimilar. The lack of similarity was shown in the processes, and the different break-down structure of the tasks and the work products in individual projects. The differences made it very difficult to find specific documentation or to compare the state of a project. At the time of the reported studies there were no plans for making the processes and documentation standards similar in any of the companies.

The differences in the process models and software engineering methodologies were a serious issue. In Case A and Case C the companies had been implementing software process improvements for several years before the acquisition. The software process improvement models used by the companies were not the same, in Case A the acquirer had been using CMM(I) and the acquired company had been using SPICE. In

Case C both of the companies had been using SPICE. Neither the acquirer nor the acquired company in Case B had been performing any specific software process improvement activities. The software process improvement models are not very easy to
combine and the lack of a transition plan caused difficulties. Additional confusion
was caused by the fact that in every case the software engineering methodologies
were based on different methodological models like RUP [7] and OMT++ [8], or
there were significant company specific modifications made into the basic model provided by RUP. In one case there was a completely home-grown methodology which
just used UML [9] as the notation. The software engineering methodology has its effects on the thinking of software engineers and the definitions of the processes of the
company.

Due to various reasons, of which some have been mentioned above, the processes
that were used for the same purpose were very different in every case. Therefore the
procedures and even the process infrastructure of the companies were surprisingly different. There were no plans to incorporate the process infrastructures and make the
processes uniform at the time of the study. In order to realize the benefits of the acquisition a situation in which there would be similar process models and methodologies used throughout the post-acquisition company must be achieved. For the reason
the promises of the acquisitions had not been achieved.

The interviews added surprising flavors to the situation. In Case A and Case B the
software engineers in the acquired organization felt that the new management had
forgotten them. The reasons for that feeling were lack of training, lack of coordination
with other development projects, and lack of information. In Case C the most prominent feeling was insecurity, the engineers thought that their jobs were not very secure
and the fate of the pre-acquisition products would be a reliable estimate of their own
fate.

Another issue that was clear from the interviews was the surprisingly large cultural
differences between the acquirer and the acquired in every case. In Case A the acquired company was the technology leader, or at least very near that position, and the
culture in that company was engineer driven. The acquiring company in Case A was,
and still is, more oriented towards thinking in which cooperation with customers and
close relations with the representatives of the customers and especially trust were val-
ued over technical mastership. Differences like that are not easy to overcome.

In Case B the acquiring company was at least as much a master of technology as
the acquired company. In that case the most remarkable differences were in the management culture. The acquiring company was, and still is, managed by people appointed by a large multinational owner that allows remarkable freedom if business
goes well, and the acquired company was managed by its entrepreneur owner who
acted as the CEO. The atmosphere of the acquiring company was very professional
and straightforward and the managerial infrastructure of the company has been tuned
to work very fast but according to the rules. In the acquired company the entrepreneur
knew everybody personally but managed the company according to his whims without any regard to the rules he had set himself.

The companies in Case C were a different story because the takeover was hostile in
the sense that the acquiring company was buying a nuisance out of the market. Both
of the companies were managed by their owners before the deal and the management

cultures were not as different as in other cases. The situation, the life after a hostile take-over, made the atmosphere awkward and the lack of trust obvious.

It was reasonably easy to propose necessary improvement steps to be taken in each case. The interesting feature of all cases is that several of those improvement steps are common. Those common features were not expected due to the fact that the settings of the cases were at least superficially different as listed in Table 1. The superficial differences were, however, only the surface and the real problems were fairly similar.

The first type of common recommendations was geared towards removing the communication deadlock between the acquirer and the acquired parts of the companies. The problem illustrated in Figure 3 was actually quite easy to remove at least in principle. The proposed improvements were to

- allow direct communication between different parts of the company;
- change the regional structure into a process oriented one in which processes are not restricted into the original company boundaries;
- reconsider the need for the manager who acted as the communication deadlock;
- create and implement a well-thought and detailed plan for incorporating the different processes and practices.

All improvement steps would cause changes in the power structures of the companies. The empowerment of software engineers makes some types of management unnecessary, which is the reason why some types of software process improvement steps are difficult to achieve [10]. Direct communication and the dismissal of the regional structure are difficult steps to implement due to the required changes in the power structure of the company. The creation and implementation of the plan for incorporating the different processes and working cultures is also fairly difficult to do because a fair and sustainable plan would include best practices selected from both the acquirer and the acquired.

It is interesting to note that the aims set for the acquisitions, as shown in Table 1, were not unrealistic, but the acquisitions had not been satisfactory the time of the study. The business aims had not been achieved. Our opinion is that the reason for the problems was that some pre-planning and reconfiguration activities had been neglected. This is contrary to the experience that successful acquisitions are results from careful planning and reconfiguration activities, and the acquired operations are not left to operate within their original boundaries [11].

Typical pre-acquisition activities are for example following: surveys of political attitudes, investigations of competitive environment, analyzing the similarities between corporate goals of the acquirer and the firm to be acquired, searching for similarities in management policies between the two firms and similar items that span the whole spectrum of the business [12]. In the analyzed cases those activities had not been performed in the way and magnitude which is required in order to perform a successful acquisition. The performed pre-acquisition activities had been able to identify viable business reasons for the acquisitions, but the other parts of the pre-acquisitions analysis had been left undone.

One of the common features of the analyzed cases was that the human issues had not been properly handled in any case. The acquisition decisions were justified, but the analysis had stopped before touching issues like the company cultures and the differences in other people-oriented aspects of the companies. It seems that the soft issues outside the hard business facts and technological issues had not been considered at all. It would be interesting to know whether such neglect is common to information technology companies or have the analyzed cases just been extraordinary bad examples.

5 Discussion

It is very difficult to get a company acquisition to work. The history of company mergers seems to be a history of failures. It is not, however, a law of the nature that mergers of companies are failures. There is no such law even in the case of information technology companies. It is possible to get a merger working, although that requires careful planning, hard work, and probably a bit of luck. All of those things are required before and after the actual acquisition.

In order to get an acquisition to work at least some typical pre- and post-incorporation activities have to be performed. Typical pre-acquisition activities include at least surveys of political attitudes, investigations of competitive environment, analyzing the similarities in management policies between the companies. The following post-incorporation activities typically include a well-thought plan to coordinate managerial activities, encouraged cooperation among employees and units, technology transfer, assessing the degree of adaptation of acquired firm to the organizational culture of the acquirer etc [12]. In the analyzed cases those activities had not been performed in any systematic way if at all.

The cases analyzed in this article make one to wonder whether it is especially common for information technology companies to neglect the considerations of soft issues when planning and implementing business restructuring. Technical issues are easier to understand and plan for, but the soft side of companies is not easy to tackle. The lack of considerations of the soft issues could explain at least some of the failed acquisitions in the software industry. It is, however, quite difficult to draw general conclusions after analyzing only three cases. Obviously additional cases have to be analyzed and if the neglect of soft issues seems to be more general, then our attitudes to managing and organizing software operations should change.

References

1. Ahonen, J.J., Sihvonen, H-M.: How things should not be done: A real-world horror story of software engineering process improvement. In Richardson, I., Abrahamsson, P., Messnarz, R., eds.: 12th European Conference on Software Process Improvement, EuroSPI 2005. Volume 3792 of Lecture Notes in Computer Science., Springer-Verlag (2005) 59-70

2. Järvinen, P.: On Research Methods. Opinpajan Kirja, Tampere, Finland (2001)

3. Karjalainen, A., Päivärinta, T., Tyrväinen, P., Rajala, J.: Genre-based metadata for enterprise document management. In: Proceedings of the 33rd Hawaii International Conference on System Sciences, HICSS'00, Washington, DC, USA, IEEE Computer Society (2000) 3013-3022

4. Ahonen, J.J., Forsell, M., Taskinen, S.K.: A modest but practical software process modeling technique for software process improvement. Software Process Improvement and Practice 7 (2002) 33-44

5. Ahonen, J.J., Junttila, T., Sakkinen, M.: Impacts of the organizational model on testing: Three industrial cases. Empirical Software Engineering 9 (2004) 275-296
6. Ahonen, J.J., Junttila, T.: A case study on quality-affecting problems in software engineering projects. In: Proceedings of 2003 IEEE International Conference on Software — Science, Technology & Engineering, SwSTE'03. (2003) 145-153
7. Jacobson, I., Booch, G., Rumbauch, J.: Unified Software Development Process. Addison-Wesley, New Yor (1999)
8. Jaaksi, A., Aalto, J.M., Aalto, A., Vättö, K.: Tried & True Object Development: Industry-Proven Approaches with UML. Cambridge University Press, Cambridge (1999)
9. Booch, G., Rumbaugh, J., Jacobson, I.: The Unified Modeling Language User Guide. Addison-Wesley, New York (1999)
10. Zahran, S.: Software Process Improvement. Addison-Wesley, London (1998)
11. Karim, S., Mitchell, W.: Innovating through acquisition and internal development: A quarter-century of boundary evolution at Johnson & Johnson. Long Range Planning 37 (2004) 525-547
12. Yeheskel, O., Newberry, W., Zeira, Y.: Significant differences in the pre- and post incorporation stages of equity international join ventures (IJVs) and international acquisitions (IAs), and their impacts on effectiveness. International Business Review 13 (2004) 613-636

Simple Indicators for Tracking Software Process Improvement Progress

Anna Börjesson

Ericsson AB and IT University of Gothenburg, Lindholmspiren 11, 417 56 Gothenburg,
Sweden
anna.borjesson@ericsson.com

Abstract. We know from the software process improvement (SPI) literature
that new technologies are often acquired, but not deployed. Fichmand and
Kemerer call this phenomenon the assimilation gap. Important prerequisites to
SPI success are SPI implementation success and SPI initiative progress. This
study presents four simple and practical indicators for SPI initiatives to stay
focused on deployment and facilitate SPI initiative progress. These practical
indicators are easy to gather, manage and evaluate and they provide an
organization with useful information to determine the progress of an SPI
initiative. The indicators focus on competence build-up, employee capabilities,
process adoption and management commitment. The result shows there are
simple and practical indicators for tracking and follow-up SPI initiatives'
progress to stay focused on deployment and decrease the assimilation gap.

1 Introduction

Already in 1978 Argyris and Schön argued there are espoused theories, a conception of
what one wants to do, and theories-in-use, action as actually performed. This theory
explains that there is a difference in what we think we do and what we actually do.
Fichman and Kemerer (1999) provide the software community with an understanding of
an existing assimilation gap similar to the difference in what we do and what we think
we do. Organizations do not manage to deploy potential improvements in the same
pace as they acquire them. Fichman and Kemerer argue an organization can err by
adopting the right potential improvements, but failing implement them in a way that
generates benefits. The successful improvement can be illusory. Organizations might
think they successfully improve, but they do something else.

Many promising reasons have been found that explain the assimilation gap, like
lack of management commitment (Abrahamsson, 2001), not understanding reactions
to change (Weinberg, 1997), knowledge barriers (Attewell, 1992), poor deployment
tactics (Börjesson and Mathiassen, 2004), and lack of agile methods (Dove, 2001;
Haeckel, 1999). The ultimate situation is of course not only to understand why there
is an assimilation gap, but also to make sure that the acquired improvements become
deployed to decrease the gap. Successful deployment requires successful software
process improvement (SPI) implementation, which then of course requires progress in
the SPI initiative.

R. Messnarz (Ed.): EuroSPI 2006, LNCS 4257, pp. 74–87, 2006.

Known SPI literature agrees on the necessity of measuring to understand and improve practice (Humphrey, 1989; McFeeley, 1996; Grady, 1992; 1997; Weinberg, 1993). Measuring is however expensive and must be considered as an investment (Humphrey, 1989). Most measurements also focus on the end result, i.e. understanding increased or decreased productivity, like costs, resources used, time spent and defects found. SPI is an approach to improve the software quality and productivity. It is therefore interesting to understand the progress in the ongoing SPI initiatives. We need to measure not only on current software practices, but also on the SPI initiatives that will provide us with our wanted future software practices. Measuring SPI initiatives' progress also keep attention to deployment, which is a prerequisite to decrease the assimilation gap (Fichman and Kemerer, 1999). It is also likely the high failure rate in SPI initiatives (SEMA, 2002) are related to this lack of progress in the SPI initiatives.

The current SPI literature provides us with little understanding of simple and practical measurements or indicators for tracking and follow-up SPI initiatives' progress. There are numerous reports on CMM appraisals (Bollinger and McGowan, 1991; SEMA, 2002), but also the CMM model and its appraisal methods are criticized for not having enough emphasize on measurements (Brown and Goldenson, 2004). Goethert and Siviy (2004) suggest a template that can help an organization to define indicators, or graphical representations of measurement data in general. The template addresses the importance of having progress indicators to know how well plans proceed. Goethert and Siviy's study provides however no actual practical suggestions for which indicators to use. Grady (1997) briefly suggests four baseline measurements for SPI programs to understand environmental aspects that have effect on the SPI initiatives' progress. Apart from this suggestion, the SPI literature provides little understanding of possible, simple and practical indicators for tracking and follow-up SPI initiatives' progress. The existing assimilation gap, the importance of measuring, the SPI initiatives' progress as a necessary prerequisite to SPI success, and the lack of simple and practical SPI progress indicators make it therefore interesting to find answers to the following question: What simple and practical indicators can be used to track SPI initiatives' progress?

The author has studied and participated in four different SPI initiatives over a five years period within the telecom company Ericsson AB in Gothenburg, Sweden, where four practical indicators for tracking and follow-up SPI initiatives' progress have been used. The indicators focus on competence build-up, employee capabilities, process adoption and management commitment. The result from the study indicates that there are simple and practical indicators to use to track and follow-up SPI initiatives' progress. The study is presented as follows. Chapter two presents the theoretical context, focusing on current understanding of indicators for software and SPI success. Chapter three describes the action-based research approach. Chapter four presents the SPI initiatives using the studied indicators and the outcome of this use. Chapter five discusses the contributions from this research and finally, chapter six presents the conclusions.

2 Theoretical Framing

It is today fairly well understood that the most effective way to improve the performance of an organization is by directly acting upon the processes it uses to achieve its results. The problem is to objectively measure the quality of a process (i.e. the ability of the process to produce good quality results) to see where you are today and to measure improvements. The first section (2.1) describes the current understanding of why measure and the second section (2.2) focuses on measuring software and SPI.

2.1 Why Measure

Software measurements play an important role in ensuring desired software quality. "As we face increasingly demanding software projects, we need to understand more precisely what we are doing and how to improve the effectiveness" (Humphrey, 1989, p. 301). Humphrey (1989) and Weinberg (1993) argue that data gathering is expensive and time-consuming, it affects the busiest people, it can be viewed personally threatening and there can be a considerable confusion on what data to gather and how to use it. It is also often a considerable delay before benefits is apparent. Grady (1992) argues software measurements are necessary to help us make better decisions. Software measurements are used to derive a basis for estimates, project progress, relative complexity, understanding when quality goals are reached, analyzing defects, and for validating best practices.

From the capability maturity model (CMM) (Paulk et al., 1995) we can further understand the difficulties measuring software implies. The key practices areas for measuring is found at level four – the managed level. Few companies ever manage to reach level four (SEMA, 2002). The maturity level four in the CMM is dedicated to explain goals, commitment, abilities and actions for measuring. To fulfil this level an organization requires having measurements for productivity and quality for the most important software project activities across all projects as a part of an organizational measurement program (Paulk et al., 1995). Despite of the known and accepted difficulties regarding measuring, there is no doubt that measuring is an important step toward increased software productivity and quality (Humphrey, 1989; Paulk et al., 1995, Weinberg, 1993). Without facts from measuring activities, presentations tend to be nothing more than yet another opinion.

2.2 Measuring Software and Software Process Improvements

Measuring software quality and productivity today relies heavily upon four distinct metrics: time, costs, size and defects found (Humphrey, 1989; Grady, 1992; Weinberg, 1993). Even though both time and cost can be measured in many different ways the major discussion within software measurements is focused on size and defects found. It has been shown very difficult to objectively measure software quality and productivity because of the subjectivity of software size (Flaherty, 1995; Humphrey, 1985; Jones, 1993; 1994) and software complexity (Albrecht and Gaffney, 1993; Albrecht, 1979).

Software measures are difficult to gather and even trickier to use and when applied on an organizational level, they are prone to misuse. It is however desirable to have some measures and we must not stop measuring (Humphrey, 1989). No literature argue for stop measuring software just because of all known difficulties, but the literature discusses what can go wrong (Humphrey, 1989; Grady, 1992) and claim when analyzing the measurements, one must understand we see indications rather than firm answers. It is therefore important to recognize indicators as satisfying measurements.

Software process implementation is a first and necessary step toward successful SPI (Börjesson and Mathiassen, 2004). Software process implementation does not alone assure SPI success, but without implementation SPI success is impossible. There are also many reports about SPI failures (Bach, 1995; Bollinger and McGowan, 1991; Börjesson and Mathiassen, 2004; Fayad and Laitinen, 1997; Humphrey and Curtis, 1991). It is therefore of highest interest to facilitate that ongoing SPI initiatives will be deployed, i.e. implemented and used. SPI initiatives need to be continuously measured to understand and communicate progress to be able to take corrective actions. To monitor the SPI programs and progress, a measurement system to evaluate progress must be in place (McFeeley, 1996). McFeeley argues the key to evaluate the SPI program will be the measurements that are selected and the ease with which they can be gathered. Grady (1997) states based on lessons learned from industry failure analysis activities, we seldom record adequate data to understand progress. This data is vital to understand environmental aspects that have effect on potential improvements (Grady, 1997). Grady suggests measuring what he calls "high-level information". These are measurements that affect the total result, not alone, but in combination with other measurements. Grady discusses the four measurements "percentage of team trained", "how extensively applied", "applied by the team before" and "team opinion value". Measuring high-level information will together with other distinguished measures contribute to understanding SPI initiatives' progress. Grady argues that these indicators are simple and cost-efficient to gather. These practical suggestions by Grady (1997) are one of the few found in the SPI literature today. The Goal Question Metric approach developed by Basili et al. (1994) can help identifying metrics for assessing new software engineering technologies and Abrahamsson's five dimensions (2000a) to measure SPI success can help identifying types of beneficial metrics. It is obvious we need to measure, but there are few simple and practical indicators guiding the SPI initiatives how to do it in practice.

3 Research Approach

This study has the dual goal of both improving how to track and follow-up SPI initiatives' progress and contributing to the body of knowledge in SPI about the same theme. The author has been actively involved in and responsible for the different discussed SPI initiatives. The author is also dedicated to a research program in a joint venture between Ericsson AB and the IT University of Gothenburg.

The study is based on action research (Baskerville and Wood-Harper, 1996; Galliers, 1992; Davison et al., 2004) with a focus on understanding how to track SPI progress. The research question is: What simple and practical indicators can be used to track SPI initiatives' progress? Baskerville and Pries-Heje (1999) argue that the fundamental contention of action research is that a complex social process can be studied best by introducing changes into that process and observing the effects of these changes.

The author collected data throughout the SPI initiatives as summarized in Table 1. Triangulation of data (Yin, 1994) has been important to avoid bias and to secure validity of the research. The combination of many different data sources has been important to make triangulation possible.

Table 1. Data collected throughout the studied SPI initiatives

#	What	Explanation
1	Direct involvement	The author has been directly involved in or responsible for the management and outcome of the discussed SPI initiatives, which gives primary access to the organization, personal opinions, coffee break discussion, etc.
2	Interviews with four SPI project managers	Each SPI project manager first answered a questionnaire with six questions about the used indicators. The SPI project managers were then interviewed for 30 min (occasionally more) to clarify and follow up on answers in the questionnaire.
3	Minutes of Meetings	The author attended steering group meetings where decisions about the SPI initiatives were taken,
4	Participatory observations	The author took the outsider role (Bartunek and Louis, 1996) at selected management and project meetings to view how data was discussed and used
5	Questionnaires to training participants	All training participants were asked a number of specific question (six grade scale answering alternatives from fully agree to fully disagree) I believe the course content and structure were clear I believe the exercises were valuable I believe I'm capable to start practicing the improvement I believe I can support and help my colleagues with the new practice
6	SPI initiative data	The author collected data from project meetings and final reports (time, participants, measurements, decisions, outcome, etc)
7	Tool data	Access to data in the tool to view who and how many that entered data in the tool and if they had followed the process

4 The Case

The first section (4.1) of this chapter describes the characteristics for the four studied indicators. The second section (4.2) describes the use of the indicators in the four studied SPI initiatives. The third and final section (4.3) describes the SPI project managers' evaluation of the use of the four indicators.

The indicators used and studied in this research project are closely related to Abrahamsson's second important dimension for measuring SPI success – the impact on the process user (2000a). Abrahamsson argues the level of success is characterized in terms of level of satisfaction with the new process and whether the new process actually is used. The indicators "training participation" and "perceived acquired know-how" map to level of satisfaction, while tool use map to actual use. The indicator "steering group participation" map to the identified need of management commitment (Abrahamsson, 2000b) to manage successful SPI projects. Table 2 shows the relation between the SPI initiatives and the used indicators.

Table 2. The relation between the studied SPI initiatives and the used indicators

		Indicator			
		Training participation	Perceived acquired know-how	Tool use	Steering group participation
SPI Initiative	Implementation of Rational Unified Process (RUP)	⬡	⬡		⬡
	Deployment of SPI principles		⬡		
	Implementation of a new change request process and tool			⬡	
	Implementation of model based software development	⬡	⬡		⬡

4.1 Characteristics of the Indicators

The training participation indicator was designed to keep exact track of who participated at which training occasion in major SPI initiatives aiming to change several competences for several different engineering roles at the same time. This indicator was also designed to make line managers committed to assure employee participation at training occasions and that it was possible to understand fulfilment of the training participation. Figure 1 visualizes the training participation indicator.

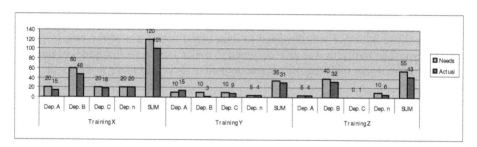

Fig. 1. Training Participation

The SPI project managers collected, from each affected line manager, the expected number of participators (needs in Figure 1) for each training occasion (training X, Y and Z in Figure 1). The SPI project managers then kept track of the number of participants at each training occasion and updated the data table after each training occasion (actual in Figure 1). This follow-up was done with help of prepared excel sheets. The training participation indicator made it possible for all interested, at all times, to follow up the progress of training participation.

The perceived acquired know-how indicator was designed to understand how valuable a given training occasion was. It was also designed to understand how well the new know-how was diffused among the participants for them to be able to start working according to the new know-how in ongoing development projects. Each training participant had to answer a questionnaire with a number of predefined questions with six grade answer possibilities (Table 1). Figure 2 visualizes the perceived acquired know-how indicator.

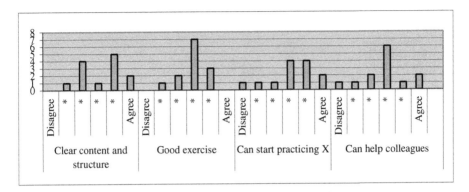

Fig. 2. Perceived Acquired Know-How

The SPI project managers assured that a predefined questionnaire (Table 1) was available at each training occasion to be filled in by all participants after the training was completed. The questions were defined as statements where the participant could both evaluate the value of the course and how he believed he could start working according to the new know-how. The SPI project managers then collected the questionnaires and updated the data table (excel sheet). This made it possible for whoever was interested, at all times, to follow up the progress of perceived acquired know-how.

The tool use indicator was designed to understand actual use of the new build up competence. The indicator was also designed to understand actual progress of the SPI initiative as tool use indicates SPI implementation success. Figure 3 shows the tool use indicator.

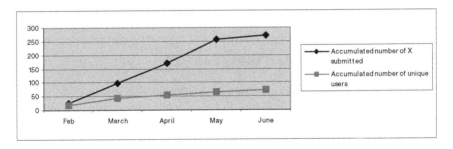

Fig. 3. The Tool Use Indicator

The SPI project manager regularly (per month) collected data through looking in the tool's databases on actual use. Figure 3 shows the number of unique users and the number of new submitted change requests in the tool. This measure makes it possible to follow-up who and how many that uses the new tool and also in some ways how they use it.

The steering group participation indicator was designed to keep track of how steering group members participated at steering group meetings where decisions about the SPI initiatives were taken. It was also designed to make it visual for the steering group members (mostly busy line managers) if they participated or not to make them understand that without participation, commitment to a decision is impossible. Figure 4 shows the steering group participation indicator.

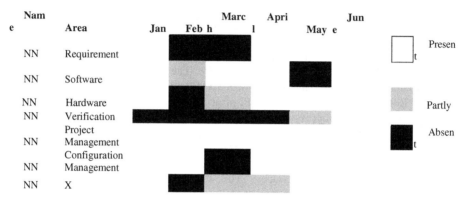

Fig. 4. The Steering Group Participation Indicator

The chairman of the SPI steering group collected data about presence and absence. This was easily done in the minutes of meetings for each steering group meeting. The chairman summarized (in excel) the data to show steering group members how they have participated. The data was also shown for other management teams to visualize how managers spend time on discussions, decisions and commitment to SPI. This measure makes it possible to follow-up managers' participation at SPI steering group meetings, which is a prerequisite for management commitment.

4.2 The SPI Initiatives' Use of the Indicators

The implementation of RUP SPI initiative was conducted during 2000-2001 in a development unit with approximately 900 employees. The SPI initiative affected requirements engineering, software engineering, verification engineering, project management, and configuration management practices. The SPI initiative was managed according to a dedicated approach (Börjesson and Mathiassen, 2004) and SPI initiative had an appointed SPI project manager with a responsibility to drive and manage the SPI initiatives' progress. During this period, approximately 15 different training courses were managed and coordinated by the SPI project manager. Approximately 500 of the 900 employees were affected by the SPI initiative. The development unit had a special steering group responsible for discussing, deciding, follow-up and solving problems for the SPI initiatives and related activities in the SPI area. The SPI project manager used the training participation, perceived acquired know-how and steering group participation indicators to track and follow-up SPI progress (see Table 2).

The deployment of the SPI principles initiative was conducted during the autumn 2003 within a development unit of approximately 550 employees. The SPI initiative aimed to raise the awareness and know-how about how to run effective SPI initiatives. The initiative was assigned to define and hold an SPI course including a dedicated part about SPI principles for conducting effective SPI initiatives according to lessons learned in previous SPI initiatives (Börjesson and Mathiassen, 2004). The SPI manager acted SPI project manager for the initiative. 550 employees were invited to attend the course and 258 employees participated. The SPI project manager used the perceived acquired know-how indicator to track and follow-up the value of the SPI initiative (see Table 2).

The implementation of a new change request process and tool initiative was conducted during 2004 in a development unit of approximately 550 employees. The initiative aimed to define and deploy a new process and tool for change request handling directly affecting nearly 200 employees. The initiative had a dedicated SPI project manager (Börjesson and Mathiassen, 2004) and the initiative was successfully diffused (Börjesson et al., 2005). The SPI project manager used the tool use indicator to track and follow-up progress of the SPI initiative (see Table 2).

The implementation of model based software development initiative was conducted during 2004 within a development unit of approximately 500 employees. The initiative aimed to increase the understanding of software architecture and software sub component interfaces. The initiative affected the requirements engineering, the software engineering, and the configuration management practices. During this period, six different training courses were managed and coordinated by the SPI project manager to diffuse the new know-how. Approximately 220 of the 500 employees were directly affected by the SPI initiative. The development unit had a special steering group to discuss, decide, follow-up and solve problems for the SPI initiative. The SPI initiative was managed according to a dedicated approach (Börjesson and Mathiassen, 2004). The SPI project manager used the training participation, perceived acquired know-how and steering group participation indicators to track and follow-up SPI progress (see Table 2). This SPI initiative used many lessons learned from the implementation of the RUP initiative, which explains the similar set-up.

4.3 SPI Indicator Evaluation

The four SPI project managers were interviewed (Table 1) about the use and value of the four described indicators. They had all either been responsible for or deeply involved in one or several of the described SPI initiatives. The SPI project managers also had experiences from similar indicators from other SPI initiatives not described in this study. Table 3 summarizes the answers from the project managers regarding the use and value of the studied indicators. The column 'positive features' shows the most positive comments from the SPI project managers. The column 'negative features' shows the most negative comments from the SPI project managers. The column 'in combination with' shows how the value of the indicators increases when combined with one or several of the other indicators.

All the SPI project managers were, in general, positive to have indicators for SPI progress. They believed the value of each indicator always could be questioned, but the value was considered high, especially compared to not having any indicators at all. The indicators made it possible to set up goals and evaluate the value of the

Table 3. Summary of answers from SPI project managers

	Positive Features	Negative Features	In Combination With
Training participation	Control of who participates and gets the new information, which is a first step towards building up new know-how. Commitment from managers to send employees to training occasions.	It does not show peoples' ability to use the new know-how. The organization might get an illusory view on what they think they know compared to what they actually know.	Perceived acquired knowledge gives a broader view on the value of the training. Steering group participation makes it possible to connect commitment and action.
Perceived acquired know-how	Understand how participants appreciate a course. Understand if people feel comfortable start working according to new know-how.	People often tend to underestimate what they learned. What people believe they can do is not necessary the same as what they can do.	Tool use (when applicable) makes it possible to relate perceived knowledge and actual knowledge.
Tool use	A strong indicator for actual process adoption. # of new users working in the tool is a good indicator for how people actually change.	Too much focus on tool use takes away focus from the process. This indicator is most effective for initiatives with a tool with a stringent process main flow.	Perceived acquired know-how makes it feasible to understand possible resistance to change to be able to take preventive actions (for instance increased support).
Steering group participation	A precondition to achieve commitment. Visualizes busy managers' focus on improvement work.	Commitment by word in a steering group does not necessarily mean commitment in action.	Training participation and perceived acquired know-how give a broad indicator of the progress of an SPI initiative.

initiative, to show progress for stakeholders and people affected by the initiative, to understand and take action to facilitate progress, and to visualize the SPI initiative's progress in general to prevent down prioritization because of unawareness. When asking the SPI project managers about other potential indicators for facilitating SPI progress, all given answers were strengthened variants of the studied indicators. One answer suggested asking employees not only what they think they are capable of, but also what they actually do. The questions should be designed according to the new process and when they had started to work, they should be asked the question(s). The weakness is that this indicator only can be performed in the later phases of the SPI initiative. Another answer suggested looking for the existence and process compliance of new process documents. This is in line with the tool use indicator, where actual use is indicated. Again, this indicator can only be performed in the later phases of the SPI initiatives.

5   Discussion

There is no doubt about the positive value of measuring software development (Humphrey, 1989; McFeeley, 1996; Weinberg, 1993) and SPI initiatives' progress (Goethert and Siviy, 2004; Grady, 1997). The majority of existing software related measurements are focused on end result. Measuring software productivity has however been proved to be difficult, especially since it requires knowledge of software complexity (Albrect and Gaffney, 1993). Humphrey (1989) and Weinberg (1993) argue data gathering is expensive, time consuming and confusing. We therefore need to find valuable indicators dealing with the difficulties Grady (1992; 1997), Humphrey (1989), McFeeley (1996), and Weinberg (1993) all pinpoint. Indicators for understanding SPI initiatives' progress needs to be easy to gather, manage and evaluate.

Making sense of gathered data is a major challenge (Grady, 1992; Humphrey, 1989). The four indicators studied in this research project have provided indications for actual progress as the indicators are based on undisputable data. None of the interviewed SPI project managers argued there had been problems regarding the trust of the data. Table 4 below summarize the usefulness of the studied indicators.

Table 4. Summary of the usefulness of the studied indicators

Indicator	Indication of	Easy to gather	Easy to manage	Easy to evaluate	Reference
Training participation	Competence build-up	Yes – a part of noting attendance	Yes – no extra time apart from data compiling	Yes – either they attend or not	A similar measurement is suggested by Grady (1997). It map well to Abrahamsson's second dimension for measuring SPI (2000a)
Percieved acquired know-how	Employee capabilities	Yes – questionnaires to training participators	Yes - no extra time apart from data compiling	Yes – what they say is what they feel	Attewell (1992) argues knowledge barriers are preventing change. It map well to Abrahamsson's second dimension for measuring SPI (2000a)
Tool Use	Process Adoption	Yes – tool database access required	Yes – having access and know-how to read the database is however necessary	Yes – either the data is in the tool database or not	The full use of this measurement can be found in Börjesson et al. (2005). It map well to Abrahamsson's second dimension for measuring SPI (2000a)
Steering Group Participation	Management Commitment	Yes – a part of noting attendance	Yes - no extra time apart from data compiling	Yes – either they attend or not	Abrahamsson (2000b, 2001) argues about the importance of management commitment

Grady (1992) argues we need to measure to estimate project progress. This is as important for development projects as for SPI projects. Key to evaluate SPI projects are according to McFeeley (1996) the selected measurements and the ease of gathering them. The selected indicators presented in Table 4 are both supported by the SPI literature (column 'Reference') and easy to gather, manage and evaluate. It is therefore likely the studied indicators are useful to track and follow-up SPI initiatives' progress.

The key practice areas for measuring in the CMM (Paulk et al., 1995) is found first at level four. This indicates the needed maturity to benefit from measuring software and how confusing measurements can be when lacking this maturity. The indicators used for understanding SPI initiatives' progress are neither expensive or confusing, nor time consuming (see Table 4). The SPI project managers believed the indicators helped them understand the SPI initiatives' progress and they were capable of taking adequate actions to address situations when the progress decreased. The indicators helped them facilitate SPI progress success, which is an important prerequisite for SPI implementation success and SPI success. SPI progress success helped decreasing the assimilation gap (Fichman and Kemerer, 1999) as the progress guided the SPI initiative towards implementation and use, i.e. the acquired potential improvements were deployed. Based on findings from this study it is fare to say there are simple and practical indicators that can be used to understand prerequisites for SPI success like SPI initiatives' progress.

As the studied indicators are independent of software specific measurements such as LoC (Flaherty, 1995; Humphrey, 1985) it is likely they could be useful to track progress of all kind of improvement initiatives. The main lesson learned from this study for practitioners and researchers are therefore to use, try-out and improve these indicators not only within the software community, but also in whatever community that needs to improve. It is of course important to understand that there are other areas than SPI progress that also affect SPI success.

6 Conclusion

This study shows the value and use of four simple and practical indicators (training participation, perceived acquired knowledge, tool use and steering group participation) to track SPI initiatives' progress to facilitate deployment and decrease the assimilation gap. The indicators indicate real competence build-up, employee capability, process adoption and management commitment. The four indicators were found to be easy and cost-efficient to gather, manage and evaluate.

References

1. Abrahamsson, P. (2000a) Measuring the Success of Software Process Improvement: The Dimensions, EuroSPI2000, Copenhagen, Denmark.
2. Abrahamsson, P. (2000b) Is Management Commitment a Necessity After All in III: Software Process Improvement? Euromicro '00, Maastricht, The Netherlands, IEEE Computer Society, 246-253.
3. Abrahamsson, P. (2001) Rethinking the Concept of Commitment in Software Process Improvement, Scandinavian Journal of Information Systems 13:69-98.
4. Albrecht, A. J. (1979) Measuring Application Development Productivity, Proceedings of the IBM Application Development Symposium, Montery, California, October, pp. 83-92.
5. Albrecht, A. J. and Gaffney, J. E. Jr (1993) Software Function, Source Lines of Code, and Development Effort Prediction: A Software Science Validation, IEEE Transactions on Software Engineering, October, Vol. SE-9, No. 6, pp.639-648.
6. Argyris, C. and Schön, D. (1978) Organizational Learning, Reading Massachusetts: Addison-Wesley.

7. Attewell, P. (1992) Technolgy Diffusion and Organisational Learning: The Case of Business Computing, Organization Science 3(1): 1-19.
8. Bach, J. (1995) Enough About Process: What We Need are Heroes. IEEE Software, 12, 2, pp. 96-98.
9. Bartunek, J.M. and Louis M.R. (1996) Insider/outsider Team Research, Qualitative Research Methods Vol. 40, Sage Publications.
10. Basili, V. G., Caldiera, G. and Rombach H.D., Goal Question Metric Approach, Encyclopedia of Software Engineering, pp. 528-532, John Wiley & Sons, Inc., 1994.
11. Baskerville, R. and Pries-Heje, J (1999) Grounded action research: a method for understanding IT in practice. Management and Information Technology 9, pp.1-23.
12. Baskerville, R. and Wood-Harper, T (1996) A critical perspective on action research as a method for information systems research, Journal of Information Technology 11, 235-246.
13. Bollinger, T.B. and McGowan, C. (1991) A Critical Look at Software Capability Evaluations. IEEE Software, Vol. 8, No. 4, pp. 25-41.
14. Brown, M. and Goldenson, D. (2004) **Measurement and Analysis: What Can and Does Go Wrong?**, presented at the 10th International Symposium on Software Metrics, 14 September 2004.
15. Börjesson, A. and Mathiassen, L. (2004) Successful Process Implementation, IEEE Software, Vol. 21, Nr. 4, pp. 36-44.
16. Börjesson, A., Martinsson, F. and Timmerås, M. (2005) Using Agile Improvement Practices in Software Organizations, Conditionally accepted to European Journal of Information Systems.
17. Davison, R., Maris, Martinsons, M. and Kock, N. (2004) Principles of canonical action research, Info Systems Journal. Vol. 14, pp. 65-86.
18. Dove, R. (2001) Response Ability – The Language, Structure, and Culture of the Agile Enterprise. New York: Wiley.
19. Fichman, R. G. and Kemerer, C. F. (1999) The Illusory Diffusion of Innovation: An Examination of Assimlation Gaps. Information Systems Research, Vol. 10, issue 3, pp 255-275.
20. Fayad, M. E. and Laitinen, M. (1997) Process Assessment Considered Wasteful, Communications of the ACM, Vol. 40, No. 11, pp. 125-128.
21. Flaherty, M. J. (1985) Programming Process Productivity Measurement System for System 370, IBM System Journal, Vol. 24, No. 2.
22. Galliers, R. D. (1992) Choosing an Information Systems Research Approach, In: Galliers (Ed.): Information Systems Research: Issues, Methods, and Practical Guidelines, Oxford: Blackwell Scientific Publications, pp.144-162.
23. Grady, R.B. (1992) Practical Software Metrics for Project Management and Process Improvement, Upper Saddle River, New Jersey, Prentice Hall.
24. Grady, R. B. (1997) Successful Software Process Improvement, Upper Saddle River, New Jersey: Prentice Hall.
25. Goethert, W. and Siviy, J. (2004) Applications of the Indicator Template for Measurement and Analysis, Technical Note CMU/SEI-2004-TN-024.
26. Jones, C. (1993) Sources of Errors in Software Cost Estimating, version 1.0, November 24, Software Productivity research, Burlington, MA 01803.
27. Jones, C. (1994) Assessment and Control of Software Risks, Prentice Hall, Englewood Cliffs, NJ 07632.
28. Haeckel, S. H. (1999) Adaptive Enterprise: Creating and Leading Sense-and-Respond Organizations. Boston, Massachusetts: Harvard Business School Press.

29. Humphrey, W. S. (1985) the IBM Large-System Software Development Process: Objectives and Directions, IBM Systems Journal, Vol. 24, No.2.

30. Humphrey, W. S. (1989) Managing the Software Process. Reading, Massachusetts: Addison Wesley.

31. McFeeley, B. (1996) IDEAL. A User's Guide for Software Process Improvement, The Software Engineering Institute, Carnegie Mellon University, Pittsburgh, Handbook CMU/SEI-96-HB-001.

32. Paulk, M. C., C. V. Weber, B. Curtis and M. B. Chrissis (1995) The Capability Maturity Model: Guidelines for Improving the Software Process. Reading, Mass., Addison-Wesley Pub. Co.

33. SEMA (2002) Process Maturity Profile of the Software Community, Software Engineering Institute, Carnegie-Mellon University.

34. Weinberg, G. M. (1993) Quality Software Management volume II – First-Order Measurement. Dorset House Publishing, New York, USA.

35. Yin, R. (1994) Case Study Research, Newburry Park, California: Sage Publication.

Investigating Suitability of Software Process and Metrics for Statistical Process Control

Ayça Tarhan[1] and Onur Demirörs[2]

[1] The Bilgi Group Software Research, Education, and Consultancy Ltd.,
ODTU Teknokent Gumus Blk No:3, 06531 Ankara, Turkey
`ayca.tarhan@bg.com.tr`
[2] Informatics Institute, Middle East Technical University,
MM Kat:4, 06531 Ankara, Turkey
`demirors@ii.metu.edu.tr`

Abstract. The application of statistical process control (SPC) techniques for software is rare due to such requirements as high maturity, rational sampling, and effective metric selection. Existing studies report results from their own implementations and provide suggestions for success. In this paper, we explain an approach used for assessing the suitability of software process and metrics for starting SPC implementation via control charts. The approach includes guidance to identify rational samples of a process as well as to select process metrics. We explain the application of the approach over a review process of a software and system development organization.

1 Introduction

Statistical Process Control (SPC) contains powerful collection of problem solving tools that are used for achieving process stability and improving process capability by the reduction of variability. It has been widely used in manufacturing domains, after proposed by Shewhart [29] and sophisticated by Deming's studies [7][8]. While benefits of SPC are proven for manufacturing companies, SPC techniques for software have not been frequently implemented by the software companies [3][9][14][21][31].

As process improvement models like CMM [26], ISO/IEC 15504 [18] and CMMI [5] have become popular during the last decade; SPC for software has gained attention. These models implicitly direct companies to implement SPC as a crucial step for achieving higher maturity levels [4][6]. Once a company invests on one of these models, it can take the advantage of following a well-founded framework to establish the infrastructure required for SPC. For other companies, however, the path to SPC implementation is not that clear. While a number of researchers provide approaches to utilize measurement and SPC techniques for software [1][10][13][15][16][20][32][33], existing implementations focus on the potential benefits of SPC results rather than on providing satisfactory guidelines based on practical evidence. We lack knowledge on the techniques for rational sampling and sub-grouping, applicability of different metrics, the means of reliable data collection and meaningful data analysis, especially for emergent development organizations.

R. Messnarz (Ed.): EuroSPI 2006, LNCS 4257, pp. 88–99, 2006.
© Springer-Verlag Berlin Heidelberg 2006

The need for such knowledge encouraged us to develop an approach to investigate suitability of software process and metrics for statistical process control. The approach includes guidance to identify rational samples of a process as well as to select process metrics. In this paper, we elaborate the approach in section 2, and demonstrate its application over an example assessment in section 3. Section 4 provides conclusions derived from the example assessment and the future work.

2 An Approach for SPC Utilization

In our approach, we address two basic requirements for SPC implementation and focus on resolving difficulties brought by them: 1) Rational sampling of process executions and data, and 2) Metric data utilization (or suitability) for statistical analysis.

The purpose of rational sampling is to obtain and use data that are representative of the performance of the process with respect to the issues being studied. If we can consider that observations are made under essentially the same conditions and that differences between the measurements are primarily due to common cause variation, then we are very likely that we rationally group the observations [12]. Since we want to sample process executions as being from a single and constant system of chance causes, we developed a clustering method based on the idea of process consistency assessment. We recommend describing each process execution in a number of process attributes such as inputs, outputs, activities, roles, and tools and techniques (Figure 1). Process consistency is assessed for similarity in process attribute values of process executions. If repetitions of a process show similarity in terms of these attributes, then we assume that the process is consistently performed among its executions.

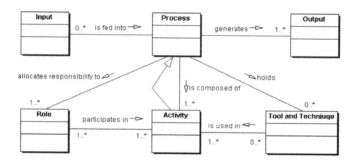

Fig. 1. Process attributes used for rational sampling (The process has a number of inputs to each execution, outputs from each execution, and activities carried out within each execution. It allocates responsibility to a number of roles participating in one or more process activities, and holds a number of tools and techniques that are used in one or more process activities.)

The second requirement is metric utilization. This includes elaboration of basic measurement practices as well as metric data existence and characteristics. Measurement practices should be performed for a specific purpose [1][25] and, metrics should have operational definitions to enable consistent implementation. Operational definitions tell people how measurements are made so that others will get the same results if they follow the same procedures. There are studies that define procedures for successfully implementing measurement practices and for incorporating measurement capability into the projects of an organization [5][19][22][25]. Also, there are high-maturity companies that developed factors to consider for measurement evaluation and to determine what measures to select for their specific use [27]. To evaluate metric utilization, we identified a number of metric usability attributes (Table 1), and developed questionnaires based on these attributes for base and derived metrics separately. Questionnaires include a rating system based on the answers of questions, and accordingly, evaluate the usability of a specific metric for applying SPC.

Table 1. Metric usability attributes used for evaluating metric utilization

Attribute	Explanation
Metric Identity	Metric should be identified including entity and attribute to measure; scale type, unit, formula; and data type and range. Measurement theory states that we cannot use nominal and ordinal scale metrics for control charting [11].
Data Existence	For any analysis, there should be measurement data. For control limits to be calculated reliably there should be at least 20 data points [2].
Data Verifiability	Metric data should be recorded at the same place in the process, by the same responsible body, and using the same method every time.
Data Dependability	Metric data should be recorded and stored as it is generated to ensure accuracy and precision; and be collected for a specific purpose. Feedback mechanisms should exist and be known by data collectors regarding data analysis and reporting.
Data Normalizability	Metric data can be normalized with a parameter or with another metric. Normalized metrics provide more insight in terms of statistical analysis. Normalizing metric-A with a parameter-P provides comparable values of metric-A in terms of the parameter-P (e.g., normalizing number of defects in a product with product size).
Data Integrability	Metric data can be integrated at project or organization levels. In practice, metric data should be integrated from individual level up to organization level for the results of statistical analysis to be effective organization-wide.

The process that we follow for rational sampling and metric utilization evaluation cannot be given here due to space limitations, but are explained in section 3 over an example assessment. We briefly describe the process assets and their usage below:

Process Execution Record: This is a form used to capture the instant values of process attributes for a process execution. Actual values of inputs, outputs, activities, roles, and tools and techniques for a specific process execution are recorded on the form. Recorded values are used to identify the merged list of process attribute values which are entered into Process Similarity Matrix for verification.

Process Similarity Matrix: This is a form used to verify process attribute values against process executions. We construct the matrix based on the values of process attributes previously entered into Process Execution Records. Process attribute values are recorded into the rows, and process execution numbers are recorded into the columns of the matrix. By going over the executions, the values of process attributes are questioned and marked if applicable for each process execution (see Figure 3 as example). The completed matrix helps us to see the differences among process executions and enables us to identify rational samples of executions accordingly.

Metric Usability Questionnaire: This is a form used to investigate the usability of a process metric in terms of metric usability attributes. The form includes a number of questions and rules for rating usability attributes as given in Figure 2.

Attributes as basis for rating		Rating rules	Weights
Metric Identity			
Q3	What is the scale of the metric data? (nominal, ordinal, interval, ratio, absolute)	If Ratio or Absolute then 1 else 0	1
Data Existence			
Q7	Is metric data existent?	If number of data points > 20 then 1 else 0	1
Data Verifiability			
Q12	Is all metric data recorded at the same place in the process? (at start, middle, end, later, etc.)	If yes then 1 else 0	1/4
Q14	Is all metric data recorded by the responsible body?	If yes then 1 else 0	1/4
Q16	Is all metric data recorded the same way? (on a form, report, tool, etc.)	If yes then 1 else 0	1/4
Q18	Is all metric data stored in the same place? (in a file, database, etc.)	If yes then 1 else 0	1/4
Data Dependability			
Q22	Are the frequencies for data generation, recording, and storing different?	If yes then 1 else 0	1/8
Q23	Is metric data recorded precisely?	If yes then 1 else 0	1/8
Q24	Is metric data collected for a specific purpose?	If yes then 1 else 0	1/8
Q25	Is the purpose of metric data collection known by process performers?	If yes then 1 else 0	1/8
Q26	Is metric data analyzed and reported?	If yes then 1 else 0	1/8
Q27	Is metric data analysis results communicated to process performers?	If yes then 1 else 0	1/8
Q28	Is metric data analysis results communicated to management?	If yes then 1 else 0	1/8
Q29	Is metric data analysis results used as a basis for decision making?	If yes then 1 else 0	1/8

(a) Metric usability questions used for rating usability of base metrics

Attributes as basis for rating		Rating rules	Weights
Metric Identity			
Q2	What is the scale of the metric data? (nominal, ordinal, interval, ratio, absolute)	If Ratio or Absolute then 1 else 0	1
Data Existence			
Q6	Is metric data existent?	If number of data points > 20 then 1 else 0	1
Data Verifiability			
Q11	Is all metric data calculated the same way? (by a tool, manually, etc.)	If yes then 1 else 0	1/3
Q12	Is all metric data calculated according to metric formula?	If yes then 1 else 0	1/3
Q14	Is all metric data stored in the same place? (in a file, database, etc.)	If yes then 1 else 0	1/3
Data Dependability			
Q15	Is metric data stored precisely?	If yes then 1 else 0	1/7
Q16	Is metric data stored for a specific purpose?	If yes then 1 else 0	1/7
Q17	Is the purpose of metric data storage known by process performers?	If yes then 1 else 0	1/7
Q18	Is metric data analyzed and reported?	If yes then 1 else 0	1/7
Q19	Is metric data analysis results communicated to process performers?	If yes then 1 else 0	1/7
Q20	Is metric data analysis results communicated to management?	If yes then 1 else 0	1/7
Q21	Is metric data analysis results used as a basis for decision making?	If yes then 1 else 0	1/7

(b) Metric usability questions used for rating usability of derived metrics

Fig. 2. Questions and rules used for rating metric usability

Both "metric identity" and "data existence" attributes have a single question as basis for rating, and each must be rated as 1 for a metric to be usable in the first place. If the scale type requirement is not satisfied or there are not enough data points, there is no need to continue the evaluation for the rest of the attributes since it will not be possible to use metric data for statistical analysis. "Data verifiability" and "data dependability" attributes have several questions as basis for rating and the weights of these questions are assigned equally to sum up 1. The resulting value for these attributes is calculated by summing the question weights shown in the rightmost column in Figure 2. The value determines the level of confidence that we should have in data analysis results, and should be as close to 1 for both attributes.

The questionnaire has two types, for base and derived metrics separately (see Figure 5 for examples). For each base metric, the answers are rated on the questionnaires according to the rules described above, and the values are formulated into a unique Metric Usability Index (MUI) by multiplying the individual values of usability attributes. For derived metrics, the calculated index is further multiplied by the arithmetic mean of the indices of base metrics that make up the derived metric.

The value of MUI is used to have a judgment on the usability of the process metric for control charting. It is interpreted in four states: Not usable ([0.00-0.25]), poorly usable ([0.26-0.50]), largely usable ([0.51-0.75]), and fully usable ([0.76-1.00]). The ranges used to distinguish these states provide a means to judge the confidence we should have on metric data for statistical analysis.

Process Execution Questionnaire: This is a form used to investigate the assignable causes for a process execution in terms of changes in process performers, process environments, and other factors if any. While working retrospectively on existing process data, answers to the questionnaire are used to understand the assignable causes for a process execution if it is an out-of-control point.

3 An Example Assessment

We applied the approach described above, as an example assessment, for review process of a system and software development organization [30]. The company, having 15 years of experience in the sector, supplies products for Turkish Armed Forces with its 45-staff development team which involves system and software engineers, project managers, and quality experts. It already has ISO 9001 [17] and AQAP-150 [24] certificates, and has been pursuing process improvement studies to achieve CMMI L3 certification for 18 months. The review process has been used by the staff to review system and software development documents as well as software code. The company did not have a specific measurement process, but was obeying policies for analyzing the data and reporting the results to high-level management. The results reported to the management were not systematically used for decision-making purposes.

While performing the assessment, we spent 12 person-days for gathering and translating review data, applying the approach, performing the analyses, and interpreting the results. We worked on existing review process data of 196 data points which were collected during two years. We translated the review data to a form that is appropriate for comparison among different projects and products.

Since the study was retrospective, we identified process attributes of review process executions by inspecting review process outputs and consulting the Quality Assurance Expert participated in the reviews. We sampled 5 reviews and filled a process execution record for each. The information on process execution records provided us typical values of process attributes, and formed an initial base to create the similarity matrix. We then verified sampled values of process attributes against 196 process executions. We recorded any new attribute value on the matrix during verification. The appearance of the matrix for the first 20 executions was as in Figure 3.

Process Attributes		PE1	PE2	PE3	PE4	PE5	PE6	PE7	PE8	PE9	PE10	PE11	PE12	PE13	PE14	PE15	PE16	PE17	PE18	PE19	PE20	....
1 Inputs																						
1.1	Product to review	o	o	o	o	o	o	o	o	o	o	o	o	o	o	o	o	o	o	o	o	o
2 Outputs																						
2.1	Review form	o	o	o	o	o	o	o	o	o	o	o	o	o	o	o	o	o	o	o	o	
2.2	Review report	o	o	o	o	o	o	o	o	o	o	o	o	o	o	o	o	o	o	o	o	
2.3	Code review report																					
3 Activities																						
3.1	Planning	o	o	o	o	o	o	o	o	o	o	o	o	o	o	o	o	o	o	o	o	
3.2	Review	o	o	o	o	o	o	o	o	o	o	o	o	o	o	o	o	o	o	o	o	
3.3	Update during meeting																					
3.4	Update after meeting	o	o	o	o	o	o	o	o	o	o	o	o	o	o	o	o			o	o	
3.5	Closure	o	o	o	o	o	o	o	o	o	o	o	o	o	o	o	o	o	o	o	o	
4 Roles																						
4.1	Project Manager	o	o	o	o	o	o	o	o	o	o	o	o	o	o	o	o	o	o	o	o	
4.2	QA Expert	o	o	o	o	o	o	o	o	o	o	o	o	o	o	o	o	o	o	o	o	
4.3	CM Specialist	o	o	o	o	o	o	o	o	o	o	o	o	o	o	o	o	o	o	o	o	
4.4	Customer																					
5 Tools and Techniques																						
	NOT IDENTIFIABLE																					

Fig. 3. Process similarity matrix for review process executions

After finalizing the matrix, we analyzed it for similarity and differences in process executions. By going over the matrix, we looked for executions with different attribute values and copied each as a separate cluster while skipping the similar ones. We identified 9 process clusters labeled from A through I as shown in Figure 4. Each process cluster we identified was a rational sample of the review process, and ideally we could chart the data for each cluster to see if it was under control. When we counted the number of process executions in the clusters, we noticed that many clusters (except A and B) had few executions. We could either remove the clusters with few data from the set and continue our study with clusters A and B only, or find a way to merge the clusters with limited data to some other cluster. We chose the latter for the purpose of experimentation.

1	Inputs	A	B	C	D	E	F	G	H	I
1.1	Product to review	o	o	o		o	o	o	o	o
2	Outputs									
2.1	Review form	o		o		o		o	o	
2.2	Review report	o	o	o		o	o	o	o	o
2.3	Code review report				o					
3	Activities									
3.1	Planning	o	o	o	o	o	o	o	o	o
3.2	Review	o	o	o	o	o	o	o	o	o
3.3	Update during meeting				o		o			
3.4	Update after meeting	o		o						o
3.5	Closure	o	o	o	o	o	o	o	o	o
4	Roles									
4.1	Project Manager	o	o	o	o	o	o	o	o	o
4.2	QA Expert	o	o	o	o	o	o	o	o	o
4.3	CM Specialist	o	o	o	o	o	o	o	o	o
4.4	Customer			o			o	o	o	
5	Tools and Techniques									
	NOT RECORDED									
Process Version		A	B	C	D	E	F	G	H	I

A-B	2								
A-C	1	B-C	3						
A-D	4	B-D	2	C-D	5				
A-E	2	B-E	2	C-E	3	D-E	4		
A-F	3	B-F	1	C-F	2	D-F	3	E-F	3
A-G	3	B-G	3	C-G	2	D-G	5	E-G	1	F-G	2
A-H	2	B-H	2	C-H	1	D-H	4	E-H	2	F-H	1	G-H	1
A-I	1	B-I	1	C-I	2	D-I	3	E-I	3	F-I	2	G-I	4	H-I	3

Cluster		Mergable To	Will Be Merged To
B	→	--	
C	→	A	A
D	→	--	--
E	→	--	--
F	→	B	B
G	→	E	E
H	→	C,F,G	F
I	→	A,B	A

Fig. 4. Initial process clusters and cluster distances

To identify possible merges among the clusters, we worked on pairs of clusters. We calculated the number of different attribute values between two clusters, and called this number as "cluster distance". For example, the distance between the clusters A and B in Figure 4 was 2, since the attribute values of these clusters differed for process attributes 2.1 and 3.4. We recorded the distances between the pairs of process clusters in the form of a triangle as shown in the upper right corner of Figure 4. Every row in the triangle showed us which clusters that a specific process cluster was the most similar to in terms of process attributes. For example, the fifth row of the triangle in the figure held distance values of process cluster F to other clusters; and when we had a close look at these values, we saw that the distance between clusters B and F was 1, meaning that B was the most similar cluster for F. When identifying possible merges, we searched for the pairs of clusters having a distance of 1. If a row included the distance values all above 1 (e.g. cluster D in row 3), we concerned the related cluster "not mergable" to any other cluster. By going over the rows of the triangle, we identified the clusters with a distance of 1, if any, for each cluster; and recorded these clusters in a table showing mergable clusters (the table shown below the triangle in Figure 4 provides this information). Here we should note that the purpose of the metric that we utilize on a control chart can affect the value of cluster distance allowed for identifying mergable clusters. If we were trying to meet customer specification limits set for code defectiveness in a project, for example, we would probably not allow a cluster distance value above 0.

We identified final process clusters (rational samples) considering mergable clusters detected and the number of data points in each process cluster. We randomly chose to merge cluster I to cluster A, and we excluded cluster H from the study due to few number of data points. As a result, we ended up with the following clusters: Cluster A (including initial clusters A, C, and I); cluster B (including initial clusters B and F); cluster D; and cluster E (including initial clusters E and G). Cluster D entirely included process executions for code review. Unfortunately, the number of data points for cluster D was so few that we excluded it from the study.

After we identified initial process clusters, we worked on process metrics to evaluate their usability for statistical analysis. We identified review opening date, review closure date, number of detected nonconformances, number of accepted nonconformances, and nonconformance resolution effort as base metrics of the review process. These were the metrics for which data was available on review records. From the base metrics, we identified derived review metrics by the formulas shown in Table 2.

For evaluating the usability, we used separate questionnaires for base and derived metrics. Figure 5 provides examples of metric usability questionnaires and calculated metric usability indices for review effort and noncompliance detection efficiency metrics. The results of usability evaluations for all review metrics are given in Table 3.

Table 2. Derived review metrics

Derived Metric	Formula
Open period	Closure date – Opening date
Open period with respect to non-conformances	Open period / Number of accepted non-conformances
Nonconformance detection efficiency	Number of accepted nonconformances / Review effort
Nonconformance resolution efficiency	Number of accepted nonconformances / Nonconformance resolution effort

Fig. 5. Example metric usability questionnaires (lefthand base, righthand derived)

Table 3. Metric usability evaluation results

Metric	MUI	Usability Status
Opening date	0.00	Not Usable [0.00-0.25]
Closure date	0.00	Not Usable
Number of detected nonconformances	0.50	Poorly Usable [0.26-0.50]
Number of accepted nonconformances	0.75	Largely Usable [0.51-0.75]
Rewiew effort	0.75	Largely Usable
Nonconformance resolution effort	0.75	Largely Usable
Open period	0.50	Poorly Usable
Open period with respect to nonconformances	0.58	Largely Usable
Nonconformance detection efficiency	0.75	Largely Usable
Nonconformance resolution efficiency	0.75	Largely Usable

We reviewed process data and used the results from process similarity assessment and metric usability evaluation to finalize process clusters and metrics prior to control charting. We intended to work with the data for derived metrics having metric usability index greater than 0.50. Open period with respect to nonconformances, nonconformance detection efficiency and nonconformance resolution efficiency were such metrics. We later included the data for open period derived metric for control charting, since it had a metric usability index of 0.50 which was very close to the lower limit for large usability. We did not intend to chart the data for any of the base metrics because they needed to be normalized for effective use. We also noticed that process cluster B (with initial clusters B and F) included process instances in which no nonconformance was detected. It would not be meaningful to chart the data for nonconformance detection efficiency, nonconformance resolution efficiency, and open period with respect to nonconformances derived metrics in this case, since all values would be zero according to their formulas. We excluded cluster B from the study.

As a result, we chose two clusters as basis for control charting with derived metrics: Process cluster A (including initial clusters A, C, and I) and process cluster E (including initial clusters E and G). We renamed these clusters as M and N, respectively, to distinguish them from their initial clusters.

We depicted review data on control charts for process clusters M and N, and for each derived metric separately. We applied variables charts for individuals of review data using Minitab Statistical Software [25]. We applied the following tests to detect the out-of-control points: 1 point > 3 standard deviations from center line, 9 points in a row on same side of center line, 2 out of 3 points > 2 standard deviations from center line (same side), and 4 out of 5 points > 1 standard deviation from center line (same side).

Figure 6 shows the charts for clusters M and N for nonconformance detection efficiency. From the figure we saw that cluster M had many out-of-control points and cluster N was under control with respect to nonconformance detection efficiency. We performed similar analyses for nonconformance resolution efficiency, open period, and open period with respect to nonconformances metrics. Accordingly, we categorized cluster M into four sub-clusters with respect to input product types to continue our analysis: Project plans (M-1), design documents (M-2), analysis documents (M-3), and the rest (M-4 including test documents, release documents, and user manuals).

We re-charted the data for derived metrics on process cluster N and sub-clusters of M, and conducted interviews with process performers in order to understand any

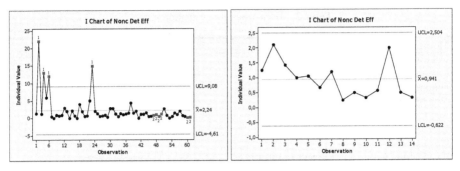

Fig. 6. Individuals charts for nonconformance detection efficiency (lefthand M, righthand N)

reasons for the assignable causes. The interviews were performed in two parts. In the first part, the experiences and dynamics of process executions were investigated in free format dialogs, and notes were taken. Here the purpose was to have an understanding of the context related to process executions, and to identify any assignable cause (probably that our approach could not detected) from the performers' point of view. During the interviews, three issues were reported by process performers as potential reasons for out-of-control points: Involvement of contractors in the review, project schedule, and product type under review. In the second part, the reasons for assignable causes detected by our approach were questioned specifically by using process execution questionnaire.

Table 4. Summary of final results from re-charted data for derived metrics

Process Cluster	Derived Metric			
	Nonconformance Detection Efficiency	Nonconformance Resolution Efficiency	Open Period with respect to Nonconformances	Open Period
M-1	1 out-of-control point	Under control	Not under control	Not under control
M-2	Under control	1 out-of-control point	Not under control	Not under control
M-3	Under control	Under control	Not under control	Not under control
M-4	Under control	Under control	Under control	Under control
N	Under control	No data	Not under control	Not under control

Based on the knowledge obtained during interviews, we re-charted the data by excluding the data points of assignable causes. Results from re-charted data given in Table 4 showed that our approach was useful as a guide for starting SPC implementation. Assessment results suggested that nonconformance detection efficiency, nonconformance resolution efficiency, and open period with respect to nonconformances metrics were largely usable for performing SPC analysis on process cluster N and sub-clusters of M, the first two being more likely to succeed considering metric usability indices. After re-charting the data we observed that all process clusters were under control with respect to nonconformance detection efficiency and nonconformance resolution efficiency metrics except two out-of-control points for which we could detect assignable causes. We also observed that the company could not use the control charts for open period with respect to nonconformances metric confidently, although the metric was suggested as usable by our approach. After the interviews we could detect that the schedule of the projects played a significant role in the open periods of review records. When the project schedule was tight, the reviews were closed more quickly. Process cluster M-4 was under control with respect to all derived metrics since it included regular documents, for which the review process was affected at minimum degree by factors as project dynamics, development maturity, and etc.

After the assessment, we concluded that nonconformance detection efficiency and nonconformance resolution efficiency metrics were usable for SPC analysis. Nonconformance detection efficiency metric could be an indicator of review process efficiency, but definitely not alone, since we had no idea on the defectiveness of the product under review. The size of the product under review was not recorded regularly, but software product's LOC data was recorded partially per month basis for year 2005. Therefore, we utilized existing LOC data to rationalize nonconformance detection efficiency for process performance. We identified reviews performed in 2005, and according to their opening dates, we recorded regarding LOC values. From the number of nonconformances accepted in these reviews and regarding software product size in LOC, we calculated nonconformance density metric by the formula "number of accepted nonconformances/KLOC" and we charted the metric data. We observed that overall process had two out-of-control points, while process clusters M and N were both under control as shown in Figure 7. That is, nonconformance detection efficiency metric could be used to judge and improve process performance since the nonconformance density metric was stable at the moment. We noted that the company should keep recording product size to continually monitor nonconformance density for possible changes in the performance.

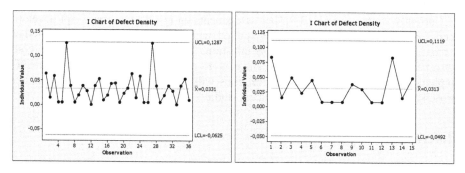

Fig. 7. Individuals charts for nonconformance density (lefthand M, righthand N)

During the assessment we observed that evaluating usability of review metrics was supporting but not enough to effectively select the metrics to be used in SPC analysis. Project context and dynamics in which the process was executed (such as project organization, schedule, development life cycle, maturity of development practices, and etc.) should also be considered while selecting the metrics. Open period with respect to nonconformances metric was such an example due to the effect of project schedule on open periods of review records. Elaboration on process metrics prior to SPC implementation requires special attention from this perspective. We can work on each process metric specifically, investigate factors that might affect its utilization, and develop guidelines for successful application.

4 Conclusions

The roles of rational sampling and metric selection practices are crucial in initiating SPC implementation for software processes. The lack of well-defined guidelines to direct these practices encouraged us to develop an approach to assess the suitability of software process and metrics for SPC. We performed an example assessment to evaluate the usability of the approach. Our experience has showed us that with established guidelines for rational sampling and metric utilization, an organization can apply SPC techniques and attain the ability to understand its processes based on quantitative data.

Before the assessment, the company had been reporting total number of nonconformances, total review effort, total nonconformance resolution effort, and ratio of total nonconformance resolution effort to total review effort metrics per project basis in high level management reviews. However, none of these metric values had been used for a specific purpose. At the end of the case study, the company initiated SPC implementations for nonconformance detection efficiency and nonconformance resolution efficiency metrics, and adopted related control charts as parts of the measurement and analysis system that it built for CMMI L3. By doing so, the company had the chance of observing and improving review process performance based on quantitative data, which is a basic requirement for achieving higher CMMI maturity levels.

The assessment was performed retrospectively on existing review records. Although it had a minimum disturbance on the work of process performers this way, we had difficulties in observing implementation details. Organizing a prospective study will support better understanding of process executions and related characteristics.

Currently we have initiated further assessments on test design, test script development and test peer review processes applied within an avionics project of another system and software development organization. The assessments will include both retrospective and prospective parts. There is no one-fits-all approach to guide SPC implementations; however, we believe trials will be beneficial to improve our approach and to fasten process improvement studies.

References

1. Basili, V.R., Caldiera, G., and Rombach, H.D., "The Goal Question Metric Approach", Encyclopedia of Software Engineering, Vol.1, pp.528-¬532, John Wiley & Sons, 1994.
2. Burr, A., Owen, M., Statistical Methods for Software Quality. Thomson Publishing Company, 1996. ISBN 1-85032-171-X.
3. Card, D., "Statistical Process Control for Software?", IEEE Software, May 1994, pp.95-97.
4. CMU/SEI, "Process Maturity Profile of the Software Community – 2000 Year End Update", Presentation, March 2001(a).
5. CMU/SEI, CMMI Product Team, "CMMISM for Systems Engineering and Software Engineering", CMMI-SE/SW V1.1 Continuous, CMU/SEI-2002-TR-001, December 2001(b).
6. CMU/SEI, "The 2001 High Maturity Workshop", CMU/SEI-2001-SR-014, January 2002.
7. Deming, W.E., Statistical Adjustment of Data, John Wiley and Sons, 1943. (Re-printed by Dover Publications, July 1984.)
8. Deming, W.E., Out of the Crisis, Massachusetts Institute of Technology, Center of Advanced Engineering, Cambridge, Mass., 1986.

9. Demirörs, O., and Sargut, K.U., "Utilization of a Defect Density Metric for SPC Analysis", 13th International Conference on Software Quality, Dallas, Texas, October 2003.

10. Fenton, N.E., and Neil M., Software Metrics: Successes, Failures and New Directions. The Journal of Systems and Software, 47, 1999, PP 149-157.

11. Fenton, N.E., and Pfleeger, S.L., Software Metrics: A Rigorous and Practical Approach, 2nd Ed., PWS Publishing Company, 1997.

12. 12.Florac, A.W., Carleton A.D., Measuring the Software Process: Statistical Process Control for Software Process Improvement. Pearson Education, 1999. ISBN 0-201-60444-2.

13. Florac, A.W., Carleton A.D., Statistically Controlling the Software Process (The 99 SEI Software Engineering Symposium), Software Engineering Institute, Carnegie Mellon University, September 1999.

14. Florac, A.W., Carleton A.D., Statistical Process Control: Analyzing a Space Shuttle Onboard Software Process. IEEE Software, July/August 2000, PP 97-106.

15. Florac A.W., Park E.R., Carleton A.D., Practical Software Measurement: Measuring for Process Management and Improvement (CMU/SEI-97-HB-003). Software Engineering Institute, Carnegie Mellon University, April 1997.

16. Humphrey, Watts, Managing the Software Process. Reading, Mass.: Addison-Wesley Publishing Company, 1989. ISBN 0-201-18095-2.

17. 17.ISO, "ISO 9001: Quality Management Systems – Requirements", 2000.

18. ISO/IEC, "ISO/IEC TR 15504: Information Tech. – Software Process Assessment", 1998.

19. ISO/IEC, "ISO/IEC 15939: Software Measurement Process", 2002.

20. 20.Kan, S. H., Metrics and Models in Software Quality Engineering. Addison-Wesley Publishing Company, 1995. ISBN 0201633396.

21. Lantzy, M.A., "Application of Statistical Process Control to Software Processes", WADAS '92, Proceedings of the Ninth Washington Ada Symposium on Empowering Software Users and Developers, 1992, pp.113-123.

22. McGarry, J., Card, D., Jones, C., Layman, B., Clark, E., Dean, J., and Hall, F., Practical Software Measurement: Objective Information for Decision Makers, Addison-Wesley Professional, 1st edition, 2001. ISBN 0201715163.

23. MINITAB Statistical Software, Release 14, http://www.minitab.com/products/minitab/14/default.aspx.

24. 24.NATO, "AQAP-150: NATO Quality Assurance Requirements for Software Development (Edition 2)", September 1997.

25. Park, R.E., Goethert, W.B., and Florac, W.A., "Goal-Driven Software Measurement", CMU/SEI-96-HB-002, August 1996.

26. Paulk, M.C., Weber, C.V., Curtis, B., and Chrissis, M.B., The Capability Maturity Model: Guidelines for Improving Software Process, Addison-Wesley Publishing, October 1995.

27. Paulk, M.C., "Practices for High Maturity Organizations", Proceedings of the 1999 Software Engineering Process Group Conference, Atlanta, Georgia, March 1999, pp.28-31.

28. Radice, R., "Statistical Process Control for Software Projects", 10th Software Engineering Process Group Conference, Chicago, Illinois, March 1998.

29. Shewhart, W.A., Economic Control of Quality of Manufactured Product, Van Nostrand, New York, 1931 (re-printed by American Soc.of Quality Control, Milwaukee, Wisc., 1980.)

30. 30.Tarhan A., and Demirors, O., "Remarks from SPC Trial for an Emergent Organization", Presentation, Europen SEPG Conference, 12-15 June 2006, Amsterdam, Holland.

31. Weller, E., Practical Applications of Statistical Process Control. IEEE Software, May/June 2000, pp.48-55.

32. Wheeler, D.J., Understanding Variation: The Key to Managing Chaos, SPC Press, Knoxville, Tenn., 1993.

33. Wheeler, D.J., Advanced Topics in Statistical Process Control, SPC Press, Knoxville, 1995.

Current Practices of Measuring Quality in Finnish Software Engineering Industry

Jari Soini[1], Vesa Tenhunen[2], and Markku Tukiainen[2]

[1] Tampere University of Technology - Pori, P.O. Box 300, FIN-28101 Pori, Finland
[2] University of Joensuu, Department of Computer Science, P.O. Box 111, FIN-80101 Joensuu, Finland

Abstract. Measurement is an important factor in Software Process Improvement, but many organizations have difficulties in establishing and utilizing metrics programs. Our ongoing research project Software Measurement (SoMe) is aimed at creating a set of tools to help in measuring and improving the quality of software products and processes. In this paper we present the current state of measurement in the Finnish software companies participating in our project and the experience they have gained. The research is based on a series of interviews and questionnaires, created to collect the experiences the companies have about individual metrics and measurement in general. These results show which process groups the measurement is focused on, and who are the beneficiaries of the measurement results in practice.

Keywords: Measurement, metrics, quality, software process improvement.

1 Introduction

Continuous process improvement has become almost a necessity for software companies, if they want to enhance their operational precondition and competitiveness in the software business [3, 17]. It is widely known that measurement is a prerequisite for improvements to process and reliability. [17].

The objective of this paper is to evaluate the focus of process and product quality measurement in practice, and how the results of measurements are used in organizations. As a part of an ongoing research project called Software Measurement, or SoMe, we carried out a series of interviews in a sample of Finnish software companies. In this paper we present the results from these interviews, concentrating on the information needs of the companies by mapping the metrics used in ISO/IEC 15504 (SPICE) [12] standard's process groups. We also looked into the beneficiaries of the data produced by the metrics. These results will give some indication of how and where to find future targets for measurement to improve the quality of software products and software engineering processes.

The structure of this paper is as follows: Firstly, the background of the study is described in Chapter 2, as well as the key concepts used and the limitations on

I. Richardson, P. Runeson, and R. Messnarz (Eds.): EuroSPI 2006, LNCS 4257, pp. 100–110, 2006.

the scope of the study. In Chapter 3, we present the research method we selected and the participants in the research. Next, in Chapter 4, we present the results obtained from the research, and in Chapter 5 their analysis and evaluation. In Chapter 6, we summarize the conclusions of the paper.

2   Background

This chapter describes the background and context of the study. We briefly describe the connection between measuring and SPI, and also give an outline of the ongoing project and in particular the interview section, which is analyzed in this paper. Finally the limitations and the key concepts of this research are presented.

2.1   Measurement – An Essential Part of SPI

There is a strong belief that SPI is essential for future success and that it can significantly improve software quality [14]. Continuous process improvement cannot exist reliably without a continuous and systematic monitoring and measurement of the company's own processes [6, 17]. Software measurement is widely recognized as an essential part of understanding, controlling, monitoring, predicting and evaluating software development and maintenance projects [6, 4, 15] and as a necessary part of any SPI program [1, 11, 8]. Two of the most fundamental reasons for measuring software are to control the processes of software production, and to indicate the quality of the product. It is also a widely accepted fact that the quality of a software product is largely determined by the quality of the process used [17].

Measurement plays an important role in process and product quality to ensure that customer requirements have been met, to provide a visible means for the management to monitor their own performance level, highlight quality problems, and provide feedback to drive the improvement effort. In practice, it has proved difficult to define the key functional process and product measurements. Especially, the utilization of the measurement results must be taken into account when developing new measurement systems in the future.

Measurement is not a goal in itself. The most effective use of data for organizational learning and SPI is to feed the data back in some form to the members of the organization. Monitoring and reporting progress has been important in creating continuing support from various levels of the organization. Measurement is meaningless without interpretation and judgment by those who will make the decisions and take actions based on them [5]. As well as management, measurement provides opportunities for developers to participate in analyzing, interpreting and learning from the results of measurements and to identify concrete areas for improvement. It is important that measurement systems are designed by software developers for learning, rather than by management for control [5].

2.2 SoMe, Software Measurement Project

In the ongoing project SoMe (Software Measurement), we are studying different practices and tools to help solve the measurement problems related to the quality of both software process development and software products. We also find out the current needs and experiences of the software companies participating in our project. As a part of the research, we have collected and analyzed project level and organizational level data about improving process and product quality, and together with measurement experiences from companies and experts we have created knowledge items from them. The final outcome of the project will be a measurement knowledge base consisting of a large metrics database. It will be released together with its support systems at the end of the project.

The project was initiated by FiSMA, the Finnish Software Measurement Association [7]. Among its members are many of the most notable software companies in Finland.

2.3 The Key Concepts and Outlines of This Study

The concepts that are central to this study are as follows: *Factor* means the objective on which the measurement is focused. *Metrics* are quantifiable attributes of the development or maintenance processes and their environment (process metrics) or quantifiable features of the software product (product metrics). *Software process improvement* (SPI) means a systematic methodology that significantly helps businesses simplify and streamline operational processes. The objective of process improvement is to ensure that business processes eliminate errors, minimize delays, promote understanding, are easy to use, are customer-friendly, adaptable, enhance competitiveness, and reduce excess capacity [10].

The research scope was limited as follows: Firstly, the research was defined so that our target group was software companies who are members of FiSMA. Of these, we sampled the companies that had previous experience and knowledge with software measurement. Secondly, the persons selected to be interviewed were people who had experience, knowledge and understanding of measurement within their respective companies – mainly quality managers, heads of departments and systems analysts. We assumed that the monitoring of their own company's internal processes and operations is part of the management's job description. Quality managers can also be considered as having a holistic view on the company's measurement activities. The third limitation is related to the research topic. In the SoMe project, our scope is to study process and product quality, because the software companies in FiSMA recognize measuring them as a challenge. Therefore, our focus in this paper is to describe the current situation related to the factors where the process and product quality measurement is emphasized in the target companies.

3   Case Study

The following two sections describe how the research was carried out. First we describe the research method and then give a short overview of the participants in the research.

3.1   Method

Our method was to conduct interviews to address research questions. The target group was FiSMA participants from all over Finland. The research material was collected with the help of personal interviews. We used the same structured interview templates in all interview sessions: one form to collect general information about the company and its measurement practices, and another spreadsheet-style form to collect all metrics the company uses or has used (see Appendix A).

When planning the interview forms, we tried to formulate the questions on quite a general level and to make them easy to answer using terminology which would be well known to all participants. In the interview sessions we asked the quality managers about the current measurement objectives related to process and product quality, and how the measurement is arranged in practice. The aim was to clarify the factors on which the current measurement is focused. For the purpose of further analysis, we also inquired detailed information about the individual metrics. From these results we can see which process groups the measurement emphasized and who are the beneficiaries.

3.2   Participants

A total of eight companies participated in this study. Three of them work in financial industry, two in software engineering, one in ITC services, one in manufacturing and one in automation systems. Five of the companies operate in Finland only, the other three also internationally. By the number of employees, the company sizes range from 195 to 15 000 (see Table 1). The common characteristic shared by these companies is that they all carry out software development independently.

Table 1. Size of participating companies by number of employees

	A	B	C	D	E	F	G	H
Company size	195	200	220	280	450	1200	3200	15000

Measurement practices and targets varied somewhat between companies. The longest systematically collected and utilized measurement history was over 12 years, but there are also companies who have only recently started to adopt this measurement work. Those who have a long experience of measurement have usually tested a wide set of metrics and measurement targets, and are today concentrating only on a limited amount of "core metrics".

The companies involved in our project were selected by their history in software measurement and by voluntarily participation. This, together with them being members of FiSMA, may create a bias in results, as these companies are more likely to perform SPI and related activities – including measurement – than the Finnish software industry in general.

4   Results

Using our interview forms, the interviewees gave us a total of 102 metrics which in their opinion were related to projects, processes, products and their quality. For the majority of metrics, they also provided descriptions of purposes, usage, effort required, and people using measurement data. Many of those metrics were not strictly in the field we required, so for the purposes of this study, we left out all those that were more geared towards measuring business, personnel and other non-software engineering areas. In addition the metrics without sufficient descriptions were discarded.

After these eliminations, we ended up with 57 metrics, which could be further mapped to 19 distinct measurement factors, derived from the interviews.

Table 2. Companies and their metrics for different measurement factors

Measurement Factors	Participating Companies								Total
	A	B	C	D	E	F	G	H	
Budget	x			x	x		x		4
Conformance to Processes (Post-Release Assessment)				x					1
Conformance to Requirements (Post-Release Assessment)				x					1
Customer Satisfaction	x	x	x		x	x	x	x	7
Defect Removal Workload	x	x						x	3
Distribution of Customer Work			x						1
# of Changes	x								1
# of Defects Found in Testing	x						x		2
# of Defects in System	x					x		x	3
# of Post-Release Customer Calls						x	x		2
# of Post-Release Defects	x	x	x					x	4
Process Assessments	x			x	x				3
Productivity	x							x	2
Progress Rate	x							x	2
Quality Assurance							x		1
Schedule	x	x	x	x	x		x	x	7
System Size		x	x				x	x	4
Validity of Testing			x	x	x				3
Workload	x	x	x	x		x		x	6
Total	12	6	7	7	5	4	7	9	57

Please note that the numbers of metrics (both the initial 102 and the final 57) are a sum of all the metrics of every company; that is, if two companies are using the same metric, it is counted twice, not just once. On the other hand, if a company measures for instance system size with two metrics, within that particular company they are counted only as one metric instead of two.

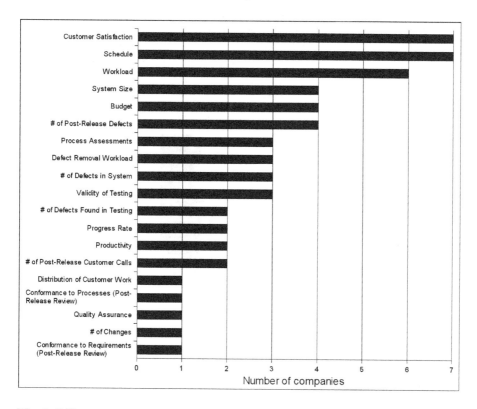

Fig. 1. Different measurement purposes and the number of companies measuring them

One key question in this study was the utilizers of measurement data and their place within organizational hierarchy. In Fig. 2 the metrics are classified according to three utilizer groups: software/project engineers; project managers; and upper management (management above project level including, but not restricted to, quality, business, department and company managers). In each group the metrics are further divided into two segments: metrics that are primarily meant for the members of that group, and those that are secondarily used by that group after some other group has had access to them primarily. Fig. 2 shows that the majority of measurement data benefits upper management. Upper management utilizes 100 % of the metrics, project managers 58 % and software engineers 26 %.

5   Discussion

To understand better what are the measurement needs of the companies, we classified the 19 measurement factors using the process groups of ISO/IEC 15504, or SPICE, reference model as a framework. The mapping of factors was carried out so that within each factor, the metrics' purpose for the company and the life cycle phase when it is used determined to which SPICE process area the factor belonged.

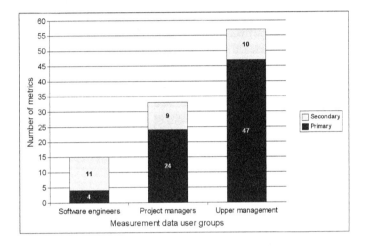

Fig. 2. Distribution of measurement results and their users in a company organization

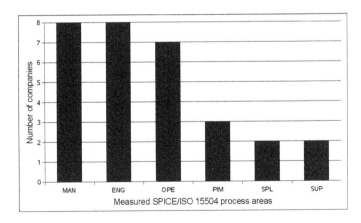

Fig. 3. The number of companies using metrics in various SPICE process groups

As can be seen in Table 3 and Fig. 3, most of the used metrics fall in the process groups of Management (MAN) and Engineering (ENG), followed by Operation (OPE), Support (SUP), Supply (SPL) and Process Improvement (PIM). Measurement is mostly focused on project management and customer satisfaction. Seven out of eight companies measure schedule keeping, the same proportion also collects feedback from customers and measure their satisfaction, and only one company less measures project workload. This is not surprising, as most of the work is done in projects. Also the customer satisfaction can be seen as an important high-level factor indicating company's business performance.

Table 3. Measurement factors mapped to SPICE process groups

Measurement Factors	SPICE Process Areas	# of Companies Measuring Factor
System Size	ENG	4
Validity of Testing	ENG	3
# of Defects in System	ENG	3
Defect Removal Workload	ENG	3
# of Defects Found in Testing	ENG	2
Distribution of Customer Work	ENG	1
Schedule	MAN	7
Workload	MAN	6
Budget	MAN	4
Productivity	MAN	2
Progress Rate	MAN	2
Conformance to Processes (Post-Release Assessment)	MAN	1
Quality Assurance	MAN	1
Customer Satisfaction	OPE	7
# of Post-Release Defects	OPE	4
Process Assessments	PIM	3
# of Post-Release Customer Calls	SPL	2
# of Changes	SUP	1
Conformance to Requirements (Post-Release Assessment)	SUP	1

However, there seems to be a distinctive lack of metrics concerning products and product quality. For example, only three companies measure the defect counts in the system, two companies measure the defect counts in testing and four the post-release defects, but only one company measures all three factors. The same phenomenon can be seen with process quality metrics, too. Less than half of the companies measure their processes, or carry out process assessments.

This bias can be explained by looking into beneficiaries, or those who utilize measurement data. Fig. 2 shows clearly, that most of the measurements are carried out for the benefit of management. All the data produced by all 57 metrics come to upper management, 82 % of them primarily. On the other hand, the engineers on the development level benefit only from 15 metrics, and of those only four are primarily meant for them. Project managers are in the middle with 33 metrics, but 73 % of them are primary.

In spite of the fact that projects are deemed important and therefore measured rather extensively, the scarcity of metrics data intended to software engineers and other project workers is surprising. Even though some of the metrics are usually regarded as tools for project teams and engineers (e.g. system size, defects found, many project metrics, etc.) [16], information they provide seems to be used only on managerial level. As the measurement data is an important means to management and decision-making, this is understandable. But the underrepresentation of engineer-level beneficiaries and the uneven distribution of information has very probably detrimental effects: if not to projects or software engineering, then at least to the validity and reliability of measurements. Much of the data needed to calculate various metrics is gathered by engineers, and the literature contains many cautionary examples of measurement programs failing because of insufficient communication as the personnel is unable to see the relevance or benefit in collecting data for the metrics.[2, 9, 13].

6   Conclusions

In order to improve the quality of software processes and products we have to find out what kind of measurement is practised currently and how to advance these practices. Measurement activities are considered successful if they help project stakeholders first to understand what is happening during their processes, and second, to control what is happening on their projects. Although this is acknowledged, many measurement initiatives have not succeeded in software industry. In many cases this has been contributed to the lack of motivation of the engineering personnel towards doing the measurements.

This paper reports a case study of Finnish software industry's measurement practices and demonstrates that the majority of the measurements is done on the purposes of financial and top-management decision support. There is obviously an imbalance of who gets the results and how the metrics are selected for communication in the organization.

However, the measurement is considered essential by the management and the practices of the measurement are carried out in most of the software organizations. With the purpose of succeeding in measurement programs we need to answer many questions, for example how to make the metrics available to the levels of organization who really need them; and are the right metrics available for upper management, project manager and software engineers? Further research could include investigating the practical means to measure the relevant metrics on different levels of a software company's organization.

References

1. Basili, V.R., Caldiera, G.: Improve Software Quality by Reusing Knowledge and Experience. Sloan Management Review, Vol. 37, No. 1 (1995) 55–64
2. Briand, L., Differding, C., Rombach, H.: Practical Guidelines for Measurement-Based Process Improvement, Software Process: Improvement and Practice, Vol. 2, Num. 4 (1996) 253–280
3. Conradi, R., Fuggetta, A.: Improving Software Process Improvement. IEEE Computer Society Press, Vol. 19, No. 4 (2002) 92–99
4. DeMarco, T.: Controlling Software Projects: Management, Measurement and Estimation. Yourdon Press (1982)
5. Dybå, T.: An Empirical Investigation of the Key Factors for Success in Software Process Improvement. IEEE Transactions on Software Engineering, Vol. 31, No. 5 (2005) 410–424
6. Fenton, N.E., Pfleeger, S.H.: Software Metrics: A Rigorous & Practical Approach. 2.Edition, International Thompson Computer Press (1997)
7. FISMA,
   Finnish Software Measurement Association. http://www.fisma.fi/eng/index. htm (13.4.2006)
8. Grady, R.B.: Successful Software Process Improvement. Prentice-Hall (1997)
9. Grady, R.B., Caswell, D.L.: Software Metrics: Establishing a Company-Wide Program. Prentice-Hall (1987)
10. Harrington, H.J.: Business Process Improvement: The Breakthrough Strategy for Total Quality, Productivity, and Competitiveness. McGraw Hill (1991)
11. Humphrey, W.S.: Managing the Software Process. Addison-Wesley (1989)
12. ISO/IEC 15504. http://www.sei.cmu.edu/iso-15504/ (13.4.2006)
13. Kan, S.: Metrics and Models in Software Quality Engineering. Addison-Wesley (2003)
14. The SPIRE Handbook. Centre for Software Engineering (1998)
15. Van Solingen, R., Berghout, E.: The Goal/Question/Metric Method: A Practical Guide for Quality Improvement of Software Development. McGraw-Hill (1999)
16. Wiegers, K.: A Software Metrics Primer.
   http://www.processimpact.com/articles/metrics_primer.html (13.4.2006)
17. Zahran, S.: Software Process Improvement: Practical Guidelines for Business Success. Addison-Wesley (1997)

Appendix A

Spreadsheet-style interview form for collecting detailed metrics information.

	A	B	C	D	E	F	G	H
	#	Name	Purpose	Type	Target	Application Domain	Formula	Values
		name of the meter	extensive description of the meter and its purpose	meter's type: Monitoring, Controlling, Predicting, Validating	what attributes of product, process and/or project are measured	in what processes, lifecycle phases etc. the meter is used	how the meter is calculated	values the meter produces and their interpretation: what's good, what's bad, what's preferred

	I	J	K	L	M	N	O	P
	Data 1	Data 2	Data 3	Data 4	Data Collection Rate	Primary Collectors	Secondary Collectors	Usage
	data used to calculate the meter	data used to calculate the meter	data used to calculate the meter	data used to calculate the meter (add more columns if needed)	how often the data is collected (e.g. X times in a day/week/month/other, please specify)	who are primarily responsible for measuring or for collecting the data	who are secondarily responsible for measuring or for collecting the data	how the data is collected and the metric calculated

	Q	R	S	T	U
	Examination Rate	Primary Beneficiaries	Secondary Beneficiaries	Workload in Establishing the Meter (1)	Workload in Establishing the Meter (2)
	how often are the meter's results looked at (e.g. X times in a day/week/month/other, please specify)	who are primarily using the meter's results	who are secondarily using the meter's results	how much resources are consumed when the meter is first introduced and established (e.g. person-hours, calendar time etc.)	estimation of the workload; scale: 1 = heavy, 2 = considerable, 3 = moderate, 4 = light

	V	W	X	Y	Z	AA
	Workload in Using the Meter (1)	Workload in Using the Meter (2)	Accuracy	Reliability	Risks	Usefulness
	how much resources are consumed when the meter is used (e.g. person-hours, calendar time etc.)	estimation of the workload; scale: 1 = heavy, 2 = considerable, 3 = moderate, 4 = light	estimated accuracy of the meter's results; scale: 1 = inaccurate, 2 = approximate, 3 = quite accurate, 4 = very accurate	estimated reliability and robustness of the meter's results; scale: 1 = unreliable, 2 = moderate, 3 = quite reliable, 4 = very reliable	risks and problems related to the meter's usage	general estimation of usefulness; scale: 1 = useless, 2 = of limited use, 3 = quite useful, 4 = very useful

	AB	AC	AD	AE	AF
	Other Information	Source	References	Author	Web Links
	free-form notes, comments and other information (e.g. meter's relation to various process models; to different sizes and types of projects or organizations; etc.)	source of the meter, any of the following: Literature, Organizations, Standards	detailed sources of the meter: - name of the author and book/article/web site/etc. - name of the company or organization - name of the standard or model	name of the author who has written the information about the meter in this table	possible links to WWW sites with related information

An Industry-Based Evaluation of
Process Modeling Techniques

Brent Cahill, David Carrington, Brian Song, and Paul Strooper

School of ITEE, The University of Queensland, St Lucia, Australia
Brent.Cahill@au.fujitsu.com,
{davec, bsong, pstroop}@itee.uq.edu.au

Abstract. There are many ways to model software development processes. This paper reports a feature analysis of four process modeling techniques using criteria specified by a software development organization. The evaluation used a single process, peer review, modeled using all four techniques. Performing the modeling activity highlighted the usefulness of the modeling activity and the usefulness of metamodels in structuring processes.

1 Introduction

This paper describes the evaluation of techniques for specifying software development processes. This evaluation forms part of a larger project to evaluate process improvement techniques supported by process modeling. Among other benefits, process modeling has the potential to allow simulation of changes or improvements made to processes. This project is a collaborative partnership between The University of Queensland and Boeing Australia. The aim of the evaluation is to select a process modeling technique based on the requirements of Boeing Australia. Similar organizations can also benefit from this research despite the specific Boeing Australia context, by following the evaluation approach described in this paper for their context.

Boeing Australia is a large software/systems development organization with a primary domain of defense systems. This research is being performed to improve the performance of Boeing Australia's software and systems development.

In related work, Henderson-Sellers et al. [1] describe a metamodel level comparison of the OPF (Open Process Framework) and the Rational Unified Process (RUP). Wang et al. [2] performed a similar comparison of different modeling techniques, but their comparison was smaller in scope and was not conducted in a commercial software/systems context.

To evaluate the different techniques, Qualitative Feature Analysis of the DESMET [3] methodology was used. Section 2 outlines the evaluation approach and details which process modeling techniques were chosen and why. Section 3 contains an application of the four modeling techniques on Boeing Australia's existing peer review process. A comparison of the techniques and the final selection are presented and discussed in Section 4.

R. Messnarz (Ed.): EuroSPI 2006, LNCS 4257, pp. 111–122, 2006.

2 Evaluation Approach

2.1 Criteria for Evaluation

Our evaluation of process modeling techniques was based on criteria identified by stakeholders within Boeing Australia. Key stakeholders were the Software Engineering Functional Manager and Chief Engineer.

Each criterion was assigned a weighting representing its importance to Boeing Australia. The weighting was on a scale of 1 – 5, one being the least important and five the most important. While it was desired that all criteria were met, the weightings were introduced to provide a clear understanding of each criterion's relevance. The following criteria were identified for evaluation:

1. **Ease of use** – *Weighting 4* since ease of use influences how readily the technique is adopted.
2. **Industry Acceptance** – *Weighting 4* since use in industry indicates the likely longevity of the technique and support.
3. **Tailoring** – *Weighting 5* since tailoring is essential for the type of projects at Boeing Australia.
4. **Mapping** – *Weighting 3* since it would be useful for the process modeling technique to be mapped to other techniques and/or approaches.
5. **Improvement Over Current Practice** – *Weighting 5* since for acceptance of the new technique, it must be better than the current technique.
6. **Measurement Data** – *Weighting 2* since it is considered desirable. If measurement data cannot be incorporated, existing methods will continue to be used.
7. **CMMI** – *Weighting 5* since attaining CMMI Level 3 is a high priority for Boeing Australia and any process initiative should support this goal.
8. **Related Elements** – *Weighting 3* since modeling the relationships between the process architecture, measurement and information architectures would increase the value of the technique.
9. **Tool Support** – *Weighting 5* since without tool support, the technique will not be used. This weighting is in agreement with Firesmith & Henderson-Sellers' [4] perspective on CASE tool support.

2.2 Selection of Process Modeling Techniques

Four process modeling techniques (PMTs) were chosen for evaluation:

1. Software Process Engineering Metamodel (SPEM) [5]
2. OPEN Process Framework (OPF) [4]
3. Business Process Definition Metamodel (BPDM) [6]
4. Specification of Coordinated and Cooperative Activities (SOCCA) [7].

The choice of PMTs was determined by an informal evaluation of how each technique would suit Boeing Australia's criteria. It was obvious to consider the two best-known modeling techniques: the Software Process Engineering Metamodel (SPEM) and the OPEN Process Framework (OPF). The SOCCA technique was included because of its ability to model elements of processes, even though it has no metamodel, and the BPDM technique was chosen due to its emphasis on business processes. However the essential feature of all these techniques is that they are able to represent processes.

2.3 Process Selection

To perform the comparative analysis within an acceptable time frame, it was decided to model a single process with each technique. Peer review was chosen for two main reasons: familiarity with the process by the first-named author and the loosely coupled nature of the peer review process.

The first-named author was involved in the development and rollout of an updated peer review process within Boeing Australia. This activity provided an intimate knowledge of the process and its requirements prior to modeling. The peer review process is loosely coupled, because its activities can be defined independently of other processes, which simplifies the modeling. The modeling activities using the four techniques were performed by the first-named author in consultation with Boeing Australia employees working on process improvement.

3 Process Modeling Techniques

Although all four techniques were evaluated, due to space limitations in this paper, only SPEM and OPF are presented in detail as they displayed the most relevant and interesting results.

3.1 Software Process Engineering Metamodel

3.1.1 Background
Developed by the Object Management Group (OMG), the Software Process Engineering Metamodel (SPEM) is intended for the development and maintenance of software processes. It conforms to the Meta Object Facility (MOF) [8], which ensures that it integrates with other models that are MOF-based.

3.1.2 Modeling Overview
SPEM 1.1, which was used in this research, uses UML 1.4 notation. There is good tool support for SPEM due to its inherent relationship with UML and a number of UML tools are able to create SPEM models. Enterprise Architect (v4.5) was the tool used in this project to produce the SPEM models.

At the simplest level, SPEM is an abstraction of roles, work products, and activities. These three concepts are related with roles performing activities on work products. Using SPEM requires that the elements to be modeled are part of the metamodel or extensions to the metamodel. Since SPEM is a UML profile, structuring of SPEM elements can be performed with further constraints that capture domain-specific semantics and modeling patterns.

Modeling using SPEM typically uses a class diagram (Figure 1), activity diagram (Figure 2), and a statechart diagram. The latter diagram is not presented here due to space limitations and also the similarity across techniques. States can also be represented in the activity diagram.

In the SPEM specification, only one role can own an activity. The role-activity rule led to several changes in the modeling of the peer review process and a re-thinking of the structure of roles within that process. Changes to the peer review roles led to a refactoring of the process model to include the role of the peer review team, a role that would not have been developed otherwise. The role of the peer review team is central to the peer review process as displayed in Figure 1. The creation of the peer review team simplified the representation of the peer review process. Rather than have multiple roles interact with peer review activities, refinement introduced the concept of a peer review team with shared role behaviors. Thus, the peer review team can also be used to distinguish between multiple roles performing an activity together and multiple roles performing the same activity individually.   Figure 2 provides further evidence of the simplification of using a peer review team. Without the peer review team role, the number of swim lanes (and hence the complexity of the diagram) would have increased, reducing readability. Activity diagrams can represent changes to work products. State changes are indicated via the names of work products as shown in Figure 2. The activity diagram shows the relationship between roles, activities and the states of the work products.

3.1.3   Technique Distinctions

A unique element of SPEM is the use of well-formedness rules. These rules provide guidance to the methodologist (process architect) as to the correct structure of methodology entities. The use of these rules provides clarity of understanding that appears to be lacking in the other process modeling techniques.

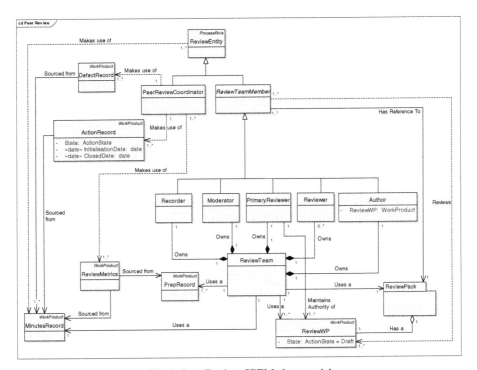

Fig. 1. Peer Review SPEM class model

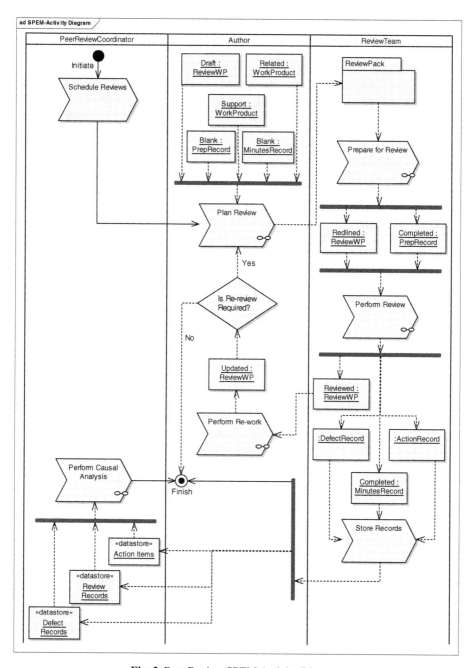

Fig. 2. Peer Review SPEM Activity Diagram

SPEM can be used with or without a UML profile, however use without a UML profile removes the ability to use <<stereotypes>> resulting in a potentially less constrained metamodel. Stereotypes allow entities to be modeled as a type of class already specified, thus reducing the number of classes that exist in the process model. The SPEM UML profile was used for this research.

3.1.4 Discussion

The use of preconditions and goals provide the criteria for entry and exit of life cycles that govern processes, goals essentially forming the post-conditions for processes. SPEM provides a simple construct using preconditions and goals to develop rules for when and how a process is performed and when it is successful in performing that function.

"WorkDefinition behavior is defined using no more than a single Activity Graph and in no other way" [5]. Although this well-formedness rule states that no more than one activity graph should be used to describe a work definition (a description of the work performed in the process), we have chosen to interpret that the iterative nature of the subwork role, WorkDefinition, allows for each work definition that constitutes the parent work definition to have its own activity graph. A result of this interpretation is that an activity graph of a work definition can have multiple levels.

Overall there is room for interpretation within the SPEM model and this is partly due to the range of SPEM's optional elements. This allows users flexibility in the creation of the model but is a weakness when considering rigorous specification of processes.

3.2 OPEN Process Framework (OPF)

3.2.1 Background

A product of the OPEN consortium, the OPEN Process Framework (OPF) provides a metamodel for defining object-oriented and component-based software development processes. The OPF was developed from prior research to advance OO and component-based software engineering processes.

As recommended by the OPEN Consortium, the OPEN Modeling Language (OML) was used. The OML notation is a recognized variant of UML, providing full UML support as well as further functionality not provided by UML [4].

From the OPEN philosophy, the weakness in UML is the poor support for responsibilities, roles, and whole-part relationships. A primary difference between OML and UML is that OML provides only unidirectional relationships between classes, thus maintaining encapsulation and information hiding in designs.

3.2.2 Modeling Overview

We are not aware of CASE tools that support OML so OML modeling was performed in Microsoft Visio™ which is a generic modeling tool. In the peer review class model using OPF/OML displayed in Figure 3, the classes remain the same, yet relationships between the classes are subtly different. Where review team was a composition under the UML notation in Figure 1, it is shown in Figure 3 as a membership. It is evident that the activity diagram of OPF/OML in Figure 4 is radically different from SPEM's activity diagram.

The OPF/OML activity diagram in Figure 4 presents a relatively simple activity diagram relating roles to work products via activities. This diagrammatic technique does not assist understanding of the order in which activities are to be performed, nor does it provide insight into the state changes of work products.

3.2.3   Technique Distinctions

Life cycles are built into the OPF allowing for the specification of life cycles separately to processes, tasks, activities, etc. OPF process constraints are represented

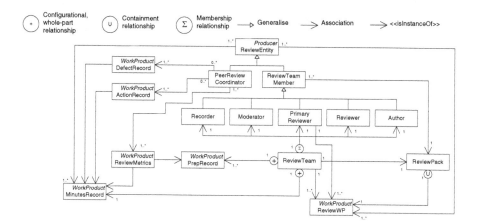

Fig. 3. Peer Review OPF Class Diagram

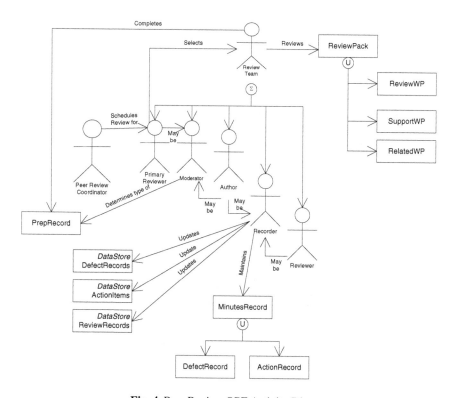

Fig. 4. Peer Review OPF Activity Diagram

as goals, objectives, purposes, pre-conditions, and post-conditions. These concepts help define processes and activities. Pre-conditions and post-conditions are heavily relied upon within the OPF.

3.2.4 Discussion

A process framework, according to Firesmith & Henderson-Sellers [4], should include a large class library of standard pre-defined process components. This philosophy is apparent in the significantly larger OPF metamodel compared to SPEM. This metamodel provides finer granularity by pre-defining a number of metamodel elements. A strength of the OPF is that it has a large class library of elements. Indeed it is not possible to provide a model of the OPF within the limits of this paper. Even though SPEM has fewer elements in the metamodel than OPF, it is possible to extend either metamodel, in accordance with certain rules.

The use of an extensive predefined class library is an advantage for OPF/OML by providing more guidance in the development of its models. Conversely this extensive predefined class library also takes more time to learn and understand, a disadvantage by comparison with SPEM which has a simpler metamodel allowing flexibility in defining its process models.

4 Technique Comparison

Table 1 summarizes the evaluation of the process modeling techniques against the criteria defined in Section 2.1. Following is the rationale for the ratings.

Table 1. Technique weighted comparison

Criteria	Weight	SPEM	OPF / OML	SOCCA	BPDM
Ease of Use	4	4	4	2	3
Industry Support	4	5	4	0	1
Tailoring	5	3	3	0	2
Mapping	3	4	1	0	2
Improvement Over Current Practice	5	5	5	3	4
Measurement Data	2	1	1	1	1
CMMI Support	5	5	5	3	5
Related Elements	3	3	3	3	3
Tool support	5	5	2	2	2
Weighted Total		149	121	59	98

1. **Ease of Use** – SPEM and OPF/OML provide a well-structured metamodel on which to base process models. The use of standard notation or the variant OML, assisted greatly in ease of use due to the availability of tools, reference material, and knowledge.

2. **Industry Acceptance** – Industry acceptance was determined by the existence of an active community for the modeling technique. SPEM and OPF scored well since SPEM has the support of the OMG and OPF the support of the open consortium, although the wide acceptance of UML provided SPEM an advantage over OPF. The OPF rating may be strengthened on two points: the use of the UML notation instead of OML and the development of the OPF into the international standard ISO/IEC WD 24744 [10]. However the current evaluation was based on the OPF with OML.

3. **Tailoring** – Those techniques based on a metamodel provide rules for the extension of the metamodel. Such extensions allow limited tailoring at the metamodel level.

4. **Mapping** – SPEM has the greatest support in terms of mapping. Derived from OMG's MOF, SPEM is compatible across the suite of OMG standards. BPDM was not given the same rating however, due to the formative status of the standard.

5. **Improvement Over Current Practice** – Each of SPEM, OPF, and BPDM provide a more detailed approach to process modeling than Boeing Australia's current practice.

6. **Measurement Data** – None of the techniques evaluated provided an obvious mechanism for incorporating metrics into process models. However, it is possible to improvise measures by representing them in the same way as work products in the class and activity diagrams of all the evaluated techniques. An example of representing metrics is shown in Figure 1 and Figure 3.

7. **CMMI Support** – The simple act of using these techniques to specify and model processes provides support for CMMI. The use of a process model also allows a standard process to be specified and tailored as required for multiple projects.

8. **Related Elements** – As identified in point 6, the capturing of measurement is a weak point for each of these techniques, however the information architecture can be captured in the work product elements of the processes modeled. Therefore each of the techniques rated moderately.

9. **Tool Support** – Modeling tools exist for the support of UML, resulting in a high rating for SPEM. OPF/OML received a low score because of the lack of tool support for OML. SOCCA uses its own notation for the modeling of processes and BPDM uses a variation of UML activity diagrams that have no tool support.

From the weighted ratings, it is clear that SPEM and OPF rate much higher than either of the other two techniques. SPEM rated higher primarily due to industry support and the portability provided through its close relationship with UML. Most of the difference between SPEM and OPF could be removed if UML had been used instead of OML for the OPF models.

The two leading techniques have a key difference in the guidance and rigor provided. OPF contains a relatively large set of elements in comparison to SPEM. Consequently OPF contains more rules and guidance for the specification and modeling of processes, while SPEM has greater flexibility for instantiating processes, allowing the user more freedom of expression in its process models, but lacking the rigid specification of OPF.

During the development of process models, the original form of the peer review process was altered based on weaknesses identified during modeling. This refactoring reinforced the benefit of developing process models using the three types of diagrams, activity, class and statechart. Iterating through the process models, the first-named author and Boeing Australia employees identified weaknesses in the existing peer review process. The result was a refined process description capturing better understanding of the roles, activities and work products required.

To some extent, OPF provides a formal description of a practice already performed in Boeing Australia. OPF's concept of a Contract Driven Life Cycle provided a framework for the use of pre-conditions and post-conditions.

Evaluation of the modeling techniques raised issues for future research. The SPEM, OPF and BPDM metamodels are evolving, thus a future evaluation of the techniques would be considered prudent. OPF forms the basis for Australian Standard (AS 4651-2004) [9] which is seeking adoption from the International Standards Organization (ISO/IEC WD 24744) [10]. OMG currently has a request for submissions for a new version of SPEM and is currently developing the Business Process Development Metamodel.

From a usability perspective, SPEM was the only technique to incorporate the state change of work products in the activity diagram and this reduces the number of diagrams that a process engineer potentially needs to develop.

5 Concluding Remarks

The evaluation of process modeling techniques within Boeing Australia was performed to identify the most appropriate modeling technique for the organization, when developing an overall process architecture. The criteria for assessing the process modeling techniques were set by Boeing Australia. Each technique was used to model a single process, the peer review process, so the effectiveness of the techniques could be readily compared. Although this research was done in the specific context of Boeing Australia, the outcome of this evaluation is relevant to similar organizations especially from the finding that process modeling can contribute to process improvement. Organizations can adopt the proposed evaluation criteria or can follow the approach presented in this paper with their own customized criteria and context.

Peer review was chosen for this evaluation because it does not require tight integration with other processes. However the activity of modeling and specifying processes to develop a process architecture will require a focus on the integration between processes. This focus will ensure that a complete picture of an organization's processes can be developed. Subsequently changes made to one process can have impacts on other processes identified and managed.

The weighted criteria identify SPEM as the most appropriate option for Boeing Australia. As a modeling technique, SPEM provides greater flexibility and support than OPF, with either OML or UML. This conclusion holds even though OPF provides more guidance and structure. SPEM has greater industry support through the OMG, which also allows for transformation of models into other descriptions. The results of this evaluation may need to be updated, given the adoption of the OPF as ISO/IEC WD 24744 [10] and should be reassessed once the standard has stabilized and gathered support.

Modeling the peer review process was worthwhile, since the refactoring performed led to a better understanding and streamlining of the process model. An improved process description was developed compared to the original. The refactoring led to new roles and new states for work products.

Measurement was not explicitly included in the techniques used for this evaluation. The lack of measurement classes/objects means that no association was made for measuring and managing processes. Support for Boeing Australia's CMMI goals was also weakened since measurement was not easily captured in the process models.

A framework is currently being developed for using SPEM to model the integration between processes starting with Requirements Analysis, which will be seen as the core process. Its integration with supporting processes and measurements will be part of the modeling scope. The contribution of this project towards Boeing Australia's CMMI initiative will continue to be a key factor in determining the value of process modeling.

Acknowledgements

We thank Boeing Australia for participating in this research and for their continuing support of collaborative software process research. We also thank those individuals at Boeing Australia who provided their time to the project, Rick Neilson, Gary Morris, Nikola Gluhajic, Kym Drummond and Derek Dominish. The Australian Research Council provided funding for the Effective Software Process Improvement project via an Australian Research Council Linkage Grant. We also thank the referees who reviewed this paper.

References

1. Henderson-Sellers, B., Collins, G., Due, R., Graham, I. A Qualitative Comparison of Two Processes for Object-Oriented Software Development. Information and Software Technology, 43 (2001) 705-724
2. Wang, A.I., Conradi, R., Thuv, C.: Framework for Evaluating Process Modelling Languages for Distributed Environments, Software Engineering and Applications, ACTA Press Phoenix, (2005) 6-9
3. Kitchenham, B. A.: Evaluating Software Engineering Methods and Tool – Part 1: The Evaluation Context and Evaluation Methods. ACM Software Engineering Notes, 21, 1 (1996) 11-15
4. Firesmith, D., and Henderson-Sellers, B.: The OPEN Process Framework. Addison-Wesley, Harlow, UK (2002)
5. Software Process Engineering Metamodel Specification v1.1 – Object Management Group (2001)
6. Frank, J., Gardner, T., Johnston, S., White, S., Iyengar, S.: Business Process Definition Metamodel – Concepts and Overview. IBM whitepaper, Object Management Group, Needham, MA (2004)

7. Engels, G. and Groenewegen, L.: SOCCA: Specifications of Coordinated and Cooperative Activities, Software Process Modelling and Technology. Research Studies Press, Taunton, UK (1994)
8. Wiegers, K. E.: Peer Reviews in Software – A Practical Guide. Addison-Wesley, Reading, MA (2002)
9. AS 4651-2004 Australian Standard – Standard Metamodel for Software Development Methodologies (2005)
10. ISO/IEC WD 24744 (2005-12-23) Information Technology – Software Engineering – Metamodel for Development Methodologies (2005)

Process Model Difference Analysis for Supporting Process Evolution

Martín Soto and Jürgen Münch

Fraunhofer Institute for Experimental Software Engineering,
Fraunhofer-Platz 1, 67663 Kaiserslautern, Germany
{soto, muench}@iese.fraunhofer.de

Abstract. Software development processes are subject to variations in time and space, variations that can originate from learning effects, differences in application domains, or a number of other causes. Identifying and analyzing such differences is crucial for a variety of process activities, like defining and evolving process standards, or analyzing the compliance of process models to existing standards, among others. In this paper, we show why appropriately identifying, describing, and visualizing differences between process models in order to support such activities is a highly challenging task. We present scenarios that motivate the need for process model difference analysis, and describe the conceptual and technical challenges arising from them. In addition, we sketch an initial tool-based approach implementing difference analysis, and contrast it with similar existing approaches. The results from this paper constitute the requirements for our ongoing development effort, whose objectives we also describe briefly.

1 Introduction

Software development organizations striving to achieve a high level of process maturity must sooner or later face the problem of process standardization, namely, guaranteeing that all organization units develop software according to one well-known, unified process. Achieving process uniformity generally requires the definition of *standard processes* (sometimes also called reference processes or generic processes) that capture organization-wide process knowledge, possibly with emphasis on a particular application domain (e.g., space software) and/or on specific development contexts (e.g., large projects). However, since they are generic, standard processes must be tailored to the particular needs of the various projects inside the organization, leading to many separate *project-specific processes.*

Both standard and project-specific processes are subject to evolving along their life cycle. Rapid technology changes, newly available useful knowledge, changes in regulations or process standards, and new project experience, to only mention a few factors, contribute to push processes in different directions. Moreover, processes need to be designed, described, introduced, and maintained in such a way that they become accepted by practitioners and thus actually used in practice. For this reason, evolution must be guided by solid, practical experience.

The problem of driving process evolution based on experience involves activities both at the organizational and at the project level. Initially, particular projects tailor

R. Messnarz (Ed.): EuroSPI 2006, LNCS 4257, pp. 123 – 134, 2006.

processes to their needs and proceed to enact them. During enactment, issues involving the process definition are typically observed, ranging from the need to refine certain process entities in order to make them more specific, to the identification of areas of the process definition that are openly inadequate and must be redefined.

Incorporating this local, project-specific experience into the standard organizational process is a potentially complex task involving at least the following two steps. First of all, local variations must be identified and characterized in order to determine if they are general enough to become part of the standard process. Afterwards, selected local variations must be generalized and added to the standard process as alternatives, together with constraints or rules limiting their use to particular cases. This, of course, requires a deeper understanding of the appropriateness of the process alternatives for different contexts and their effects on these contexts.

Additionally, before the start of a new project, a characterization of the project context and its goals must be produced, providing the information needed to select adequate process alternatives for the project. This closes the experience cycle, opening opportunities for experience reuse.

We believe that the first step can be effectively supported by so-called *process model difference analysis*, namely, finding, analyzing, and displaying the differences between variants of a single process model in ways that are meaningful, and thus useful, to the people maintaining and using the process. The second step addresses the so-called *variability analysis*, i.e., identifying which context characteristics and project goals differ among a family of projects, and determining the corresponding process variation points and the rules associated to them. The concept of variability analysis originally comes from product line engineering [1].

This paper presents our current steps towards an effective, practical approach for process model difference analysis. The rest of the paper is structured as follows: In Section 2, we present two process management scenarios derived from our experience with process modeling and implementation, analyze the possible role of difference analysis in them, and derive a set of basic interesting difference analysis operations. In Section 3, we discuss the conceptual and technical challenges of process model difference analysis, and contrast them to existing procedures like the standard longest common subsequence algorithm used by diff. Section 4 discusses the basic concepts of our ongoing implementation work. Section 5 presents some related work and Section 6 concludes the paper by discussing open challenges and plans for realizing our view.

2 Application Scenarios for Difference Analysis

In the following, we sketch two scenarios that demonstrate the need for process model difference analysis. These scenarios are based on the authors' experience in defining and managing the evolution of process standards (such as the SETG [2] of the European Space Agency) and implementing compliance management in organizations. The scenarios are used to identify a set of basic operations involved in difference analysis. For each one of the two scenarios, we describe the problem at hand and identify the process stakeholders (or rather, stakeholder roles) involved in it. In a second step, we list the questions that each stakeholder must answer in the context of the scenario, together with the difference analysis operations that can be used to support the stakeholders in answering these questions.

2.1   Scenario 1: Definition and Evolution of Process Standards

In principle, there are two main approaches to the definition of process standards: *top-down* and *bottom-up*. In the top-down approach, a standardization board collects individual experiences, methods found in literature, or requirements enforced by other standards, and creates a prescriptive process model, which is then provided to the development organization and empirically optimized later on. The ECSS [3] standards for space software, or the German national V-Modell XT standard [4] are examples of the top-down approach. In the bottom-up approach, standards are mainly developed based on observation and descriptive modeling. The WISEP reference process for wireless Internet services [5] and the LIPE reference model for e-business software development [6] illustrate this approach. It is important to observe that, independently of how process evolution is managed, observing processes in practice, identifying variations in them, analyzing these variations, and feeding them back into the standard process model [7] are fundamental activities for actual improvement. This feedback cycle can be supported by process model difference analysis.

One typical scenario is that a large software organization distributes a single process model to several of its development units, which is intended to be used as the main software process description for conducting independent software development projects. Since the defined process has not been widely tested in the context of the organization, and since conditions differ from one project to the next, individual projects are allowed to adapt the process description in an ad-hoc manner to better suit their particular needs.

After a few months, the independently tailored process models have diverged significantly. This poses a number of challenges:

– The central organization wants to make sure that, despite project differences, a unified basic process is followed by all projects, and that the customization of this process is done in a systematic way. In other words, it is important to prevent local processes from diverging too much from the established organization standard.
– Additionally, practices introduced by individual projects may turn out to be useful to other projects. It would be valuable to identify such practices, abstract them, and eventually integrate them with the generic organization-level process definition.
– Furthermore, it would be valuable to identify areas of the current process that adequately fit the organization's environment, as well as areas that may be difficult to enact in the current environment. It would also be important to identify areas that, although adequate, may require improvements in their documentation.
– Software managers, software developers and, generally, personnel working on software projects, may be moved between projects based on changing organizational needs and priorities. People used to one project's process definition may have problems getting acquainted with new, slightly different processes between their previous and new projects. Process difference analysis could help to identify these differences and provide guidance for working in the new project.

A similar scenario arises when a reference process model (e.g., V-Modell XT or ECSS) is adopted and further tailored by separate organizations. The standards body responsible for the reference model may be interested in collecting feedback from process users in order to determine how the reference model should evolve.

The following table lists involved stakeholders, their questions, and the way process model difference analysis can support them in answering their questions:

Stakeholder	Question	Helpful difference-analysis operations
Software Process Group	Are there any structural changes (new/deleted activities/products, different relations) in project processes with respect to the organization's process?	Visualize structure with differences.
	Do structural changes affect the general process structure or only the detailed structure of particular process areas?	Provide different views into process structure and structural differences: general, per process area, per role, etc.
	Which entity descriptions were modified? What sort of modifications happened?	List changed descriptions. Highlight entities in the general structure whose descriptions changed. Measure the extent of changes and visualize it based on the structure (i.e., map trees.) Apply text comparison to descriptions.
	Which areas of the process were changed by many projects? Are the changes similar?	Present differences with respect to the main model in parallel. Apply similarity detection algorithms to common changed areas.
Project Manager	Which process changes have we made until now? Can we justify them based on our concrete project needs and requirements?	Visualize structural differences, including views. Visualize description differences on top of the structure. Visualize recorded rationales for changes [17].
Developer (process agent)	What is different between the process I used to follow in my old project and the process defined for my new project?	Compare processes from the old and the new project with common ancestor (main organizational process is the ancestor.)
	What's special in my new project's process with respect to the general organization's process I learned in my training?	Compare process with ancestor.

2.2 Scenario 2: Process Compliance Analysis

Nowadays, more and more organizations are subject to regulatory constraints requiring the existence of explicit processes, as well as adherence to them (see, for example, the IEC 61508 standard for safety-related systems [8].) Being compliant typically requires maintaining traceability information that captures the relationships between the actual and the prescribed development processes, a difficult task since, for a variety of reasons, it is possible for both models to evolve, thus leading to deviations. Difference analysis can help to characterize the evolution in order to determine whether action is necessary to stay compliant. In addition, traceability information needs only to be updated for those process parts of the models that changed.

The following is one typical scenario: A development organization adopts a reference model as a base definition for its development processes. As usual with reference models, although they provide a good framework for process definition, some aspects of them must be adapted to the unique needs of each organization. For this reason, a tailoring effort is launched, which concludes several months later with a process definition adequate for being used by new development projects at the organization. Some time afterwards, and independently from all internal process efforts, a new version of the reference model is published. There is pressure from inside and outside the organization to use this new version of the reference model. However, the organization does not want to lose the significant effort invested in tailoring the old version. The transition poses a number of difficulties:

- It is hard to determine which tailoring changes can be moved to the new version of the reference model directly, which of them can be adapted, and which must be discarded because either they are now covered by the new model or they conflict with it.
- Moreover, since it is difficult to reliably identify the areas that must be changed, even estimating the effort necessary to produce a tailored variant of the new reference model version can be very hard.
- In addition, standardization organizations typically do not give sufficient information about the detailed changes. Often, differences between new versions are only described on an abstract level (e.g., the new standard focuses more on reliability), but it is unclear which process elements have changed.

The following table is similar to the one included in the previous scenario:

Stakeholder	Question	Helpful difference-analysis operations
Software Process Group	How exactly were the structure and contents of the reference model modified? Which actual elements were affected and how?	Compare process with ancestor (old version of the reference model is the ancestor.) Visualize structure with differences.

Stakeholder	Question	Helpful difference-analysis operations
	How exactly did we tailor the structure and contents of our current process model? Which actual elements were affected and how?	Compare process with ancestor (old version of the reference model is the ancestor.) Visualize structure with differences.
	Which areas did we tailor that remained essentially untouched in the new reference model version? Which areas were modified in the reference model that we did not touch? Which areas were changed in both cases (conflicts)?	Compare processes with common ancestor (old version of the reference model is the ancestor.) Visualize structure with differences.
	How big are the conflicts? Were do the most complex conflicts lie?	Measure the extent of changes. Compare and visualize.
	Are there structural or content related similarities between our changes and the changes made to the reference model?	Apply similarity algorithms to selected portions of the model.

2.3 Further Applications

Analyzing and visualizing differences between process models can be used in many other situations: An example application is the collaborative design of development processes. Here, difference analysis can be used during the integration of parallel designed processes. Another example for the use of process difference analysis is the development of systems for process versioning and configuration management. Here, differences between process models can be determined and used as deltas to calculate previous versions of process models.

3   Difference Analysis Challenges

Based on the set of useful operations presented above, this section discusses the main challenges we observe in process difference analysis. These challenges cover various conceptual and implementation issues.

3.1 Filtering and Presenting Results for a Multitude of User Groups

Practical process models used in real-world development organizations are often very complex, comprising a large number of interrelated process entities (activities, artifacts, roles, etc). For this reason, a large majority of process stakeholders have to deal with only one portion or aspect of the process model (e.g., only the analysis or the testing process; only administrative or technical portions of the process; only high-level process descriptions; etc.) while performing their daily work.

As shown in the scenarios, the need arises to provide such users with difference analysis operations that are particularly tailored to their needs. This requires a flexible notation for specifying comparisons that is able to express the composition of a variety of filtering, transformation, and visualization algorithms, among other possibilities, to produce the difference analysis results.

Figure 1 shows a graphical comparison of two variants of a hierarchical structure (for example, an activity hierarchy in a process model) that we kept intentionally small for illustration purposes. Such a difference analysis would require filtering the model variants to extract the desired hierarchy, comparing them, and producing an adequate visualization with a graph layout algorithm.

3.2 Genericity

Our experience shows that organizations tend to have very specific, idiosyncratic ways to speak about software development and software development processes. Even if the general concepts used to model software processes tend to be similar, the way they are exactly defined as well as the terminology used to refer to them may vary widely among different software organizations, or even between divisions of a single organization.

Such a variety of process model schemata further complicates difference analysis. Even if we do not try to support comparing models structured according to different schemata, comparison must often make use of schema information in order to produce meaningful results. For example, particular attributes (e.g, long text descriptions) of certain entities belong to data types that require comparison with specialized algorithms (e.g., LCS-based text comparison). Also, the model may contain portions that, based on the schema, may be known to correspond to sequences, trees, or some other known structures that can benefit from being processed with more specialized algorithms.

3.3 Multiple Comparison Algorithms (or, Why Diff Is Not Enough?)

Comparing source code versions and analyzing the resulting differences (often referred to as *patches*) is a task software developers perform on an almost daily basis. Source code comparison serves a variety of purposes, like sharing of changes; review and analysis of changes done by others; space-savvy storage of multiple versions; and measurement of the extent and scope of changes; among others. Such comparisons can be performed using widely available software, like the well-known Unix diff utility, and similar programs.

An obvious question when speaking about model difference analysis is whether the problem is not solved by just storing the models in files and comparing them using diff. Although this is usually possible, it is almost always the case that the results delivered by diff are practically unusable. Diff relies on interpreting files as being composed of text lines (sequences of characters separated by the newline character) and then finding the *longest common sequence* (LCS) of lines by using an efficient algorithm (see [9] for example). The underlying practical assumption is that the material in the file can be read and understood sequentially.

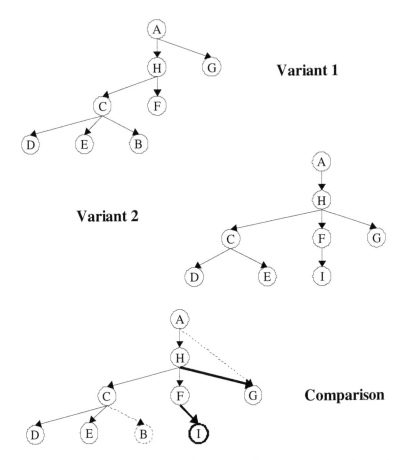

Fig. 1. Hierarchy difference analysis. The first two graphs represent two variants of the same hierarchy (for example, with nodes corresponding to process activities and arrows corresponding to a *has-subactivity* relationship.) The third graph displays the differences between the two hierarchies: dashed elements are present only in the first variant, whereas elements drawn in bold are only in the second one. Other elements are common to both variants. Such a display can be very useful to quickly identify differences between complex structures.

Although this assumption holds true for source code files, process models usually follow patterns that resemble trees or, more generally, graphs instead of plain sequences. They are often heterogeneous in nature, being composed of pieces of data that follow different structural patterns and are represented in diverse ways. Of course, it is always possible to use LCS-based algorithms to compare certain portions of a process model (like text descriptions). It is also possible to store complete models in a line-oriented format (i.e., a text-based formal process model notation) and compare that representation. Although such an approach can be useful for determining differences in particular denotations of a model, we deem it insufficient to cover the wider range of abstract, task-oriented comparisons we are considering.

3.4   Detailed Change Histories Versus Difference Analysis

It is also possible to determine version differences along the evolution of a process model by simply recording every change as it is done. Keeping such a change log manually, however, is very hard, unreliable work that often prevents people from concentrating on their main tasks. For this reason, the only viable alternative is to embed support for recording changes in process modeling tools (similar to the "track changes" function available in common word processing programs).

Even if that is the case and although such change traces can be useful for certain purposes (e.g., auditing) they often contain too much information for most other purposes. For example, changes must often be undone, or they get superseded by larger modifications. Most difference analysis users are not interested in such minutiae. Proper difference analysis requires expressing the differences in a condensed, targeted form, which frequently can be obtained by directly processing the models instead of looking at their detailed change history.

4   A Preliminary Architecture for Difference Analysis

At the time of this writing, we are taking the first steps to produce a practical implementation of the vision presented in the previous chapters. In this section, we briefly discuss the elements that, according to our current vision, should comprise an adequate process model difference analysis system.

A block diagram for our architecture is shown in Figure 2. It is comprised of the following components:

– A *model importer,* which purpose is reading model variants in diverse formats and storing them in a common, comparable format in the model database.

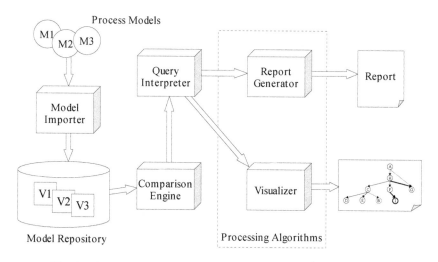

Fig. 2. Block diagram for a preliminary difference analysis architecture

- A *model database*, containing a number of model variants. The database stores process models using W3C's Resource Description Framework (RDF) [18] as a generic notation. RDF is able to represent internal model structures like graphs, trees and sequences. Data attached to such structures, like text descriptions and graphics, can also be stored as RDF literals. Currently, we are testing a trial implementation of such a database, based on a standard relational database system.
- A low-level *comparison engine*, which calculates raw differences between model variants. This engine takes two variants of a model and produces a single model (called the *comparison model*) that contains the elements from both variants decorated to indicate whether they are common to both variants or exclusive to one of them. Our intent is to also use RDF to express such unified comparison models.
- A specialized *query language interpreter*, able to direct the above engine to build a comparison model from two given model variants, and further filter and process it in a variety of ways. This language is also able to feed the (potentially filtered) comparison model to other algorithms for further processing or visualization.
- A number of *visualization and display algorithms* intended to provide a high–level view of the comparison results.

5 Related Work

Although no previous work we know about specifically deals with analyzing and visualizing differences between process models, other research efforts are concerned in one way or another with comparing model variants and providing an adequate representation for the resulting differences.

[10] and [11] deal with the comparison of UML models representing diverse aspects of software systems. These works are generally oriented towards supporting software development in the context of the Model Driven Architecture. Although their basic comparison algorithms are applicable to our work, they are not concerned with providing analysis or visualization for specific users.

[12] presents an extensive survey of approaches for software merging, many of which involve comparison of program versions. Most program comparison, however, occurs at a rather syntactic level, and cannot be easily generalized to work with more abstract structures like process model graphs.

[13] provides an ontology and a set of basic formal definitions related to the comparison of RDF graphs. [14] and [15] describe two systems currently in development that allow for efficiently storing a potentially large number of variants of an RDF model by using a compact representation of the differences between them. These works concentrate on space-efficient storage and transmission of difference sets, but do not go into depth regarding how to use them to support higher-level tasks.

Finally, an extensive base of theoretical work is available from generic graph comparison research (see [16]), an area that is basically concerned with finding isomorphisms (or correspondences that approach isomorphisms according to some metric) between arbitrary graphs whose nodes and edges cannot be directly matched by name. This problem is analogous in many ways to the problem that interests us, but applies to a separate range of practical situations. In our case, we analyze the differences (and, of course, the similarities) between graphs whose nodes can be reliably matched in a computationally inexpensive way.

6 Summary and Future Work

Process model difference analysis helps to determine the differences between two variants of a process model, and offers flexible mechanisms to filter, analyze, and display those differences in specific ways, with the intent of supporting software process evolution. This type of analysis relies on the fact that the compared models contain a sizable common portion that can be used as a base for the comparison.

We have described two process management oriented scenarios where difference analysis can be used to support the tasks of many of the stakeholders involved in process improvement. The analysis of these scenarios allowed us to identify a number of concrete comparison operations that would arguably be useful while performing many of the discussed tasks.

Taking the scenarios and the particular comparison operation types into account, we discussed the main conceptual and technical challenges we think we have to overcome in order to implement a practical difference analysis system. We also presented a preliminary sketch of the software architecture for such a system.

Our aim is to completely implement a working difference analysis system, in order to validate its utility in practical scenarios. The main objectives for the validation are guaranteeing that our system allows us to specify a wide variety of useful comparisons with reasonable effort, and that the produced comparison results constitute useful support for the process improvement tasks at which they are targeted.

Acknowledgments. We would like to thank Sonnhild Namingha from Fraunhofer IESE for proofreading this paper. This work was supported in part by the German Federal Ministry of Education and Research (V-Bench Project, No.01I SE 11 A).

References

1. Rombach, D.: Integrated Software Process and Product Lines: Unifying the Software Process Spectrum. In: International Software Process Workshop, SPW 2005, Revised Selected Papers (Mingshu Li, Barry Boehm, Leon J. Osterweil, eds.) LNCS 3840. Springer-Verlag, (2006)
2. European Space Agency, Board for Software Standardisation and Control (BSSC): Tailoring of ECSS Software Engineering Standards for Ground Segments in ESA. BSSC document 2005(1) Issue 1.0. (2005)
3. European Cooperation for Space Standardization (ECSS), standards available at http://www.ecss.nl (last checked 2006-03-31)
4. V-Modell XT. Available from http://www.v-modell.iabg.de/ (last checked 2006-03-31).
5. Ocampo, A., Boggio, D., Münch, J., Palladino, G.: Towards a Reference Process for Wireless Internet Services, IEEE Transactions on Software Engineering, vol. 29, no. 12 (2003) 1122-1134

6. Zettel, J., Maurer, F., Münch, J., Wong, L.: LIPE: A Lightweight Process for E-Business Startup Companies Based on Extreme Programming. In: Proceedings of the 3rd International Conference on Product Focused Software Process Improvement (Profes 2001). LNCS 2188, Springer-Verlag (2001) 255-270

7. Basili, V. R.; Caldiera, G.; Rombach, H. D.: Experience Factory. In: Marciniak, J. J. (Ed.): Encyclopedia of Software Engineering. Volume 1. A-O. John Wiley & Sons (2002) 511-519

8. International Electrotechnical Commission (IEC): IEC 61508: Functional safety of electrical/electronic/programmable electronic safety-related systems   .
   http://www.iec.ch/zone/fsafety/ (last checked 2006-03-31)

9. Algorithms and Theory of Computation Handbook, CRC Press LLC: Longest Common Subsequence. From Dictionary of Algorithms and Data Structures, Paul E. Black, ed., NIST (1999)

10. Alanen, M., Porres, I.: Difference and Union of Models. In: Proceedings of the UML Conference, LNCS 2863Produktlinien. Springer-Verlag (2003) 2-17

11. Lin, Y., Zhang, J., Gray, J.: Model Comparison: A Key Challenge for Transformation Testing and Version Control in Model Driven Software Development. In: OOPSLA Workshop on Best Practices for Model-Driven Software Development, Vancouver (2004)

12. Mens, T.: A State-of-the-Art Survey on Software Merging. IEEE Transactions on Software Engineering, Vol. 28, No. 5, (2002)

13. Berners-Lee, T., Connolly D.: Delta: An Ontology for the Distribution of Differences Between RDF Graphs. MIT Computer Science and Artificial Intelligence Laboratory (CSAIL). Online publication http://www.w3.org/DesignIssues/Diff (last checked 2006-03-30)

14. Völkel, M., Enguix, C. F., Ryszard-Kruk, S., Zhdanova, A. V., Stevens, R., Sure, Y.: SemVersion - Versioning RDF and Ontologies. Technical Report, University of Karlsruhe. (2005)

15. Kiryakov, A., Ognyanov, D.: Tracking Changes in RDF(S) Repositories. In: Proceedings of the Workshop on Knowledge Transformation for the Semantic Web, KTSW 2002. (2002) Lyon, France.

16. Kobler, J., Schöning, U., Toran, J.: The Graph Isomorphism Problem: Its Structural Complexity. Birkhäuser (1993)

17. Ocampo, A., Münch, J.: Process Evolution Supported by Rationale: An Empirical Investigation of Process Changes. In: Proceedings of the 2nd Software Process Workshop and 7th International Workshop on Software Process Simulation and Modeling, SPW/ProSim 2006. (2006)

18. Manola, F., Miller, E. (eds.): RDF Primer. W3C Recommendation, available from http://www.w3.org/TR/rdf-primer/ (2004) (last checked 2006-03-31)

Changing Role of SPI – Opportunities and Challenges of Process Modeling

Antero Järvi, Tuomas Mäkilä, and Harri Hakonen

University of Turku,
Department of Information Technology,
FI-20014 University of Turku, Finland
{antero.jarvi, tuomas.makila, harri.hakonen}@utu.fi

Abstract. Software process modeling is gaining acceptance because of the evolving Software Process Engineering Metamodel (SPEM) language. While carrying out empirical process research in software companies in order to model reusable process components with SPEM, we have faced issues that concern Software Process Improvement (SPI) more generally. To understand the general context we have structured these issues into five important aspects of SPI. In this paper we present each aspect through its challenges and opportunities from the process modeling point of view. Consequently, we claim that by overcoming the challenges, process modeling will bring new concrete opportunities for SPI.[1]

1 Introduction

During the last year we have worked on modeling software process frameworks into reusable process components using Software Process Engineering Metamodel (SPEM) process modeling language [1]. The aim of this modeling task has been to identify process content that can be encapsulated as process components and to define guidelines for reusing and tailoring the components for different process contexts. Although the modeling language has the needed expressive power, we constantly ran into situations where we faced many different modeling alternatives, but could not find decisive arguments for choosing between them. This is evidently due to our narrow focus on the modeled process framework as an isolated system; we lacked the software development context where the modeled process framework would be used in. This inspired us to conduct an empirical study on the process needs in different types of software companies, aiming at defining the missing process modeling context. Especially, we concentrated on the variation in processes within the software development companies. We wanted to understand the extent of process variation, and how the companies currently manage to provide process support for different types of projects. It turned out that except for the largest companies, process variation

---

[1] This paper is based on work done during the ReProCo research project (Sub-project of the E!3320 project) in co-operation with Genestia Group Inc. - Neoxen Systems and Devera Software Development Center.

had not been studied. Typically the companies had a single process that was generic enough to fit any project.

Software process modeling has a long research history, but industrial adoption has been slow [2]. The reason for this is twofold. First, SPI itself is complex and evolving issue that still faces many improvement needs [3]. Second, process modeling has a more comprehensive effect on SPI than is generally understood. Process modeling does not simply enhance SPI by making process definition and communication more efficient and increasing process presentation clarity, but it also brings a qualitative change to SPI widening its role in the organization.

Based on our experience in process modeling and the empirical study, we have identified areas that have an important role in realizing the potential of process modeling. This paper is structured along these areas: (i) business, project and process coherence, (ii) process frameworks, (iii) process definition, (iv) SPI cycle, and (v) organization's capability. For each area, we discuss the basic challenges that must be overcome and present opportunities for process modeling technology. The areas are illustrated in Figure 1.

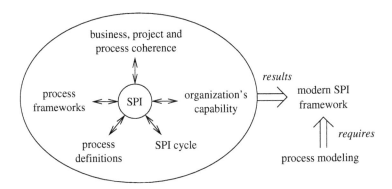

Fig. 1. The areas of concern in realizing the potential of process modeling in a successful SPI function

2   Business, Project and Process Coherence

The fundamental task of the SPI function is to constantly take care of the software processes so that they match the needs of the company's current business objectives. The relevant business goals are company specific and typically involve a mixture of issues of profitability, time-to-market, market share, product strategy, sufficient product and operations quality, and cost efficiency of software development. Also, issues like organizational learning, skills management, core competence and outsourcing management relate to the software development processes. In order to meet the business goals, SPI typically targets process structure and work practices, tooling, quality assurance, compliance to various quality standards or maturity frameworks, software reuse for accumulating long term value, and risk management.

While the fitness of specific processes or methodologies to a certain business context is a common topic in SPI literature, we have found only few cases where the discussion is brought down to practical level where business objectives, described as business factors, are mapped to concrete software process properties. The situation can be clarified by categorizing business factors with respect of stability and volatility, as presented in Figure 2. Stable factors are those that remain unchanged across projects, e.g. organization structure, market situation or product roadmap. Volatile factors vary from project to project including issues like uncertainty of requirements, customer relationship, timeliness requirements, and expected product life span. Traditionally, SPI focuses on stable business factors while volatile project dependent factors are summarized as typical project factors of an average project. This is adequate with similar projects, but fails to provide sufficient process support when the volatile factors vary substantially.

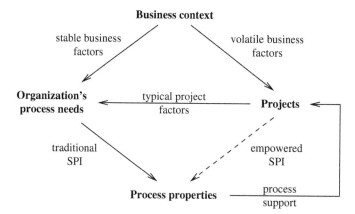

Fig. 2. The stable and volatile business factors map differently to process properties of a project

Coping with the volatile business factors requires empowering SPI with the ability to customize processes for each project based on the project's unique needs. Many popular process frameworks include mechanism for this kind of two-level process tailoring [4,5,6]. However, the frameworks do not explicitly define any business factor taxonomies to guide process tailoring. The required taxonomy consists of (i) business factors and process properties that are categorized and (ii) a mapping from business factors to process properties.

Several business factors have been proposed as the basis for process selection and process customization. We present briefly the approaches of Cockburn and Boehm&Turner. However, neither of these consider the stability of involved factors, instead their work defines common project factor combinations.

Cockburn's Crystal methodology family is adapted to a project in two steps [7]. First a 'methodology type' is selected according to project size and criticality of the developed system. Other factors are taken into account in the second step as priorities that reflect the business objectives that the project faces, e.g.

productivity, repeatability and correctness. The rationale for the first step is that a larger crew needs a more formal methodology and that a more critical system needs more publicly visible correctness in its construction. While this kind of methodology family and selection framework can certainly support high versatility of projects, it is fair to ask how much effort is needed to develop and maintain possibly a few dozen separate processes. Also, the development team's capability to carry out this many methodologies is questionable. However, the factors and priorities are expertly chosen and they certainly capture significant causes of project specific process needs.

Boehm and Turner define two opposite home grounds; one where agile approach is likely to pay off, and another which favors plan-driven methods [8]. They present five critical factors that position a methodology or project with respect to these two home grounds, and also a risk based tailorable method for balancing between them. The positioning factors are system criticality, number of project personnel, skills and capabilities, project dynamism, and organization culture. These factors are used for analyzing the risks of employing agile or plan-driven approach. The process is then tailored to mitigate the risks.

2.1   Challenges

It appears that there is no universal way of choosing which business factors to use as the basis for process variation and the issue is organization and business dependent. For example, the size of the project is generally an important factor, but in some cases other factors like geographical distribution of the development organization can dominate over mere project size.

Thus, the first challenge is to identify the stable and volatile business factors by systematically analyzing the company's business context and projects. Understanding which factors have high priority creates a basis for process design, and is beneficial also for its own sake: The forces that are present can be balanced, risks mitigated and long term business value secured.

The second challenge is supporting the relevant business factors with the software process. This involves selection and adaptation of the process framework, discussed in Section 3, and mapping the business factors to process properties to provide the basis for process tailoring. Mapping the factors to software process properties ties business factors together with development aspects so that they can be resolved together.

2.2   Opportunities

The main opportunity lies in being able to take volatile project factors into account by creating a customized process for a particular project. This is clearly the motivation behind the Crystal methodology family which aims at tailoring a methodology for a project fast enough to get the benefits of customized process before the project is over. Boehm and Turner propose that methods and processes should be built-up, not tailored-down. This should be supported by a repository of 'plug-compatible' process assets that could be quickly adopted, arranged, and used to support specific projects. We share these views and believe that process modeling will provide mechanisms (i) for defining core process structure and content that capture the stable business factors and (ii) for encapsulating the volatile project factors into process components or other reusable or tailorable process assets.

3   Process Frameworks

From the process modeling viewpoint, a process framework describes what must be managed when organizing work, work products, and teams in a given context. The context allows us to have constraints from which, for example, best practices, standardization, and cost-efficiency arise. The most crucial constraints are called dominant assumptions because they define the fundamental characteristics of the process framework. For example, in IBM Rational Unified Process (RUP) it is assumed that Elaboration phase establishes and stabilizes the architecture of a system, and this property is relied on the succeeding Construction phase [5]. In Extreme Programming (XP) process it is assumed that a customer with proper skills and knowledge is constantly available [9]. This is imperative since most of the work in XP relies on instant customer feedback.

Incorporating a new process framework to a company has initiation and managing phases. The initiation of the framework begins with determining and adapting it from the perspective of the company's organization and business context. After this, the process framework is institutionalized to ensure that the organization is able to run it: The skill sets of the company's personnel are supplemented so that the process's practices become organizational process capabilities. This gives concrete means to manage the institutionalized process framework issues, such as project wise tailoring and co-existing frameworks. Figure 3 illustrates the situation where a company initiates projects with agile, RUP, and Microsoft Solution Framework (MSF) [10] process frameworks.

3.1   Challenges

A process framework should be initiated in steps, as described in [11]. In the first step, the process framework is selected and in the second step this company level process is institutionalized. These steps form the two principal challenges of framework adoption.

The first challenge, selecting the framework to fit the company's stable business factors and context, requires understanding the dominant assumptions of the framework under consideration. These assumptions set the limits for the modification of the framework. For example, considering the modifiability, XP is a more specific process than RUP. The applicability of XP is narrow with specific demands, e.g. a single co-located team. Furthermore, the fundamental rules and practices of XP are entwined so that they cannot be altered or removed without in depth analysis of the consequences. On the other hand, the standard RUP is more modifiable but can only be enacted with adaptation. The

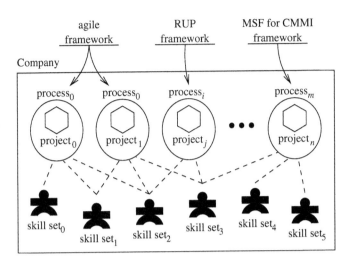

Fig. 3. Initiating process standard frameworks for projects. The projects can run in sequence or in parallel.

goal should be the most specific process framework with respect to the dominant assumptions and modifiability that does not cause foreseeable conflicts. The second challenge in the initiation phase is to institutionalize the selected process framework. This requires that SPI is able to model, manage and utilize personnel skills and organizational capabilities.

A more serious challenge lies in project specific framework adaptation that takes the volatile business factors into account. If the SPI cycle does not keep up with the change rate of the main project factors, it is inevitable that either the work in the project will not conform to the process or the process is used to coerce the work to become inappropriate. This can be an indication of that in terms of dominant assumptions and modifiability a more general or totally different process framework should be used.

Adjusting, adapting, or tailoring an institutionalized process framework is only rarely about including or excluding process elements. For example, it seems unlikely that just removing artifacts, tasks, or roles from a complex framework we get a simpler but still applicable process. If this kind of scalability is possible, it should be defined as a feature in the framework itself. Thus, the SPI's challenge is to cope with the nontrivial management of the company's process frameworks.

A company runs multiple projects in sequence or even in parallel. Because the projects are highly cohesive but rather decoupled, this introduces the continuity problem: How to handle process related know-how, learning, and innovation? It is in the SPI's domain to clarify relationships between the projects that utilize different process frameworks. Process modeling can be used for providing concepts to express explicitly the strategic in-house requirements that affect every process. Process modeling should make SPI more cross-cutting to projects.

All of the preceding challenges call for common conceptualization of the process frameworks. In order to manage multiple institutionalized process frameworks at the same time there must be unifying vocabulary that can describe the processes' similarities and differences. For example, see [12] for various frameworks and [13] for framework attributes taxonomy.

3.2   Opportunities

In a complex problem domain the introduction of common understanding of concepts, relationships, and terminology has often advanced both the research and commercial use. We believe that process modeling will affect SPI similarly, and it will benefit and widen the area where SPI operates successfully. The following process modeling opportunities can contribute to more advanced SPI.

Process modeling separates the definition and use of the process. This means that on one hand, process models can be structured from the perspective of managing large process libraries with efficient tools and practices. On the other hand, the defined processes can be presented in various formats and integrated tightly to project work using tools that are independent of process management.

The opportunity of process management is to achieve specificity and generality at the same time. In practice, process definitions must be structured according the stable and volatile factors using e.g. process components, composition and tailoring mechanisms. This opportunity is materializing rapidly with the appearance of process authoring tools, e.g. Eclipse Process Framework [14] that implements needed process management features.

The opportunity of process usage involves presentation media independence, more interactive ways of presenting the processes, coupling process models to project management for providing automated managerial instruments for planning, monitoring and control, and incorporating processes into integrated development environments for offering a rich process support for the developers.

4   Process Definitions

In every organization a process exists that defines the daily work. In immature or small organizations, the process can be implicitly defined by the culture, tools, document templates and guidelines. This kind of process adapts to the emerging problems in an ad hoc manner with unpredictable results. More mature organizations have explicitly defined processes, forming the basis for continuous process improvement. Process definitions offer a way to analyze the current state of the processes and enable design and communication of process changes.

According to the Capability Maturity Model Integration (CMMI), defined processes are tailored from the organization's process assets [4]. These process assets consist of process descriptions, process element descriptions, life-cycle model descriptions, process tailoring guidelines, and process-related documentation and data. The process elements can be further divided, for instance, into process roles, work products, and applicable procedures. Every process definition should include all of these elements.

There are various business process modeling languages available e.g. traditional flow chart notation, *Business Process Modeling Notation (BPMN)* [15],

Integrated Definition Methods (IDEF) [16], or *Event-Process Chains (EPC)* [17]. However, software processes have slightly different characteristics than business processes. Where business process modeling is more activity based, the software processes emphasizes the work product flow between the activities. Although there is no de facto standard for software process modeling available, the Software Process Engineering Metamodel (SPEM) [1] is gaining support in the software industry and academic world. With the introduction of SPEM 2.0 in the near future and the ongoing Eclipse Process Framework project [14], we expect to see an accelerated adoption of process modeling.

4.1 Challenges

The SPEM provides a fairly extensive notation for modeling software processes. However, it does not give actual guidelines on how the software processes should be modeled. A challenge is to find out the appropriate accuracy and level of detail of the process definitions. Of course, this is somewhat dependent on the actual purpose of the process modeling. Becker et al. define possible uses for process models, e.g. continuous process management, and identify the required modeling characteristics correspondingly [17].

Second challenge with the process modeling is the creation of models that are equivalent to the actual process. This is not only a question of modeling notation but also about supporting the process implementation with the process definition. It can be argued if too much effort is usually put to the process definition. Better results could be achieved by implementing simple processes and improving them based on the appropriate measurement feedback [18].

Lack of the de facto standard of process modeling causes several challenges to the process definition during the SPI: Tool development becomes slow and expensive, and the absence of the "common language" between process model users also makes maintaining and comparing the process definitions difficult.

All software development stakeholders should be taken into consideration during all parts of the SPI cycle. Fulfilling the different needs of the stakeholders poses a challenge to process definition practices and languages. This challenge is further discussed in Section 6.

4.2 Opportunities

A standard process modeling language that is widely adopted in the software industry and in the research community would yield many benefits. The SPEM could become this kind of de facto process modeling standard. With common process definition notation and guidelines, software process participants could focus on the process definition and modeling itself. In addition the models would be more comparable and interoperable. Reuse of processes within an organization and even between organizations would become possible.

The common modeling notation would be a well-founded start but not sufficient by itself. Process definition conventions should be developed as well. As an example we have proposed a method for increasing re-usability of process definitions by dividing process models into reusable process components [19]. It should be noted that the underlying process framework defines the interfaces and the feasible organization of the process components. Therefore, reuse of process content seems to be restricted to a process framework — process content from different process frameworks are not generally compatible.

5   SPI Cycle

There is a consensus on the basic steps and workflow of SPI cycle in the literature [6, p.46] [20, p.2] [17, p.239] [5, p.253]. The terminology can vary, but basically the continuous software improvement loop always contains the same steps. First the current processes have to be assessed, then the improving changes have to be designed, followed by the implementation of the processes into the organization, and finally the effects of the changes have to be analyzed. The loop is repeated at an appropriate pace.

5.1   Challenges

There are no actual challenges in the general structure of SPI cycle. The consensus on the topic is very firm. The content of the various steps varies greatly, i.e. there are several different methods for assessment of the current processes, designing the changes, implementation of new processes, and analyzing of the results. However, process modeling will affect these SPI steps, as discussed throughout this paper.

5.2   Opportunities

With a proper use of the software process modeling, the SPI cycle could become faster and more efficient. Notably the feedback from process enactment is enhanced. The ideal situation would be that the SPI cycle would not pose any extra overhead to the organization, instead SPI activities would be integrated to other process related activities and to the project management.

6   Organization's Capability

The organizational structure, management practices, culture, responsibility definitions and employees' skills are all constituent elements of SPI. Adopting process modeling techniques raises challenges in all these organizational areas.

6.1   Challenges

The first challenge is to get SPI related responsibilities clear and ensure that SPI's role is understood as a supportive function to operational activities. Different process stakeholders have varying motivators and de-motivators for SPI, reflecting their dissimilar process interests [21,22]. To be successful, SPI should take into account the needs of business management, offer the process as a tool for the project management, and help the development teams to achieve and maintain the needed capabilities. If this is not understood, there is a danger that SPI becomes too detached from the rest of the organization. The process views of these key roles are illustrated in Figure 4. The business management's role is to define the strategic goal of SPI, to provide for the necessary resources, and show managerial commitment to achieve the SPI goals. Process engineers take care of process definition, tailoring, monitoring and improvement. Project management executes projects using the defined processes, and operates as a two way channel between the development teams and the process engineers, relaying feedback and instruction. The development teams' main responsibility is to develop and maintain capabilities required to carry out the process tasks.

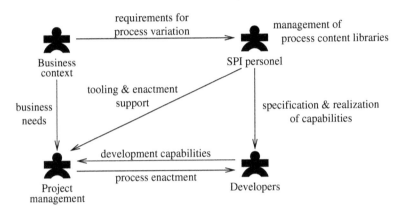

Fig. 4. The roles and relationships of the process stakeholders in a company

The second challenge is to analyze which SPI tasks require special expertise and thus should be allocated to dedicated SPI roles, and which tasks should be carried out by other roles, i.e. project managers, developers or business managers. This can be seen as balancing between centralized and distributed SPI work. The challenge of centralized SPI is its integration to development, whereas the challenge of distributed SPI is to keep SPI coherently working towards the business goals.

Many of the benefits attainable by the use of process modeling are due to speeding up the SPI cycle and defining SPI cycles at various levels, e.g. main SPI cycle for maintaining organization level process libraries, and project level cycles for taking care of project variations. Defined and efficient communication channels both within a cycle and between cycles in different levels are needed.

6.2 Opportunities

Role specific process views can be generated from formally defined process models. This supports the process work of all key roles in the organization. Process modeling technology can be used to explicitly express the balance between centralized and distributed SPI and thus facilitate responsibility allocation in the organization. For example, process components could be used to implement a process variability point linked to a project specific variation. In this way the volatile factors can be tailored locally in the project level without violating organizational level process requirements, such as quality goals. In addition, the above organizational challenges must be considered in realizing any of the opportunities presented in this paper.

7   Discussion

Software process modeling technology is maturing; useful first generation modeling language standard exists, first commercial tools based on the standard language are available, as well as open source solutions. Process modeling is a versatile technology that should not be taken only as a new tool for process engineers. To release the full potential of process modeling, a comprehensive approach on software engineering is needed. In this paper we have discussed how process modeling will affect five important areas of SPI.

The main findings can be summarized as follow. Process modeling enables encapsulating fragments of process content and reusing it to efficiently create customized processes. Identification of business and project factors and taxonomies of process properties are required in order to promote company's business goals with increased process capabilities. Process modeling, specifically a standard modeling language, defines common concepts and terminology, and therefore provides a unifying background for process frameworks. This makes it possible to compare, select from and even deploy several process frameworks for supporting projects with different dominant process assumptions.

The SPI cycle can be accelerated with the use of process modeling technology. More importantly, SPI can be organized as several nested cycles, corresponding to the different levels of process tailoring. Most of the attainable benefits of process modeling require a decentralized SPI function. This requires a clear definition of organizational roles and disseminated process responsibilities.

Both theoretical and applied research on process modeling is clearly needed. As examples, further research should consider existing organizational issues, structure of process libraries, and tooling for all stakeholders. Any research on software process modeling should be tightly connected to practical software development context to ensure pragmatic value. We believe that a comprehensive approach is needed to make process modeling into a mainstream SPI practice in software industry.

References

1. Object Management Group. *Software Process Engineering Metamodel Specification - Version 1.1*, January 5 2005. formal/05-01-06.
2. Alfonso Fuggetta. Software process: A roadmap. In *ICSE - Future of SE Track*, pages 25–34, 2000.
3. Reidar Conradi and Alfonso Fuggetta. Improving software process improvement. *IEEE Software*, 19(4):2–9, 2002.

4. CMMI Product Team. CMMI for systems engineering and software engineering (cmmi-se/sw, v1.1) - staged representation. Technical Report CMU/SEI-2002-TR-002, Software Engineering Institute, Pittsburgh, PA, USA, December 2001.

5. Philippe Kruchten. *The Rational Unified Process: An Introduction (Second Edition)*. Addison-Wesley Professional, March 14 2000.

6. ISO/IEC, Geneva, Switzerland. *ISO/IEC 12207, Information technology - Software life cycle processes*, August 1 1995. ISO/IEC 12207:1995.

7. Alistair Cockburn. Selecting a projects methodology. *IEEE Software*, pages 64–71, July / August 2000.

8. Barry Boehm and Richard Turner. *Balancing Agility and Discipline, A Guide for the Perplexed*. Addison-Wesley, 2003.

9. Don Wells. Extreme programming: A gentle introduction. `http://www.extremeprogramming.org/`, 2006. Accessed on June 22 2006.

10. Msf homepage. `http://msdn.microsoft.com/vstudio/teamsystem/msf/`. Accessed on June 22 2006.

11. Backlund et al. Transfer of development process knowledge through method adaptation and implementation. In *Proceedings of the 11th European Conference on Information Systems (ECIS 2003)*, June 2003.

12. The frameworks quagmire. `http://www.software.org/quagmire/`. Accessed on June 22 2006.

13. Christian Printzell Halvorsen and Reidar Conradi. A taxonomy to compare SPI frameworks. *Lecture Notes in Computer Science*, 2077, 2001.

14. Eclipse process framework project homepage. `http://www.eclipse.org/epf/`. Accessed on June 22 2006.

15. Object Management Group. *Business Process Modeling Notation Specification - Final Adopted Specification*, 2006. dtc/06-02-01.

16. Knowledge Based Systems Inc. Integrated definition methods home page. `http://www.idef.com/`. Accessed on June 22 2006.

17. Becker et al., editor. *Process Management - A Guide for the Design of Business Processes*. Springer, 2003.

18. John Davenport. Don't write another process. *Methods & Tools*, 12(3):2–14, 2004.

19. Antero Järvi and Tuomas Mäkilä. Observations on modeling software processes with SPEM process components. In *Proceedings of The 9th Symposium on Programming Languages and Software Tools*, Tartu, Estonia, 2005.

20. Bob McFeeley. *IDEAL: A Users Guide for Software Process Improvement*. Software Engineering Institute, Pittsburg, PA, February 1996. CMU/SEI-96-HB-001.

21. Nathan Baddoo and Tracy Hall. De-motivators for software process improvement: an analysis of practitioners' views. *The Journal of Systems and Software*, 66:23–33, 2003.

22. Nathan Baddoo and Tracy Hall. Motivators for software process improvement: an analysis of practitioners' views. *The Journal of Systems and Software*, 62:85–96, 2002.

Mentality Patterns: Capturing and Dealing Explicitly with Recurring Turns of Mind in Software Development

Georgios Koutsoukos[1,2]

[1] ATX Software S.A, Rua Saraiva de Carvalho, 207C,
1350-300 Lisbon, Portugal
[2] Department of Computer Science, University of Leicester,
Leicester LE1 7RH, UK
georgios.koutsoukos@atxsoftware.com

Abstract. The increasing adoption of agile methods for software development is amplifying the message that people are one of the most critical success factors of any software project. This paper addresses two fundamental questions that arise in that context: How can we capture, make explicit and effectively communicate human attitudes, beliefs and ways of thinking that influence individual and team work in projects? How can we supplement software process methods and support tools in order to take into account such human factors explicitly, systematically and effectively?

1 Introduction

The importance of human factors for the success of software projects has been historically emphasized by many authors: Weinberg in "Psychology of Computer Programming" [16], DeMarco and Lister in "Peopleware" [7], Curtis et al with the development of the People Capability Maturity Model [6], just to name a few. With the advent of Agile Software Development Methodologies [1], [3] this message has been significantly further amplified. As stated in [4]:

> *"People's characteristics are a first-order success driver, not a second-order one. [...] Most of my experiences can be accounted for from just a few characteristics of people. Applying these on recent projects, I have had much greater success at predicting results and making successful recommendations. I believe the time has come to, formally and officially, put a research emphasis on what are the characteristics of people that affect software development, and what are their implications on methodology design"*

In this paper, we take stock of several years of experience of software development and project management at ATX Software and make concrete proposals for making certain characteristics first-class concerns of software development methods and support tools. First, we present the notion of *mentality pattern* as an abstraction through which we can capture, systematise, communicate and reason about recurring human attitudes, beliefs, ways of thinking and respective acting that can have a decisive impact on the quality of work of individuals and the interactions within teams. These

R. Messnarz (Ed.): EuroSPI 2006, LNCS 4257, pp. 147–158, 2006.

patterns are formulated in a way that is independent of the development process that is followed and the technical profile of the individuals. In a second stage, we use this notion to define what we call the *Mentality Innovation Sub-Process* – an organized way to supplement and enhance software development methods and processes with means for "managing" such human-related factors explicitly and improving the effectiveness of individual work and the way teams blend together.

Having these goals in mind, the paper proceeds as follows. In section 2, we expand on and give examples of the proposed notion of mentality pattern. In section 3, we explain how mentality patterns can be used to improve software development methods and processes. Section 4 provides a justification for these proposals that builds on the theory of cognitive dissonance and the theory of self-perception. We review related work in software process methodology in section 5. Finally, in section 6, we summarise the lessons that we have learned in applying our innovation sub-process in real projects and discuss lines for further research.

2 Mentality Patterns

The Oxford Advanced Learners Dictionary defines mentality as "*the particular attitude or way of thinking of a person or group*". Based on the previous definition, we put forward the notion of mentality pattern as "*a recurring attitude [state of mind or predisposition to act], belief or way of thinking of a person or group, observed independently of any specific project or technical context*".

An example is what we call "Fear to Admit Ignorance" – Many people do not like to make known explicitly that they have only limited knowledge of the concepts, technologies, solutions or other aspects that are essential for the work in which they are engaged either individually or within a team. It is not difficult to imagine the consequences that such an attitude can have on the output of a task on or the rest of the team if that person is relied upon for his/her expertise.

In Table 1, we list some examples, applicable to both individuals and teams, which we have identified during several years of experience. The goal is not to be exhaustive but just to provide enough examples that illustrate the point. On the other hand, we are not claiming any originality in identifying those patterns: some are probably as old as mankind! In fact, many (if not all) of the patterns that we capture in Table 1 are not necessarily specific to software engineering but can also be found in other human activities as studied in the context of social sciences. However, we are not aware of any work within social sciences that uses in a similar way the notions of "mentality" and "pattern". Nevertheless social and psychological studies have been extremely useful for guiding our work and in section 4 we relate some of our arguments to conclusions drawn in such studies.

In what concerns software engineering, we can find some justification for the notion of mentality pattern on Weinberg's observation and invention of the term "egoless programming": in [16], he stresses the importance of having programmers that do not attach their ego to their code, what can be regarded as one of the first "paradigmatic" mentality patterns in the history of software. In [8], DeMarco identifies "can-do" attitudes as a major factor for escalating minor setback into true disasters. In [13], McConnell states that many problems in software development boil

Table 1. Examples of Mentality Patterns

Mentality Pattern	Description
Fear To Admit Ignorance	Not explicitly admitting of having limited or no knowledge of something (theory, technology, solutions etc).
Better Is The Enemy Of Good	Fear or resistance of further improving or modifying something that already works.
Experience Driven Optimism	Thinking that a problem is easy to solve because it seems similar to something you have done in the past.
Subject Guru	The belief of having incontestable expertise on a topic.
Legacy Person Mentality	The belief that something cannot be done without you or the desire that something cannot be done without you.
It Works! (but I do not know why)	Accepting a result without having a solid explanation of how it was reached.
I Will Do It My Own Way!	Tendency to "reinvent the wheel" instead of using existing solutions of others. Also known as the "Not Invented Here" mentality.
Have The Right To Make Assumptions	Making assumptions and not validating them with anybody (colleague, user) or explicitly stating them in deliverables.
The Best Is The One I (We) Am Comfortable With	The attitude of trying to impose a solution that a person or team is more comfortable with, for instance due to technical or other background.
"Opportunistic" Listening	The attitude of not paying attention to others words or work and in particular defining the level of attention according to the others' position, age or experience.
It Is Not My Fault!	The attitude of not admitting error or blaming others for failure.
Negativism	The attitude of looking for any negative points on others' approach, opinions or solutions instead of possible positive aspects.
"Secretivism"	Reluctance in sharing information or knowledge.
No Coding = Useless	The belief that when people are doing non-coding work (e.g. design, documentation, administration) they are contributing less to the project.

down to what he calls "wishful-thinking" i.e. *"hoping something works when you have no reasonable basis for thinking it will"*.

The existence of such recurring mentality is also known among software development practitioners. Many colleagues from different organizations have directly confirmed to us the existence of the patterns listed in Table 1. Similar comments can also be found in discussions within the software community: copying from a weblog discussion [15]: *"Programmers, in general, are extremely secretive. I remember one group had to kick out one of their members because he had like 12 pages of code and wouldn't let anyone else in the group see the printout. Otherwise, this guy was talkative and open."* Unfortunately, such observations are currently scattered in books, scientific papers, web pages, project notes and, mostly, people's minds. Moreover, they are often hidden in texts about project best or bad practices, guidelines and recommendations, or they are discussed in redundant and inconsistent ways. Our goal in putting forward the concept of mentality pattern is to provide a systematic way of capturing such human factors and making them explicit through a representation primitive that can be used as a common vocabulary to communicate and share experiences accumulated within and across projects and organizations.

Therefore, for mentality patterns to be applied in practice there must be a way of documenting and using them effectively. For this purpose we are developing a representation language, an example of which is given in Table 2 for the "Fear to Admit Ignorance" pattern. The proposed template is inspired on design patterns as used for developing code [11]. Actually, references to design (anti-)patterns may be included in the description of a mentality pattern as in the example below to describe the impact that it can have on software development practice. A selective, but not necessarily exhaustive, list of possible causes for a given pattern can also be included in order to guide the actions to be taken when dealing with it. We are currently developing a support system through which a repository of mentality patterns and associated practices can be built and shared. This system will include heuristics, rules of thumb, and guidelines for developers and project managers to share experiences and make effective use of this knowledge in projects as discussed in section 3.

Table 2. The "Fear To Admit Ignorance" Mentality Pattern

Pattern Name	Fear To Admit Ignorance
Other Names	None Known
Related Patterns	Subject Guru, It Works! (but I do not know why)
Symptoms	-Silence when one should give an opinion. -Talking about something else or moving the discussion to another point when one should comment on something.
Representative Quotes	*"Is it X... that you mean by Y...?"*
Consequences	Programming practices according to the "TowerOfVoodoo" and "VoodooChickenCoding" anti-patterns
Anecdotal Stories and Examples	*"In a project we were supposed to use an external API. Most of the people knew very well its functionality. However, there was a colleague that did not. He did not say anything even when the manager asked if everybody was comfortable with the work or there were anything to be taken care before we start. When the team started working, our colleague was, apparently, trying to understand what each piece of the API was doing judging by the method names! Result: It was taking him ages to write a piece of code that was working properly, not to mention the code that seemed to be working but in fact was not."*
Possible Causes	-Feeling of superiority e.g. due to position or experience -A shy person reluctant to ask questions

We should make clear that mentality patterns are about recurring human attitudes, beliefs and ways of thinking not to be confused with guidelines or good and bad practices of software projects. For instance, statements such as "undermined motivation" or "not sufficient automated source-code control" are bad practices that may have their origins in mentality patterns but are not themselves mentality patterns.

3 The Mentality Innovation Sub-process

In order to make effective use of the notion of mentality pattern, we propose what we call the "Mentality Innovation Sub-Process" as a sub-process that can be incorporated in but is independent of the specificities of any particular development method, framework, or project management method. The sub-process was put together based on our experience and has been refined over several development projects. It consists of 3 elements: two phases and one continuous activity as outlined below.

3.1 Mentality Principles Setup Phase

This phase occurs typically during the team building activity at the start of the project. It consists of a collective exercise whose basic structure is described below:

- The team manager or another team member prepares a list of mentality patterns of his/her choice.
- For each mentality pattern in the list, each team member acknowledges whether he/she has observed the pattern in his/her previous experience. If so, he/she explains in an anecdotal manner how the pattern contributed negatively or positively in projects. If possible, such "contribution" of the pattern is considered both in the context of individual work and team interaction.
- Team members are asked to communicate other mentality patterns they believe they have identified in their past projects experience. If the team agrees that a proposed pattern actually exists, the pattern is accepted, further discussed, analysed and documented based on the template presented on Section 2, and added to the initial list.
- After the list of patterns has been completed and evaluated, the team discusses and prepares what we call the team's Mentality Principles Manifesto. This is a description of the principles, directly derived from the list of mentality patterns, according to which the team will operate during the project. For instance, a manifesto principle, derived from the "Fear to Admit Ignorance" mentality pattern, could state something like:

> "Whenever we are not confident that we have enough knowledge of a subject of any nature (technical, project related or other) in order to perform our work with the highest quality standards, we will ask whoever we feel necessary until we are confident. All project participants commit to answering the questions of fellows in the most comprehensive way possible".

In general, the manifesto principles should be simple, straightforward, understandable and non-ambiguous. They may also include some implications on the team's actions. The manifesto itself should not be lengthy: as Cockburn puts it in [3], "people can keep only a small amount in their heads". Space limitations prevent us from giving more details on the structure, guidelines for creating or the specific content of such project manifestos.

3.2 Mentality Feedback Activity

During this activity, project team members provide evaluation and corrective information to each other with respect to the mentality patterns and mentality principles already established. This should occur regularly and definitely whenever symptoms of patterns are observed that could lead to problematic situations.

Mentality feedback is also an important component between project phases and milestones, especially if there exist aspects or deliverables of the project that are not satisfactory. Moreover, feedback should always be provided in an organized way: that is, with respect to the project mentality principles manifesto that everybody has agreed on. Any other principles or individual impressions of mentality patterns that have not being agreed a-priori should not be considered. If, however, throughout the project, team members believe that new mentality patterns are being observed, the whole team should update the manifesto in the same way it was created during the setup phase.

Finally, mentality feedback can be provided freely per individual or per team basis: individuals can provide feedback to individuals, the team can provide feedback to individuals or individuals can provide feedback to the team. However, the team managers are responsible for dealing with specific situations of team members being "sensitive" to specific forms of feedback and decide what is the most effective way of providing mentality feedback to them.

3.3 Mentality Learning Phase

During this phase, the team learns from its experience by reflecting on the following:
- Have the mentality principles been followed during the project? If not, why?
- Have any (and which) mentality patterns been observed during the project? Was feedback given on those patterns? Was it effective? If not, why? What could have been done to make it more effective? What were the problematic aspects of the project that could have their origins on those or other mentality patterns?
- Have any new mentality patterns being discovered? Which? How can they be incorporated in the initial list and on the manifesto?
- How can the whole sub-process be improved in future projects?

In order to be more constructive, the Learning Phase should preferably occur whenever the project team is "relaxed": that is, when there are no further project details to be taken care of and people have already got some rest after the project effort. This is because it is on relaxed conditions that people are more willing to contribute to the learning task, discuss in an open manner, accept points of view or even criticism from others and contribute new ideas.

4 Foundations and Rationale

In the previous section we have outlined the *When, What and Who* of the Mentality Innovation Sub-Process. In this section we focus on its foundations – the *Why*. The rationale behind the sub-process is in the realization, based on our many years of experience, that in what concerns attitudes, beliefs and ways of thinking of persons or groups, one can distinguish two different cases:

1. There are individuals and groups that, in many occasions, are very conscious of what attitude, belief or way of thinking will have a positive impact on the success of projects in general, and specific tasks in particular. However, for several reasons, the analysis of which is outside the scope of this paper, they choose not to follow that particular "constructive" attitude or way of thinking. For instance, many people are aware of the fact that they fear to admit ignorance but often choose to continue operating and acting according to that state of mind.
2. There are cases in which people are not conscious of the particular attitudes or way of thinking they follow, and just assume they are thinking in the "right way" or doing the "right thing". "Experience Driven Optimism" and "Have the Right to Make Assumptions" are possible examples of this case.

Our objective is not to identify which mentality patterns belong to one or the other case, but to explain why and how the sub-process deals effectively with both.

4.1 The Theory of Cognitive Dissonance

As far as the first case is concerned, we believe that this phenomenon should be considered and can be explained by the widely accepted socio-psychological theory of Cognitive Dissonance [10], [12] whose basic arguments are outlined as follows.

Humans dislike inconsistency between two cognitions (knowledge, belief, attitude, way of thinking) or between a cognition and a behaviour. Such inconsistency causes the arousal of an unpleasant psychological state, called cognitive dissonance. According to Cooper and Fazio [5], the arousal of such a psychological state depends on the degree of aversive consequences to us or those we like and the personal responsibility we take for attitude-discrepant behaviours. Personal responsibility consists of two factors: freedom of choice and the belief that potential negative consequences of the actions were foreseeable. Humans need to reduce such dissonance and there are 4 different available paths in order to do so:

  i. When two cognitions are in conflict, change one or the other cognition.
  ii. When two cognitions are in conflict, make one cognition more important or reduce the importance of the other, possibly by adding new cognitions.
  iii. When cognition is in conflict with behaviour, change behaviour.
  iv. When cognition is in conflict with behaviour, change cognition.

The choice of moment and path to reduce dissonance has been a matter of psychological debate [12]. As far as the choice of path is concerned, psychological studies conclude that we tend to choose the path of *least resistance*. The degree of such resistance is determined, among others, by factors such as threats to self-concept (the perception we have for ourselves) or self-presentation (our concern for the perception of others for us), possible rewards, the degree to which cognitions are consonant with many other cognitions, the extent of pain or loss that must be endured for changing a behaviour, and the satisfaction obtained from a behaviour.

Coming back to mentality patterns and the first case identified at the beginning of this section, we believe that the previous discussion on Cognitive Dissonance explains why people do not always follow constructive attitudes and ways of thinking even if they are conscious of them:

– either they do not experience dissonance arousal, that is, based on Cooper and Fazio remarks above, either the inconsistency between attitudes, beliefs and behaviour does not have aversive consequences for them or those who they like, or they do not take personal responsibility for such inconsistency because they may feel that they do not have freedom of choice or because they think that potential negative consequences of the actions were not foreseeable;
– or the "constructive" attitudes and ways of thinking that they are aware of have a degree of low resistance, making it easier to reduce dissonance by following paths (i), (ii) or (iv) (change cognition) than (iii) (change behaviour). In other words, they tend to change or diminish the importance of the "constructive" cognition. For instance, "Fear to Admit Ignorance is a problematic attitude" could become "Sometimes it is good not to admit ignorance". This is particularly true when such a cognition change, altering or diminishing the importance of "constructive" mentality, does not impose a threat to self-concept, self-presentation or possible rewards. We are convinced that in the context of teamwork the self-presentation factor in particular has a very significant contribution to the degree of resistance of "constructive" mentality.

Guided by the socio-psychological theories and observations above, the Mentality Innovation Sub-Process is therefore designed to achieve the following goals. The Mentality Patterns and Principles Setup phase and the associated manifesto stimulate the experiencing of *dissonance arousal*: people agree to what constitutes "constructive mentality" and commit to following it. This implies that they will take personal responsibility for possible inconsistencies between what has been agreed and how they may operate. Moreover, the power of the possible argument that they do not have freedom of choice is diminished; they have participated on the principles setup phase and the mentality principles manifesto was not imposed to them. Finally, they cannot argue that potential negative consequences of actions were not foreseeable because the use of anecdotal stories in mentality patterns implicitly forces individuals to apply the story metaphors to their own situations, hence considering the gains or pitfalls of following a certain mentality.

The Mentality Innovation Sub-Process also attempts to *raise the resistance* of "constructive" mentality, thus making it more likely, when dissonance arouses, that a choice be made for changing behaviour instead of changing or diminishing the importance of "constructive" cognitions. This effect is achieved in two ways:

– people agree with and commit to the fact that mentality is an important factor for the success of projects; this implies that the specific "constructive" attitudes and ways of thinking identified during the setup phase become part of their system of values and principles (the Manifesto), a fact that significantly raises the resistance of such "constructive" attitudes and ways of thinking.
– people become aware that not following the agreed "constructive" mentality would be a threat for their self-presentation: the team will constantly observe whether "constructive" mentality is followed during the project and continuous feedback on this matter will be provided.

4.2 Self-perception Theory

As far as the second case is concerned, in which people are not conscious of particular attitudes and ways of thinking, we need to consider another psychological paradigm – Bem's Self-Perception theory [2].

According to the Self-Perception theory, we develop our attitudes by observing our own behaviour and concluding what attitudes must have caused them. For instance, "if I often eat Indian food, I like Indian food". In other words, people use inferential processes to determine the attitudinal significance of their actions. It should be noted that, for many years, this view seemed to challenge Cognitive Dissonance in the sense that according to Self-Perception we do not necessarily change our attitudes in response to our behaviour. However, more recent studies, for instance by Fazio et al [9], concluded that both theories are right – it all depends on the circumstances: inferential processes postulated by self-perception theory are especially likely to influence attitudes that are not pre-existing and well-established, or when the discrepancy between attitude-behaviour is fairly small. At the same time, there is substantial evidence that larger attitude-discrepant actions do produce effects described in the Cognitive Dissonance theory. Therefore, the use of Cognitive Dissonance for Case 1 above – people conscious of constructive mentality but do not follow it – is justified and supported; and so is the use of Self-Perception theory for Case 2 – people with no pre-existing notion of attitude or way of thinking.

We still have to discuss how the Mentality Innovation Sub-Process, guided by the Self-Perception Theory, deals with Case 2 of mentality patterns. In our view, when people are not conscious that they follow a particular attitude or way of thinking, we need to devise ways in order to explicitly stimulate and guide Bem's inferential processes that people apply to determine the attitudinal significance of their actions. In other words, with respect to mentality patterns, we need to explicitly guide people in order to become conscious of a particular mentality, and subsequently change it if it leads to problematic practice or continue following it if proven to be constructive. For instance, if people operate according to the "Have the Right to Make Assumptions" mentality, we need to explicitly trigger the inference mechanism so that they can become aware of the mentality of making assumptions without validating them. In our view, there are mainly two ways in which this can be achieved.

The first consists in increasing the levels of what we call "self- enlightenment": stimulating people to look inside themselves, judge their own past and present actions, the underlying attitude and way of thinking-related reasons for those actions, and how those contribute to their personal development and work results. The Setup Phase aims to explicitly serve this goal.

The second way is stimulating interpersonal communication: only when the people around communicate with and alert individuals (and teams) on specific attitudes and ways of thinking, can they become aware of possible problematic or constructive attitudes, and adjust accordingly. It should be noted that interpersonal communication is by itself a way of stimulating "self-enlightenment". However, mere communication exhibits a problem: often people are not willing to hear the comments and opinions of others. The main cause is that people tend to judge comments from others as being "their particular view" and, hence, tend to just ignore them. This is particularly true for "ad-hoc" comments that come from fellows that people either do not know well or on whom they do not have a positive opinion. Only when there is an agreed by all basis on the established aspects upon which communication will be performed and feedback will be given, can people be willing to accept more and think about the views of others. The purpose of the mentality principles manifesto is, precisely, to act as such a team-agreed, mentality-related communication and feedback basis.

Similarly, the Feedback Activity and Learning Phase are also about communication and "self-enlightenment": stimulating individuals and teams to consider their attitudes and ways of thinking, become aware of the current negative and positive cases, improve their project-related practices, and use those experiences in the future.

5 Relevance to Software Engineering

Our work is based on and guided by proven concepts, methods and sound observations found either in the specific context of software process methodologies or in software engineering and other human activities in general. In what follows we outline some of the evidence that justifies the relevance of our proposal.

Although different in its nature and goals, the notion of mentality pattern capitalizes on the proven expressive power and communication benefits of the design pattern concept. Such power and benefits have been observed and realized for many years and in various areas, the most notable of which probably being OO design [11].

In [3], Cockburn argues that a properly performed software team-building phase and relevant exercises are very advantageous for achieving team morale and effective communication. The PMBOK Guide [14] also refers to team-building activities as a crucial component of effective project management. Sharing this view, we have "injected" the Mentality Principles Setup to the team-building phase, but in a narrower context and with different objectives in mind: to use the mentality patterns in order to trigger a collective culture and commitment to mentality innovation.

As far as the Mentality Principles and Manifesto are concerned, one should observe that the existence of principles is found implicitly or explicitly in all software process methods and the notion of a manifesto is also found in Agile Process Methodologies. Those principles form the basis upon which each process is explained and organized, provide the rationale for prescribing certain practices and ruling out others, and guide the way each process should be executed. Therefore, projects adopting specific process methods implicitly adopt, at least to a good extent, the principles defined by those methods. Being only complementary to and an independent component of software process methods, the Mentality Innovation Sub-Process adopts a project-specific, team-created and mentality-oriented notion of principles that is more appropriate for the objectives it is designed to meet.

The Mentality Feedback Activity and the Mentality Learning Phase are also not entirely novel: feedback, learning and effective communication are also important components of Agile Process Methodologies. However, in those methods, the importance of feedback is considered more in the sense of feedback given by users-clients after deliverable portions of software. Moreover, the feedback, learning and communication aspects of those methods do not target explicitly and in a systematic way the mentality-related innovation as presented in our work.

6 Results and Outlook

The Mentality Innovation Sub-Process has been applied in small to medium size projects over several years with very encouraging results. The process was applied in an "informal" way in the sense that the project team was not aware of it.

The sub-process proved to be simple and relatively straightforward to apply in the sense that it does not impose any significant overhead to process methods already in place. In our first view, it also seems to improve the way people think on problems and on team cohesion and interaction. For instance, we have observed that after applying the process people are more careful in making and stating assumptions, are more willing to admit their ignorance and to accept responsibility for mistakes.

On the other hand, there exist mentality patterns, for instance "Opportunistic" Listening and "Secretivism", which tend to persist even after following the sub-process with the same team in several projects. This leads to the conclusion that some mentality patterns are more difficult to deal with. Moreover, as we were actually expecting, the degree that specific persons exhibit a specific pattern varies. Therefore for obtaining better results faster, the execution of the sub-process should sometimes be adapted to account for specific persons and associated mentality pattern variations. Providing "formal" support on how this can be done is part of our ongoing work.

Another lesson learned is what we call "mentality patterns interference". That is, people and their associated mentality patterns influence one another, either negatively or positively. For instance, in the former case, the "Negativism" of one person tends to amplify the "Secretivism" of others, whereas in the latter case, people that are willing to admit ignorance affect in a positive way their peers that do not. This observation is of high importance for guiding decisions on the way people should be distributed in teams or perform tasks jointly, for instance pair programming. Moreover, even when certain distributions are inevitable due to technical, team size or other constraints, being aware of such interference is essential for a more effective team management.

Finally, our focus so far has been on obtaining qualitative rather than quantitative results. The main obstacle for quantitative results is that the sub-process targets mentality innovation, an aspect that is difficult to measure in a comprehensive way. However, to this end, it is clear that a fair assessment of the impact of the sub-process in projects as well as more reliable results can only be obtained once it is applied by other people and in different organizations. We are currently looking for partners for a wider experiment.

Acknowledgements

The author would like to thank Prof. J.L Fiadeiro (Univ. of Leicester) for his encouragement to pursue this research and his numerous comments and suggestions.

Prof. M. Holcombe (Univ. of Sheffield), L. Andrade and P. Dimenza (ATX Software), Dr A. Lopes (Univ. of Lisbon), T. Kotridis (Credit Suisse First Boston, UK), Dr J. Pissarra (ISCTE, Portugal) and D. Vallianos (KB Implus Hellas) have all provided valuable insights that must be gratefully acknowledged. Finally, this work would not have been possible without the many colleagues that over the last 10 years, with their associated mentality patterns, have triggered the author's interest in this matter.

References

1. Agile Alliance: http://www.agilealliance.org
2. Bem, D. J.: Self-perception theory. In L. Berkowitz (ed.): Advances in experimental social psychology, Vol. 6. Academic Press, New York (1972)
3. Cockburn, A.: Agile Software Development. Addison-Wesley, Boston (2002)
4. Cockburn, A.: Characterizing People as Non-Linear, First-Order Components in Software Development. In 4th Int. Conf. on Systems, Cybernetics, and Informatics, June (2000)
5. Cooper, J., and Fazio, R. H.: A new look at dissonance theory. In: L.Berkowitz (ed.): Advances in experimental social psychology, Hillsdale, NJ Erlbaum (1984) 229–262
6. Curtis, B., Hefley, B. and Miller, S.: The People Capability Maturity Model. Addison-Wesley, Boston (2001)
7. DeMarco, T. and Lister, T.: Peopleware: Productive Projects and Teams. Dorset House, New York (1999)
8. DeMarco, T.: Why Does Software Cost So Much. Dorset House, New York (1995)
9. Fazio R. H, Zanna, M. and Cooper, J.: Dissonance and Self-perception: An Integrative View of Each Theory's Proper Domain of Application. Journal of Experimental Social Psychology, Vol. 13 (1977) 464–479
10. Festinger, L.: A Theory of Cognitive Dissonance. Stanford University Press, (1957)
11. Gamma, E., Helm, R., Johnson, R. and Vlissides, J.: Design Patterns: Elements of Reusable Object-Oriented Software. Addison-Wesley Professional (1995)
12. Harmon-Jones, E. and Mills, J. (eds.): Cognitive Dissonance: Progress on a pivotal theory in social psychology. American Psychological Association (1999)
13. McConnell, S.: Rapid Development. Microsoft Press, (1996)
14. Project Management Institute: Guide to the Project Management Body of Knowledge, A (PMBOK Guide). Project Management Institute (2004)
15. The Joel on Software Forum: Programmers Attack. http://discuss.fogcreek.com, May 2003
16. Weinberg, G.: The Psychology of Computer Programming. Van Nostrand Reinhold (1971)

Improving by Involving: A Case Study in a Small Software Company

Nils Brede Moe and Tore Dybå

SINTEF ICT, NO-7465 Trondheim, Norway
{nils.b.moe, tore.dyba}@sintef.no

Abstract. One way of implementing Software Process Improvement (SPI) is to empower employees to carry out decisions made by management. An alternative way is to invite developers and project leaders to participate in all phases of planning and implementing SPI projects. Such participation has always been a central goal and one of the pillars of organization development and change, and has also been shown to be one of the factors with the strongest influence on SPI success. However, there are few studies reporting how participation can be done in practice in software companies doing SPI. In this paper, we describe how long-term participation can be realized in various SPI initiatives using several participation techniques like search conferences, survey feedback, autonomous work groups, quality circles, and learning meetings. The research has been carried out in a small Norwegian software company called Kongsberg Spacetec, over a period of eight years.

1 Introduction

Participation and involvement has been one of the most important foundations of organization development and change, and has always been a central goal and one of the pillars of organizational learning [12].

Employees should as a minimum be given a say in organizational decisions, since they have much to gain and lose from organizational changes [30]. They should be able to help create and shape changes as well as seeing the results of changes and acting upon them. Participation involves sharing the difficulties and jointly overcoming the barriers of change, as well as experiencing both its negative and positive aspects. Participation should be offered and managed in such a way as to allow all employees to improve their work and feel a sense of contribution to the organization and its mission. Within the context of software process improvement (SPI), Dybå [12] defined employee participation as *the extent to which employees use their knowledge and experience to decide, act, and take responsibility for SPI.* When members of an organization feel they are excluded from participation by the leadership, they will find ways, often unhealthy, to express themselves [30]. As a result of not being able to participate, employees may ultimately leave the company. Therefore organizations need to provide a climate of participation if they are to remain healthy. By doing so, they increase not only the learning capacity of employees, but also their ability to influence organizational outcomes. Another potential effect of participation is increased emotional attachment to the organization, resulting

R. Messnarz (Ed.): EuroSPI 2006, LNCS 4257, pp. 159–170, 2006.
© Springer-Verlag Berlin Heidelberg 2006

in greater commitment, motivation to perform and desire for responsibility. As a result, employees care more about their work, which may lead to greater creativity and helping behavior, higher productivity and service quality [16].

Participation itself does not ensure that an organization will be successful in achieving its goals, and participation includes some degree of risk, as seen by management. For participation to be successful, however, organizational members must know how to participate effectively [30].

The idea of SPI is to change work practices to become more effective or predictive, or to develop software with higher quality. The underlying idea is that the way software is developed affects the final product. When all key people and employees actively take part in process improvement, the companies can more easily focus on how things can be done better, faster or cheaper. There are several reasons why involvement is of high importance for small software companies, especially in the field of SPI:

- Small and medium-sized enterprises (SMEs) are often more vulnerable of people leaving than large companies.
- SMEs seldom have the possibility of maintaining an SPI department of their own or people dedicated to work with SPI. So to have a continuous SPI focus and to have a possibility to succeed with SPI, they need to involve employees in planning and executing SPI projects.
- Small software organizations have also shown that they can implement SPI at least as effectively as their large counterparts by capitalizing on their relative strengths in employee participation and exploration of new knowledge [11, 12].

So for small companies to be successful in SPI they need to focus on participation. But how does an SME achieve participation? Everyone who uses the term participation thinks of something different. There are several techniques available, and which technique to choose is maybe not so important [28], as long as participation is a long-term initiative. Cotton *et al.* [6] found that long-term forms of participation appear to be more effective than short-term forms. For example search conferences [24], survey feedback [5], autonomous work groups [18], quality circles [18, 20], and learning meetings [13] are all predicated on the belief that increased participation will lead to better solutions and an enhanced organizational problem-solving capability.

In software engineering research, we find several frameworks aimed at (quality) improvement, and past process improvement studies have concentrated on process improvement frameworks. As a result, process maturity models like Capability Maturity Model Integration (CMMI) [26] and Software Process Improvement and Capability dEtermination (SPICE) have been developed. The use of such models for improving the process can be viewed as part of a top-down approach to SPI. This approach finds weak points in the organization by comparing its current process against the maturity model and sets goals on the basis of its alignment with the model. However these frameworks are not participation oriented because improvement is defined as an adjustment towards a normative model, even though CMMI is supposed to have its origin in Total Quality Management (TQM) [7] where participation is one of the fundamental ideas.

As opposed to a top-down, model-driven approach, a bottom-up approach assumes that process change must be driven by the organization's goals, characteristics, product attributes, and experiences. Every development organization must first understand its process, products, software characteristics, and goals before it can select a set of changes that are meant to improve its process [21]. Therefore this approach requires leadership and involvement by management, supported by the knowledge and expertise of developers. The Quality Improvement Paradigm (QIP) [3] and the Goal Question Metric (GQM) method [27] are examples of such bottom-up approaches.

The work described in this paper is motivated by the growing evidence that long-term participation in SPI is necessary for company success, especially for SMEs. To the best of our knowledge there are no studies that describe how this can be done in practice. Therefore our research question has been: How can an SME achieve participation when doing SPI? In the next section we describe the research methods that have been used. Then we describe how SPI initiatives have been implemented in a Norwegian SME, focusing on long-term participation, followed by a discussion and conclusions.

2 Research Method

2.1 Research Context

The work described in this paper has been carried out in a Norwegian software company called Kongsberg Spacetec ("Spacetec") from 1998-2005. Spacetec has been involved in three large Norwegian SPI research projects in this period. In these projects, Spacetec has cooperated with other companies, research institutions and universities in improvement activities. The collaboration has been based on finding common improvement and learning goals, and working together to achieve these goals. TQM, GQM and QIP have been central in all these research projects.

Spacetec is one of the leading producers of receiving stations for data from meteorological and Earth observation satellites. Spacetec has expertise in electronics, software development and applications. 80% of the 50 employees in the company have a master's degree in physics or computer science. At the start in 1984 the main task of the company was engineering through customer specific projects, and the main customer was the European Space Agency [15]. Because of this, the ESA PSS-05 [15] software engineering standard was adopted. This standard follows the traditional waterfall approach. During the 1990s the market situation changed, and a new kind of customer became increasingly important. These customers were not interested in how the product was developed nor how the quality assurance was performed. Instead of providing detailed requirements specifications, they expected off-the-shelf products that could be delivered at short notice. In return for lack of uniqueness, the new customers expected a much lower price, so it became impossible to charge enough for a product to cover the complete development costs. This made it necessary to develop generic products through internally financed and managed projects, but also to have a continuous focus on SPI.

2.2 Action Research

We have participated in collecting experience from Spacetec, and we used the participative research method *action research* [2]. Action research has been described as "a post-positivist social scientific research method, ideally suited to the study of technology in its human context" [4](p.235). Action research merges research and practice thus producing extremely relevant results. Together, the researchers and the stakeholders define the problems to be examined, co-generate relevant knowledge about them, learn and execute social research, take actions, and interpret the results of action based on what they have learned [17]. In other words, the researchers have assisted Spacetec by not only suggesting and planning the introduction of the various participation techniques, but also assisted Spacetec in applying them. The cyclical process model proposed by Susman and Evered [29] was central in this work:

- *Diagnosing* – identifying the present problems and their underlying causes and formulating a working hypothesis.
- *Action planning* – specifying the actions that can improve the problem situation.
- *Action taking* – implementing the interventions specified
- *Evaluating* - jointly assessing the interventions by Spacetec and researchers.
- *Specifying learning* - documenting and summing up the learning outcomes of the action research cycle.

These learning outcomes from a SPI initiative, like introduction of a technique, gave knowledge contributions to both theory and practice, but also served as the starting point for a new cycle. When we collected the data needed in the evaluating of the various actions, we relied on several data sources to strengthen our case study. Interviews, usage logs, participant-observation from workshops and document inspection have all been important data sources.

3 Long-Term Participation in Spacetec

Spacetec has focused on improvement initiatives in projects as well as on a company level. First we describe the framework Spacetec has used for organizing SPI-projects, and then how participating techniques have been used in various SPI initiatives.

3.1 Organizing Process Improvement in Spacetec

The process improvement initiatives in Spacetec consist of three main phases: *initiating*, *executing* and *project closure*. Executing was organized according to three levels - plan, do, check - and was used to carry out continuous improvement on all levels. A last step in the traditional improvement cycle is act [13] – describe the new or improved process and make use of it. In Spacetec this corresponded to a new improvement level including planning, doing and checking. These levels spanned from simple activities or processes to iterations, releases or even to the project or company as a whole. Spacetec has 2 people working partly with quality assurance. These two persons are responsible for coordinating the SPI initiatives. In Table 1 we have specified examples of various participation techniques used in SPI projects at Spacetec.

Table 1. Participation techniques used in initiation, execution and closing of different SPI projects

	Three phases of SPI projects in Spacetec		
	Initiation	Execution	Closing
Search conference	Defining a strategy for a new development processes		
Survey feedback	Defining scope of a process assessment, and who to involve.	Developing, conducting and evaluating the assessment.	Initiating improvement plan based on assessment results
Learning meeting		After action review/ Postmortem review in projects, feedback meetings	Review of development processes, Postmortem review after projects
Quality circle		Planning, prioritizing and execution of improvement actions, process workshop	Establishing the project-closure committee
Autonomous workgroup			Developing an improvement plan

3.2 Search Conference

The search conference [24] is a method for participatory, strategic planning in turbulent and uncertain environments, which makes it a method suited for small software companies. All the work is conducted in self-managed teams that are responsible for the entire planning process. The search conference process is based on democratic participation, which gives those employees most affected by the change more control. The intended result of the conference is to produce a committed group of knowledgeable people who have a deep understanding of the challenges confronting their organization, agreement about the ideals the strategy is supposed to serve, action plans that are aligned with those ideals, a social method for participation, and a process for engaging the whole system in the strategy implementation.

Spacetec possessed several meter of software lifecycle descriptions, and these descriptions did not always correspond to the process that was actually performed during development. Therefore, Spacetec decided to improve and document their development methodology according to the new process approach of ISO 9001:2000 [19]. They arranged a search conference were the goal was to discuss the present situation before looking into the future. Brainstorming was used to make sure that the whole group (managers and project leaders) generated ideas, and to make it possible for the group to free themselves from the old way of thinking. An important result from the conference was the decision to define the new processes based on the company's existing best practices, and to publish them on the intranet through an Electronic Process Guide [25]. This would include developing different tools that would help carrying out the processes, and the possibility to tailor the process for each project. A number of process workshops [9] (se section 3.4) were planned for involving marketing and sales personnel, developers and project managers, and for defining best practice.

3.3 Survey Feedback

Survey feedback is a process of systematically collecting and feeding back data for individuals and groups at all levels of the organization to diagnose, interpret meanings, and design corrective action steps [5]. The process involves two major components; the use of an attitude survey and the use of feedback workshops.

Because Spacetec wanted to discover potential improvement areas and the areas they did not need to improve, they performed a survey feedback process consisting of the following six steps: Assessment initiation, focus area delineation, criteria development, assessment design, assessment implementation, and data analysis and feedback. How this process was conducted is described in more detail in [14]. In the initiation of the assessment Spacetec clarified the respective roles and the objectives of the assessment, by answering the following questions:

- What are the purposes of performing software process assessment?
- Who are the users of the assessment, and how will the results be used?
- What is the scope of the assessment in terms of organizational units and issues?
- To what extent is there a commitment to using scientific methods (e.g. psychometric principles) to design and implement the assessment?
- Who should conduct the assessment, and what resources are available?

Three developers, three project leaders and three managers were invited to participate in the process. This group was responsible for designing and conducting the process including discussions of the results. For defining the assessment, a standard questionnaire was used as a starting point for internal discussions and for the development of the tailor-made questionnaires. The group was encouraged to edit the questionnaire by both removing and adding questions, but only new questions were added. Spacetec's problem of focusing was probably caused by the fact that they had experienced several challenges but had not been able to identify their causes. The questionnaires were answered by the nine participants, and analyzed by the researchers. The results were then presented to the participants, and discussed in the form of a feedback meeting (se section 3.4). Findings regarding the scores on current strengths and future importance were presented in terms of a gap analysis. After the presentation of the results, the nine participants formed an autonomous group (see section 3.6) for developing an improvement plan. Conducting an additional assessment was also considered, but this was skipped since the discussions of the results clearly revealed what the company needed to focus on (learning from experiences) for the next period.

Spacetec also developed another survey were everybody participated, to examine if the process guide offered the needed support in the different process areas. The results were analyzed by the researchers and presented together with process guide usage logs, in company plenary sessions for management, project leaders and developers. The results were discussed in the form of a company feedback meeting (se section 3.4).

3.4   Learning Meeting

During execution of SPI projects, Spacetec used various forms of learning meetings [13]. The purpose of such meetings is to learn from others in order to contribute to the project. Spacetec arranged learning meetings in the form of so-called post Postmortem review [8], After Action Reviews, and feedback meetings [13].

Postmortem reviews are originally intended to be used after the project is finished, but Spacetec found them useful also after major activities and project milestones. Everyone in the project was invited in addition to a person from outside the project to chair the meetings – typically 4-10 people. The meetings lasted from 2-5 hours and typically had the following steps:

- What has gone well so far in the project?
- What caused the success? The success factors were identified in order to be repeated in the rest of the project.
- What has not gone well so far in the project?
- The problems where then identified, to avoid the same pitfalls and obstacles in the rest of the project.
- Finally improvement actions where identified and documented. Without action – no improvement. Typically, the actions involved incorporating the new knowledge into updated processes, procedures, checklists and models.

After the postmortem review, the improvement actions where distributed to a quality circle consisting of project participants, and the actions were conducted in "live" projects.

Another way of learning from experience was to use GQM [27] to collect project data, analyze them and present them in regular feedback meetings. The purpose of these meetings was to present the data for those who collected them in order to get their interpretations. Since Spacetec combined the participants' knowledge and understanding of the development process with the collected data, it was possible to make better decisions based on less data than if they had only based the decision on pure statistical analyses. The initial measurement plan was also presented to the management-group.

A learning meeting was also initiated for revising the electronic process guide. The process guide provided four different basic projects types, and for this learning meeting two persons working with each project type were invited. In the beginning of the meeting each pair revised the entire guide with the perspective of one of the project types. They documented:

- What should be removed?
- What should be changed?
- What should be added?

In the next step, each pair presented its results to the other participants with a subsequent discussion. Through enthusiastic discussions about best practices, the participants found processes that were not perceived as necessary, created new processes, clarified misunderstandings about the meaning of processes, and processes where simplified. The learning meeting also identified several SPI actions, e.g.

creating new checklists and the need for more training and knowledge sharing. The whole process guide was revised in 7 hours, and after the meeting the results were implemented by the persons responsible for the process guide.

Spacetec has institutionalized postmortem review as an activity performed at the end of each project. As opposed to the learning meeting during the project, this type of postmortem review focuses on reflecting on experiences that could be made available to future projects.

3.5 Quality Circles

A quality circle is composed of volunteers who arrange regular meetings to look at productivity and quality problems, and discuss work procedures [20]. The strength of such circles is that they allow employees to deal with improvement issues that are not dealt with in the regular organization. They generate solutions that may or may not be implemented by the organization [18]. The quality circles used in Spacetec have all been temporary, and created with a relatively well-bounded mandate to be fulfilled. Once the task was accomplished, the circle was disbanded. The kind of quality circle used at Spacetec is also known as "Task force" [18].

Quality circles have been important in the SPI work at Spacetec for detailed planning, prioritizing and execution of improvement actions related to project work, e.g. specifying an experience database (how to collect the experiences, how to use the databases, tool requirements, and a plan for infusion). After the improvements actions were resolved, the group was normally dissolved. New groups with new members were formed when new improvement actions were suggested.

The quality circle in the form of a process workshop [9], was central in specifying and developing Spacetec's electronic process guide. During this work five main processes were defined, and for each process one or two process workshops were arranged. For Spacetec to achieve realistic descriptions with accurate detail as well as company commitment in an efficient manner, all relevant employee groups (developers, project leaders, sales and marketing personnel) were involved in defining the processes. In the workshops the attendees discussed how they work, which fostered learning even before the process guide was available on the intranet. Participation also assured quality, since the process guide was developed by people who actually perform the work; it did not describe how consultants or senior staff imagined the development processes to be like. The workshops usually lasted half a day, had 4-6 participants, and in total more than 20 persons participated in one or more workshops.

Another more permanent quality circle has been the project-closure committee, where all the project leaders participate. This forum discusses e.g. the postmortem review reports from the projects. These discussions function as a learning meeting as well as a foundation for improvement actions on a company level.

3.6 Autonomous Working Group

Autonomous working groups [18] are often used as a synonym for "self-managing teams" and for "empowered teams." These are teams of employees who typically perform highly related or interdependent jobs, who are identified and identifiable as a social unit in an organization, and who are given significant authority and responsibility for many aspects of their work, such as planning, scheduling, assigning tasks to members, and making decisions.

In Spacetec such a group was used e.g. to produce a detailed improvement plan from the results of the first process assessment. Their mandate included planning improvement actions on a strategic company level, and presenting the plan to the management before the group was disbanded. Important actions suggested from this group were the foundation of the project-closure committee and an initiative for learning from own experiences, resulting in the introduction of the postmortem review and the development of the experience database.

4 Discussion

It is well documented that involvement is necessary for achieving success, and that employee participation in SPI projects is particularly important for small companies. Several studies report the benefit of such involvement [1, 11], but they do not describe how the involvement was planned and executed in the companies participating in the studies. There are however several case studies on different involvement techniques, e.g., quality circles and learning meetings. These are mainly single technique studies, mostly from large companies, few of them in the area of SPI. As far as we now, there are no case studies reporting how involvement is done in SPI work for small software companies.

We have shown how a small software company has used various techniques for long-term participation in SPI projects over a period of eight years. Spacetec has also conducted several other improvement initiatives with and without broad participation, but we have focused on showing those initiatives that best illustrate how they have used participation in their SPI strategy. Since the effect of involvement is well documented (e.g. [11, 12]), it was not our goal to document this effect in the work described here. However, when introducing the process guide in Spacetec, we found that those involved in creating the EPG had a much higher usage level than those who were not involved [22]. We also found this effect after two years, indicating a long term effect. After introducing the postmortem review, the postmortem review reports were compared with project experience reports (the traditional way of documenting project experience). We found that the postmortem review report identified more experience that was useful for future projects than experience reports that were seldom read [10]. Several initiatives, e.g., the process assessment, identified the need for collecting experiences and making them available, resulting in planning and specifying an experience databases. Even though there was a strong need for this experience database, this initiative failed since the tool was never implemented. The reason for this was that Spacetec never allocated the necessary resources for implementing it. Maybe the initiative was not strongly enough anchored among the management, or those participating in specifying it never really believed in the idea. However, when the EPG was implemented some years later, it was implemented in a way that also made it an experience database [23].

Involvement is not the only factor for achieving success in SPI. Another important success factor is business orientation [12], and an SPI project needs to be aligned with the companies' business goals and strategies if it is to succeed.

A high level of participation [1, 11] and a long-term focus are important [6]. Through the various techniques, Spacetec has involved a substantial share of the employees. The improvement actions performed at Spacetec can be classified into:

1. Those that were terminated after achieving relatively short-term goals, e.g., development of an experience database and an electronic process guide, and process assessment.
2. Those that were institutionalized, e.g. post mortem reviews and project-closure committees.

Participation in SPI initiatives like 2) happens regularly and continuously as long as the initiative is prioritized in the company. Since postmortem reviews are performed frequently, almost every developer will participate in one or several feedback meetings during a year. Participation in these initiatives is not voluntary since they participate by virtue of their position (e.g. project participant, project leader in project-closure committee). Participation in activities like 1) also had a high level of participation among the employees. The development of the EPG involved 40% of the employees, and feedback-meetings on EPG usage involved all of the 50 employees. It was voluntary to participate in the development of the EPG, but in the feedback-meetings on the EPG usage everyone was asked to participate. Even though SPI initiatives like 1) were ended after they reached their goals, they have been considered long-time initiatives since they have consisted of several sub-activities and been the starting point of other SPI meetings.

5   Conclusion and Further Work

Several studies show that participation is important for a company to be successful, and especially when small companies are to succeed with implementing SPI. We have given examples on how a small software company has used various techniques for achieving long-term participation among a broad number of employees in SPI projects. We will also continue to study how both new and old involvement techniques are used in Spacetec. Spacetec is at the moment considering trying out SCRUM, an agile method, which requires a high level of participation. We will also study how large companies can achieve a higher level of involvement in SPI, particularly at the team and project level.

Acknowledgement

This work was supported by the SPIKE project, partially funded by the Research Council of Norway.

References

1. Ahire, S. L. and Golhar, D. Y., "Quality management in large vs small firms - An emperical investigation," Journal of Small Business Management, vol. 34, no. 2, (1996) 1-13

2. Avison, D., Lau, F., Myers, M., and Nielsen, P. A., "Action research," Communications of the ACM, vol. 42, no. 1, (1999) 94-97

3. Basili, V. R., "Quantitative Evaluation of Software Engineering Methodology," The First Pan Pacific Computer Conference Melbourne, Australia, (1985)

4. Baskerville, R. L. and WoodHarper, A. T., "A critical perspective on action research as a method for information systems research," Journal of Information Technology, vol. 11, no. 3, (1996) 235-246

5. Baumgartel, H., "Using employee questionnaire results for improving organizations: The survey "feedback" experiment," Kansas Business Review, vol. 12 (1959) 2-6

6. Cotton, J. L., Vollrath, D. A., Froggatt, K. L., Lengnickhall, M. L., and Jennings, K. R., "Employee Participation - Diverse Forms and Different Outcomes," Academy of Management Review, vol. 13, no. 1, (1988) 8-22

7. Deming, E. W., Out of the Crisis. Cambridge, Massachusetts: The MIT Press (2000).

8. Dingsøyr, T, "Postmortem reviews: purpose and approaches in software engineering," Information and Software Technology, vol.47, no.5,(2005) 293-303

9. Dingsøyr, T., Moe, N. B., Dybå, T., and Conradi, R., "A workshop-oriented approach for defining electronic process guides - A case study," in *Software Process Modelling, Kluwer International Series on Software Engieering,* S. T. Acuña and N. Juristo, Eds. Boston: Kluwer, 2004, pp. 187-205.

10. Dingsøyr, T., Moe, N. B., and Nytrø, Ø., "Augmenting Experience Reports with Lightweight Postmortem reviews," in *Third International Conference on Product Focused Software Process Improvement,* LNCS 2188, F. Bomarius and S. Komi-Sirviö, Eds. Kaiserslautern, Germany: Springer Verlag, 2001, pp. 167 - 181.

11. Dybå, T., "Factors of Software Process Improvement Success in Small and Large Organizations: An Empirical Study in the Scandinavian Context," Proceedings of (ESEC) and 11th SIGSOFT Symposium, Helsinki, Finland, (2003) 148-157

12. Dybå, T., "An empirical investigation of the key factors for success in software process improvement," IEEE Transactions on Software Engineering, vol. 31, no. 5, (2005) 410-424

13. Dybå, T., Dingsøyr, T., and Moe, N. B., Process Improvement in Practice - A Handbook for IT Companies. Boston: Kluwer, 2004.

14. Dybå, T. and Moe, N. B., "Rethinking the Concept of Software Process Assessment," Proceedings of the European Software Process Improvement Conference (EuroSPI), Pori, Finland, (1999)

15. ESA, "ESA software engineering standard," European Space Agency 1991.

16. Fenton-O'Creevy, M., "Employee involvement and the middle manager: evidence from a survey of organizations," Journal of Organizational Behavior, vol. 19, no. 1, (1998) 67-84

17. Greenwood, D. and Levin, M., Introduction to action research: social research for social change. Thousand Oaks, Ca: Sage, 1998

18. Guzzo, R. A. and Dickson, M. W., "Teams in organizations: Recent research on performance and effectiveness," Annual Review of Psychology, vol. 47 (1996) 307-338

19. ISO, "ISO 9001:2000 Quality management systems -- Requirements," 2000.

20. Lawler, E. E. and Mohrman, S. A., "Quality Circles - after the Honeymoon," Organizational Dynamics, vol. 15, no. 4, (1987) 42-54

21. McGarry, F., "Process Improvement Is a Bottom-up Task," IEEE Software, vol. 11, no. 4, (1994) 13-13
22. Moe, N. B. and Dingsøyr, T., "The Impact of Process Workshop Involvement on the Use of an Electronic Process Guide: A Case Study," EuroMicro, Porto, Portugal, (2005) IEEE: 188-195
23. Moe, N. B., Dingsøyr, T., Nilsen, K. R., and Villmones, N. J., "Project Web and Electronic Process Guide as Software Process Improvement," EuroSPI 2005, Budapest, Hungary, (2005) LNCS 3792, pp. 175 – 186
24. Purser, R. E. and Cabana, S., "Involve employees at every level of strategic planning," Quality Progress, vol. 30, no. 5, (1997) 66-71
25. Scott, L., Carvalho, L., Jeffery, R., D'Ambra, J., and Becker-Kornstaedt, U., "Understanding the use of an electronic process guide," Information and Software Technology, vol. 44, no. 10, (2002) 601-616
26. SEI, "Capability Maturity Model ® Integration (CMMI), Version 1.1," 2002.
27. Solingen, R. v. and Berghout, E., The Goal/Question/Metric Method - A practical Guide for Quality Improvement of Software Development. London: McGraw-Hill 1999.
28. Stalhane, T., "Root cause analysis and gap analysis - A tale of two methods," in *Software Process Improvement, Proceedings*, vol. 3281, *Lecture Notes in Computer Science*, 2004, pp. 150-160.
29. Susman, G. and Evered, R., "An assessment of the scientific merits of action research," Administrative Science Quarterly, vol. 23, no. 4, (1978) 582-603
30. Zajac, G. and Bruhn, J. G., "The moral context of participation in planned organizational change and learning," Administration & Society, vol. 30, no. 6, (1999) 706-733

Trust Facilitating Good Software Outsourcing Relationships

Kerstin V. Siakas, Dimitri Maoutsidis, and Errikos Siakas

Alexander Technological Educational Institute of Thessaloniki,
Department of Informatics, P.O. Box 141, GR-57400 Thessaloniki, Greece
siaka@it.teithe.gr, dimao@it.teithe.gr, serik@mailbox.gr

Abstract. Offshore outsourcing and teams working across national borders have become a fact. Management experiences difficulties when applying traditional management approaches, because of the increased complexity of global organizations and global partnerships and their dependency on people with different underlying norms, values and beliefs. Cultural sensitivity is a core issue. Trust, an issue embedded in culture, is utmost important for global organizations and global outsourcing partnerships. In this paper we investigate the phenomenon of trust by analyzing the characteristics, their interconnection and identification in the software outsourcing context. Our findings reveal the importance of trust in software outsourcing relationships and the recognition that trust is culture bound and therefore prompts for special caution and cultural awareness. The advantages gained in outsourcing relationships which could demonstrate trust between partners were improved communication, efficiency and output of Information Systems (IS) development projects, as well as mitigation of opportunistic behavior.

Keywords: Trust, Outsourcing, Global Organizations.

1 Introduction, Motivation and Perspectives

Since the Industrial Revolution companies have struggled with how to exploit their competitive advantage in order to increase profit and extend their markets. In today's rapidly changing and highly competitive global environment organisations face more challenges than ever. The evolution of the internet has endorsed organisations to establish business partnerships beyond geographical boundaries. Organisations increasingly delegate Information Technology (IT) intensive business activities, such as resource demanding operational tasks and projects, as well as critical strategic business processes to external service providers outside the home country.

The countries involved as customers / clients are mainly North America and Europe with Japan following [1]. The prevailing software service supplier is India, dominating 80–90 percentage of the total offshore development revenue worldwide [2]. Other software service provider countries are shown in table 1, classified by status in the global market.

Offshore outsourcing can decrease some costs, but it usually adds expenses, such as partner (service provider / customer) selection and the cost of transitioning work to

R. Messnarz (Ed.): EuroSPI 2006, LNCS 4257, pp. 171–182, 2006.

Table 1. Outsourcing Software Service Provider Countries [1]

Leaders	India
Challengers	Canada, China, Czech Republic, Hungary, Ireland, Israel, Mexico, Northern Ireland, Philippines, Poland, Russia, South Africa
Up Comers	Belarus, Brazil, Caribbean, Egypt, Estonia, Latvia, Lithuania, New Zealand, Singapore, Ukraine, Venezuela
Beginners	Bangladesh, Cuba, Ghana, Korea, Malaysia, Mauritius, Nepal, Senegal, Sri Lanka, Taiwan, Thailand, Vietnam

outsourcing service providers. Additionally outsourcing creates challenges in cross-cultural management including communication, cultural differences and a lack of common internal processes [3].

According to a survey [4] including 101 IT professionals, the benefits of offshore outsourcing were considered as following:

- Lower cost (78%);
- Increased IT department productivity (44%);
- Reduced project timeline (37%);
- Competitive advantage (30%);
- Internal customer satisfaction (20%).

On the other hand the challenges of offshore outsourcing were:

- Managing communication (67%);
- Cultural differences (51%);
- Lack of internal processes for specifying work (40%);
- Lack of internal customer management skills (32%);

The most striking findings from the above survey are cultural differences (51%) and management of communication (67%), which both are important success factors in outsourcing relationships. In outsourcing relationships, which usually include virtual collaboration and virtual teams, the main difference found between collated teams and virtual teams was within communications and trust [5]. Our interpretation of these findings is that communication in virtual teams is much harder due to constraints such as language, time and distance and this in turn leads to inadequate communication and subsequently to difficulties in building trust.

2   Why Is Trust so Important in Outsourcing Relationships?

Globalisation expanding worldwide beyond domestic boundaries is a business fact, which is creating an interconnected world economy, in which companies do their business and compete with each other anywhere in the world, regardless of national boundaries [6]. Saee [7] states that globalisation has been beneficial to nearly all countries around the world. However, globalisation does not imply homogeneity of cultures [8]; diverse cultures dependency on people with different underlying norms, values and beliefs either favour or suppress different behaviours and cultural values [9]. Organisations are dependent on people with different work values norms and attitudes and therefore cultural awareness in global organisations and outsourcing relationships is of utmost importance for improving and sustaining competitive advantage.

All IT outsourcing relationships contain elements of cooperative agreement and requirements of increasingly complex systems [10]. In order to effectively manage an outsourcing contract in today's dynamic business environment, both the service provider and the client must value and nurture the relationship. Recent research undertaken by the Warwick Business School in the UK regarding 1200 outsourcing contracts around the world, has found that outsourcing relationship can be either power- or trust-based and that relationships based on mutual trust rather than punitive service level agreements and penalties, benefit from a 'trust dividend' worth as much as 40% of the contract's total value [11]. Real trust has to be nurtured and comes from planning, structures, processes and measurement. Good relationships are strategic assets and demand on-going management investment and attention. Ignoring the value of outsourcing relationships will have a huge impact on return on investment and the potential added business value gained from outsourcing. Only management can ensure that the mechanisms, people and incentives are in place to build the desired relationship and create an environment in which to foster the trust relationship. Trust also mitigates perception of opportunistic behaviour between outsourcing partners and thus enhances knowledge, resource and asset transfer [12].

Challenges for managers of distributed organisations and outsourcing relationships are enquired to build trust though communication instead of controlling [13]. Integrity, the ability to build trust and keep promises [14], has to be cultivated. In order to build trust and shared commitment personal contact time is needed [5]. Trust contributes to the ability of team members to collaborate [15], which in turn leads to easier adaptation of complexity and change [16, 17].

However, trust is culturally embedded and since offshore outsourcing involves different national cultures we need to understand differences in cultures and to have cultural awareness in order to build trust. Cooperation between outsourcing partners and project team looms as an important factor for success. Trust is important for cooperation and the slightest cultural misunderstanding can create serious cultural damage [18]. Outsourcing companies are reluctant to transfer key knowledge to outsourcing providers, because of the risk of the providers becoming competitors in the future. Organisations may also have trade secrets or vital customer information they want to protect. Some organisations have chosen to open subsidiaries, and thus transferring the organisational culture into the local company (e.g. Siemens and Bosch in India and China), whilst other organisations try to find the balance between the portion of outsourcing, the context of outsourcing for the creation of added business value. In all these case trust is an important factor and will be a facilitator for increasing outsourcing relationships both in depth and breadth.

In the literature there is agreement that trust will develop only when there is some kind of risk and interdependence between partners [19]. When contractual hazards are high (easy to switch to another client) management of outsourcing relationships become increasingly based on trust, because every future contingency can not be known at the time the contract is signed [20] and trust develops over the course of a relationship. Frequent direct contact through face-to-face meetings is a key factor to developing trust between the client and the service provider [21].

Hofstede [22] provided strong evidence that national cultural differences shape organisational behaviour at a local level, and that differences in national and regional cultures affect work values. He argued that culture is a collection of characteristics possessed by people who have been conditioned by similar socialisation practices, educational procedures and life experiences. Krishna et al. [23] affirm that major differences in norms and values cannot be harmonised since they derive from deep-rooted differences in cultural background, education and working life. In offshore outsourcing relationships there is a customer / client and a service provider both from a different national culture. Companies / customers may also have multiple sourcing relationships in different countries and service providers may have their own service providers. This is a very complex relationship and may involve many different countries with different cultural values. The recognition of differences in national cultures can be beneficial for progress in a variety of ways [24].

The organisation culture, in the form of assumptions, beliefs, attitudes and values are shared by existing members and taught to new members of the organisation. By promoting a strong organisational culture within global organisations, without disproving and demolishing local converging values and attitudes, success is more likely to occur. Organisational culture affects directly individual behaviour by imposing guidelines and expectations for the members of the organisation. One of the key issues for managers in global organisations is integration across geographic distance and cultural diversity [25].

Organisational culture is mainly created and maintained in existing frameworks by the founders and the leaders of an organisation through their value system [26, 27]. Three of the most important sources of organisational cultures are according to Brown [28]:

- societal or national cultures within which an organisation is physically situated;
- the vision, management style and personality of the founder and other dominant leaders of the organisation;
- the type of business an organisation conducts and the nature of its business environment.

The challenges globalisation offers, originates from social, economical, legal, political and technological differences between nations, together with cultural differences regarding work values, attitudes and preferences both of employees and customers. Shared stakeholder values are considered to be important for the success of organisations that work in a global context [22, 27, 29]. Management of global organisations that can take account of the cultural context of their endeavours experiences better success. Even though the very act to deliberately create trust can lead to mistrust, results from previous studies indicate that certain social mechanisms can be used to create an environment in which trust can gain a foothold and flourish [30, 31]. Evidence shows that from a cultural point of view Eastern cultures compared to Western view trust as an important factor in any transactions and therefore choose to have longer-term relationships built on basis of trust with the client. Contracts are considered less important and are viewed with scepticism [32].

Regarding IT outsourcing there seems to be relative high awareness of cultural issues in the literature, which seems to propose:

- Recognition of the fact that cross-cultural training is needed both in advance and continuously [33];
- Use of 'cultural bridging staff' (people rooted in the country of the sourcing service provider as well as in the country of the client) for informal sharing of experiences [23];
- Use of common systems, common processes and common compatible technologies [34];
- Recognition of the importance of the communication language [33];
- Use of trust-building mechanism [34].

All the above cultural issues are important for understanding and building trust in different cultural settings. In the following section we investigate the phenomenon of trust in more detail by unfolding the characteristics of trust.

3   The Notion of Trust

The notion of trust has been studied by a number of disciplines, each emphasizing different aspects: *"researchers in different disciplines have viewed trust along different dimensions"* [35]. Economists tend to view trust as calculative, psychologists emphasize the personal attributes and sociologists stress the institutional properties [19]. In this paper, ideas from all these three disciplines are drawn upon because aspects from economics, sociology, and psychology are seen to be relevant in software outsourcing relationships. All disciplines seem to agree that trust is a complex phenomenon with many meanings, difficult to identify, and no widely acknowledged definition of the term exists [1] and that the notion of trust generally is associated with one party having confidence in another and an implication of alignment between relevant value systems [15, 31].

Building a successful relationship with stakeholders in global outsourcing relationships, where engagements often span several years, is a critical success factor [36, 37, 38, 39]. This refers in particular to the global outsourcing partners, such as the client and the service provider, but is also important to all other suppliers and partners involved in the sourcing relationship. By managing expectations and effectively responding to stakeholder needs both the client and the service provider establishes trust with its stakeholders and help to sustain long term relationships and to avoid internal resistance.

Handy [40] points on seven principles of trust to be kept in mind:

- *Trust is not blind*, which means that it is unwise to trust people whom you do not   know well;
- *Trust needs boundaries* and confidence in someone's competence and commitment to common goal;
- *Trust demands learning.* Every individual has to be capable of self renewal;
- *Trust is tough.* When trust proves misplaced people have to go;
- *Trust needs bonding.* The team must adhere to the organisational vision and mission;

- *Trust needs touch.* A shared commitment requires personal contact to make it real;
- *Trust requires leaders.* Trust-based organisations hardly have to be managed, but they do need a multiplicity of leaders.

In outsourcing relationships self-management in the distant location is needed in order to get high performance. Self-management can only be realised in an environment where the leader displays trust through delegation. On the other hand the team members must trust that the leader is committed to support collaboration and manage the team boundaries [5].

As people from different countries and organisations work together on project teams and outsourcing relationships there will be a technology transfer through personal and business interests which will also will create a closer relationship and enhance trust levels [18]. Trust within organisations exist on three levels [41, 42], namely deterrence-based trust (when both parties can be trusted to keep their word, based on intuition), knowledge-based trust (is based on predictability of the other party developed through knowledge of the other party) [1, 19, 42] and identification-based trust (when one party has fully internalised the other's performance [42]. The longer the outsourcing relationship the better will the outsourcing partners know each others advantages and disadvantages and thus the predictability rises together with trust or eventually distrust. The three levels are believed to be linked in a sequential iteration in that one level enables trust on the next level along with the evolvement and maturity of the relationship [41].

In order to relate the attributes of trust to the software outsourcing context, some factors about trust are considered important. The attributes are discussed below and in the end the attributes are evaluated.

4   The Complexity of Trust

Because companies involved in outsourcing are geographically dispersed, a risk factor stems from lack of information about what the distant partner is doing. In software outsourcing relationships establishing trust is suggested to have several advantages, such as mitigating opportunistic behaviour, improving communication, facilitating knowledge transfer [12], improving efficiency and output quality of Information Systems (IS) development projects [34].

In software outsourcing relationships trust is important within and between organisations, and is different in these two settings [19]. Trust within the organisation refers to differences in trust at the individual, group, and institutional level [19]. Trust has been found to differ regarding which organisational level is studied [1]. The setting within organisations is influenced by the organisational culture. The setting between dispersed organisations is influenced by the national cultures in which the organisations (client / service provider) are situated. This paper looks at trust in both these settings (organisational and national environment) and will consider trust at different levels too.

Trust has not only to do with relationships between humans, but also concerns systems. While trust in humans stems from interaction, trust in abstract systems puts its faith in the correctness of principles [43]. Both personal and system related trust is addressed in this paper. Trust has been found to change over time. Usually, three phases are identified: building, stability, and dissolution [19].

Trust is not a button switch but it exists in varying levels. The degree of trust in a relationship may vary not only over time, but as well between different relationships. Trust exaggerations (over- or under-investments in trust) are undesirable behaviours both from a strategic and a moral point of view [16]. Because it is possible to trust little or more, trust is considered to have a dynamic nature [19]. Trust cannot be present in every aspect of a relationship, because some of motives of the partner can be trusted and some may be questionable [44]. Especially in offshore outsourcing relationships trust cannot be present in every aspect; a sceptical approach is required. Since cultural awareness is difficult to create, we need to be cautious and critical to our feelings of trust; independent of if they are based on intuition or on knowledge. We also have to stress here that trust has to be present in both parties. The trustor must trust the trustee and vice versa, it is a mutual relationship.

Finally, trust depends on social conditioning. In the World Value Survey (WVS) [45], undertaken 1990-1993 across 43 societies covering around 60000 respondents that completed a questionnaire with more than 360 questions. The responses to the question: *Generally speaking, would you say that most people can be trusted or that you can't be too careful in dealing with people?* showed variances from 7% in Brazil, can be trusted, to 66% in Sweden.

5 Attributes of Trust

In order to understand trust its characteristics have to be analysed. These characteristics can be identified by studying relevant literature. Imsland [1] proposes seven identifiable attributes of trust, namely predictability, competence, structure, calculation, goodwill, knowledge and betrayal, which we will analyse in more detail below. A discussion of the attributes will help to provide a better understanding of trust, and their interconnection for identification and visibility.

Predictability: The expectation of something from someone else is essential for the existence of trust. Giddens [43] stresses the notion of trust as faith in predictability. Trust is more likely to be established if an ability to predict another person's or organization's behaviour exists. Predictability is achieved through monitoring and influencing the behaviour of the partner. In the beginning of an outsourcing relationship the partners know little or nothing about each other. They look for indications that will enable them to build trust. Finding more information about the future partner, such as studying web-pages, tracing history and reputation, as well as observing how the organisation works (preferable over a period of time) will help in determining the organisation's way of functioning. Control mechanisms can be introduced to make the behaviour predictable. There is evidence that predictability is considered to be an important trust-building mechanism [34]. However, trust is not necessarily present when predictability is present, but as a general rule, trust is difficult to build if one cannot predict behaviour [46].

Competence means having the ability to efficiently perform something that the partner requires [44]. It also includes capacity to learn new tasks and technologies

[34]. Competence is especially important in the IT outsourcing context. One key argument for an organisation to outsource can be the lack of competence within its own organisation [47]. A client that has chosen a service provider with good competence reputation will feel more confident about the outcome of the project. However, competence trust on its own does not ensure trust on all levels.

Structure is a way of formal control of the procedures used to achieve something. Examples of structures can be written contracts, reporting mechanisms, and rules for response time on written messages [12]. Also, the use of standards, such as ISO 9001:2000 [48] and Capability Maturity Models, such as CMMI (Capability Maturity Model Integrated) [49, 50] and the eSourcing Capability Maturity Model eSCM –SP for Service Providers [37, 38, 39] and eSCM-CL for Client Organisations [36] are considered structural attributes [1]. In particular the practices of these frameworks are well adaptable for any virtual organisation as the high capability level of outsourcing cooperation of service clients and providers implement a real knowledge based virtual organisation [51].

Considering predictability as an attribute of trust, and structure as a way of achieving this, structure also has flaws, in respect to trust. Very tight structural control harms performance, because much time has to be spent on reporting and providing feedback to the controller [19]. Hofstede [22] found that Power Distance is a basic cultural dimension related to power and control and Uncertainty Avoidance another cultural dimension related to the degree societies want to create structures and rules to protect them against ambiguous situations. The studies of these two dimensions in depth will enable the client organisation to understand the degree of structures suitable to be implemented in another country. Siakas and Hyvarinen [52] have developed an on-line self-assessment tool that finds the fit between national and organisational culture. The tool is based on Hofstede's two dimensions, namely Power Distance and Uncertainty Avoidance, and from the results the client will get an indication about if more or less structures are desirable in a certain country context.

Calculation: The idea of calculation refers to the ability to predict whether the trustee is capable to accomplish the requirements successfully [19]. If calculations show that there is a risk factor of the trustee not being able to fulfil the requirements, there is no reason for the relationship to begin. The company also has to compare the potential risks with the possible advantages of the relationship. A distinction between objective and subjective risk is valuable [53]. Objective risk is based upon the objectively calculated consequences of different alternatives when making a decision. Subjective risk is the decision makers' estimate of objective risk. Every decision has both an objective and a subjective risk, but because of complexity and lack of information, only subjective risk is possible to determine.

Goodwill is trust based on intuition. In every new relationship people use their intuition and experience to figure out if someone is trustworthy. It can be about any characteristics of someone, whether personal characteristics like honesty and benevolence, or more general attributes like competence and predictability [44]. Even if trust in organizations, as opposed to trust in individuals, concerns faith in the correctness of principles more than interaction [43], such trust is also dependent on a general goodwill between the organizations.

Knowledge about the partner(s) in a relationship is seen to be important when building trust. The most important outcome of such interaction is predictability. It is important to notice that gaining rich knowledge about the partner is difficult to achieve, and emerges only after longer-term interaction [19]. However, Hertzum [53] identifies four ways of building knowledge-based trust: first-hand experience, reputation, surface attributes (visible artefact, such as language, symbols, heroes, behaviour patterns, rules and procedures), as well as stereotypes. The two last ones, surface attributes and stereotypes are actually manifestations of cultures [25] and thus training of outsourcing partners in each others cultures would make an important input for understanding cultural differences and improving cultural awareness, which also will be an important factor for building trust. Regarding reputation Lander et al. [34] undertook a case study with four primary stakeholder groups, namely upper management, project team members, users and employees of the client. Upper-level management considered that reputation was an important determinant for trust regarding selection of client and for employing team members into the projects, while project team members and users were less focused on reputations since they assume that upper-level management has exercised due diligence in this regard. Clients did know little or anything of the service provider's reputation and thus had not reporting anything about its importance in creation of trust.

Since members of software outsourcing projects are dispersed geographically, these four ways of building trust (first-hand-experience, reputation, surface attributes and stereotypes) must be supported by bringing together key personnel [1]. We extend by stating that face-to-face meetings and the use of 'cultural bridging staff' (people rooted in the country of the sourcing service provider as well as in the country of the client) improves communication, cultural understanding and knowledge about each other, thus slowly facilitating creation and sustaining a trust relationship.

Betrayal: In every relationship exists a risk factor, of someone acting opportunistically and by so doing breaking the trust that has been built. This is called betrayal, and is defined as *"a voluntary violation of mutually known pivotal expectations of the trustor by the trusted party (trustee), which has the potential to threaten the well-being of the trustor"* [55]. Examples of betrayal are theft, lying, braking of contract and promises. In research regarding trust building mechanisms Lander et al. [34] found that senior management and team members at the outsourcing provider reported that the fulfilment of promises is crucial to the development of trust, whilst the client did not share this view. For the client, fulfilment of promises is an artefact of a contractual relationship. This result indicates that it would be valuable if outsourcing partners appreciate what the other party value in trust-building processes and in project related actions in order to find a mutual ground of commitment.

Each one of these seven attributes has its own important role in the software outsourcing context. Some characteristics of the above attributes may be similar and this brings the conclusion that the attributes of trust are interconnected together up to a point and partially overlapping. If some of the above attributes exist up to a certain degree that implies essentially that all of the attributes are present [1]. If for example *competence* is present in a company, there will also be predictability, calculation and knowledge based on the competence. Thus you can also have goodwill and not expect betrayal.

6 Conclusion

Globalisation today is a reality having created numerous of challenges for managers worldwide. Increased and improved capabilities of ICT facilitate continuous expansion of globalisation today's IT outsourcing activities have shifted to involve much greater range and depth of services than in the past and an increasing number of IT functions are transferred to IT service providers. Outsourcing and virtual collaborations prompt for cultural sensitivity, flexibility and adaptability, together with high awareness of risks and dangers due to cultural differences. Globalisation is a competitive advantage if handled in a right manner.

In this paper the emphasis was on trust, which was analysed in relation to the software outsourcing context. Trust was found to be a complex phenomenon and a critical success factor. Trust is slowly built through communication and experience of attitudes and behaviours of stakeholders. Advantages of trust in outsourcing relationships was found to be improved communication, efficiency and output of IS development projects as well as the mitigation of opportunistic behaviour.

References

1. Imsland, V.: The Role of Trust in Global Outsourcing Relationships, Candidate Science Thesis, Oslo University, Department of Informatics (2003)
2. Khan, N., Currie W. L., Weerakkody, V., Desai, B.: Evaluating Offshore IT Outsourcing in India: Supplier and Customer Scenarios. In Proceedings of the 36th Annual Hawaii International Conference on System Sciences, January (2003) 239–248
3. Siakas, K. V., Balstrup, B.: Software Outsourcing Quality Achieved by Global Virtual Collaboration, Software Process: Improvement and Practice (SPIP) Journal, John Wiley & Sons, Vol. 11, no. 3 (May-June, 2006)
4. Ware, L.C.: Weighing the Benefits of Offshore Outsourcing, CIO Research Reports (2003), retrieved at 23.03.2006 from http://www2.cio.com/research/surveyreport. cfm?ID=62
5. Balstrup, B.: Leading by Detached Involvement – Success factors enabling leadership of virtual teams, MBA Dissertation, Henley Management College, UK (2004)
6. Cullen, J. B.: Multinational Management: A strategic Approach, Cincinatti, Ohio, South Western College Publishing (1999)
7. Saee, J.: Strategic Global management: Cross-Cultural Dimension, France, Normedia Publishing House (2002)
8. Walsham, G.: Making a World of Difference: It in a Global Context, Wiley, Chichester (2001)
9. Siakas, K.V, Berki, E., Georgiadou, E.: CODE for SQM: A Model for Cultural and Organisational Diversity Evaluation, EuroSPI 2003 (European Software Process Improvement Conference), Graz, Austria, 10-12.12.2003, IX 1-11
10. Willcocks, L., Choi, C. J.: Co-operative Partnership and "Total" IT Outsourcing: From Contractual Obligation to Strategic Alliance? European Management Journal, March, Vol 13, No 1 (1995) 67 - 78
11. Willcocks, L. P., Cullen S.: The Outsourcing Enterprise, The power of relationships, Warwick Business School white paper (2005), retrieved 26.03.2006 from http://www. prnewswire.co.uk/cgi/news/release?id=159034

12. Sabherwal, R.: The role of trust in outsourced IS development projects, Communications of the ACM, 42 (2) (1999) 80
13. Maguire, S.,Phillips, N., Hardy C.: When 'silence= death', keep talking: Trust, control and the discursive construction of identity in the Canadian hiv/aids treatment domain. Organization Studies 22(2) (2001) 285–310.
14. Yukl, G.: Leadership in Organisations, New Delhi, Pearson Education (2002)
15. Costigan, R. D, Ilter, S.S, Berman, J. J.: A multi- dimensional study of trust in organizations, Journal of Managerial Issues, 10 (3) (1998) 303 -318
16. Wicks, A. C., Berman S. L,   Jones T. M.: The structure of optimal trust: Moral and strategic implications, The Academy of Management Review, 24(1), (1999) 99–116
17. Zaheer, A., McEvely, B., Perrone, V.: Does Trust Matter? Exploring the Effects of Interorganisational and Interpersonal Trust on Performance, Organisational Science, 9 (2) (1998) 141-159
18. Cleland, D. I, Gareis R.(eds): Global Project Management Handbook, McGraw-Hill, Inc. US (1994)
19. Rousseau, D. M, Sitkin, S.B. Burt, R.S, and Camerer, C.: Not so different after all: A cross-discipline view of trust. The Academy of Management Review 23(3), (1998) 393–404
20. Barthelemy, J.: The Hard and Soft Sides of IT Outsourcing Management, European Management Journal, October, Vol. 21. No. 5, (2003) 539-548
21. Dyer, J. and Ouchi, W. (1993): Japanese-style partnerships: giving companies a competitive edge, Sloan Management Review, 34, 51-63
22. Hofstede, G. (2001): Culture's consequences: comparing values, behaviours, institutions, and organisations - 2nd Ed. - Thousand Oaks California, Sage Publications
23. Krishna, S., Sahay S., Walsham, G. (2004). Managing Cross-cultural Issues in Global Software Outsourcing, Communications of the ACM, April Vol. 47, No 4
24. Biro, M., Feher, P.: Forces Affecting Offshore Software Development, EuroSPI 2005 (12th European Software Process Improvement Conference), Springer, Budapest, Hungary, Nov. (2005) 187-201
25. Siakas, K.V.: SQM-CODE: Software Quality Management – Cultural and Organisational Diversity Evaluation, PhD Thesis, London Metropolitan University, UK (2002)
26. Bryman, A.: Charisma and leadership in organisations, London, Sage Publications (1992)
27. Schein, E.: Organisational Culture and Leadership, London, Jossey-Bass Ltd. (1985)
28. Brown, A.D.: Organisational Culture, Financial Times Management, Pitman Publishing (1998)
29. Land, F.F.: The Management of Change: Guidelines for the Successful implementation of Information of Information Systems, in Brown, A. (eds): Creating a Business Based IT Strategy, Chapman & Hall (1992)
30. Bigley, G.A, Pearce, J. L.: Straining for shared meaning in organizational science, problems of trust and distrust, Academy of Management Review, 23 (3) (1998) 405-422
31. Blois, K.J.: Trust in business to business relationships: an evaluation of its status, Journal of Management Studies, 36 (2), (1999) 197
32. Samaddar, S., Kadiyala, S.: Information systems outsourcing: Replication an existing framework in a different cultural context, Journal of Operations Management, Nov, (2005) 458-460
33. Foster, N.: Expatriates and the impact of Cross-Cultural Training, Human Resource Management Journal, Vol. 10, No 3, (2000) 63-78
34. Lander, M. C., Purvis, R. L., McCray, G. E., Leigh, W.:Trust-building mechanisms utilized in outsourced IS development projects: a case study, Information & Management, 41, (2003) 509-528

35. Kim, K., Prabhakar, B.: Initial trust, perceived risk, and the adoption of internet banking. In Proceedings of the twenty first international conference on Information systems, Association for Information Systems (2000) 537–543
36. Hefley, W.E, Loesche, E.A.: The eSourcing Capability Model for Client Organisations (eSCM-CL), Draft for public view, Working paper, 28, Feb, (2006)
37. Hyder, E.B, Heston, K.M, Paulk, M.C.: The eSourcing Capability Model for Service Providers (eSCM-SP) v2, Part 1: Model Overview, CMU-ISRI-04-113, Pittsburg, PAL Carnegie Mellon University (2004)
38. Hyder, E.B, Heston, K.M, Paulk, M.C.: The eSourcing Capability Model for Service Providers (eSCM-SP) v2, Part 1: Practice Details, CMU-ISRI-04-114, Pittsburg, PAL Carnegie Mellon University (2004)
39. Hyder, E.B, Kumar B., Mahendra V., Siegel J., Heston K.M, Gupta R., Mahaboob H., Subramanian P.: The e-Sourcing Capability Maturity Model (eSCM-SP) for IT enabled Service Providers, v1.1, CMU-CS-02-155, School of Computer Science, Carnegie University, Pittsburg (2002)
40. Handy, C.: Trust and the Virtual Organization, HBR OnPoint enhanced edition, OnPoint, June (2000)
41. Lewicki, R. , Bunker, L.: Developing and Maintaining Trust in Work relationships, in R. M., Kramer, T. R. Tyler, Frontiers of Research and Theory, Sage, Thousand Oaks, CA (1996) 114-459
42. Sharipo, D.L., Sheppard B.H., Cheraskin, L.: Business on a Handshake, Negotiation Journal 8 (4) (1992) 365-377
43. Giddens, A.: The Consequences of Modernity, Stanford University Press (1990)
44. McKnight, D. H., Chervany N.L.: Trust and distrust definitions: One bite at a time. Lecture Notes in Computer Science 2246 (2001) 27–54.
45. Inglehart, R. Modernization and postmodernization: Cultural, economic, and political change in 43 societies, Princeton, NJ: Princeton University Press (1997)
46. Brenkert, G. G.: Trust, Morality and International Business, Business Ethics Quarterly, April 8(2) (1998) 293–317.
47. Carmel, E., Agarwal, R.: Tactical Approaches for Alleviating Distance in Global Software Development. IEEE software 18(2), (2001) 22–29
48. ISO: Retrieved 26.3.2003, from http://www.iso.org/
49. Herbsleb, J., Carleton, A., Rozum, J., Siegel, J., Zubrow, D.: Benefits of CMM-Based Software Process Improvement: Initial Results, Technical Report, CMU/SEI-94-TR-13, August (1994)
50. CMMI: Retrieved at 26.03.2006 from http://www.sei.cmu.edu/cmmi/ems
51. Biro, M, Deak G, Ivanyos, J., Messnarz, R., Zamori, A.: Using the eSourcing Capability Model to improve IT enabled business process outsourcing services. EuroSPI 2003 (European Software Process Improvement Conference), Graz, Austria, 10-12.12.2003, III.1-III.16
52. Siakas, K.V, Hyvarinen, J.: On-line Assessment of the Fit between National and Organisational Culture; A new tool for Predicting Suitable Software Quality Management System, The 14th Software Quality Management Conference, SQM 2006, April 2006, Southampton, UK
53. Das, T.K., Teng, B-S.: Trust, Control, and Risk in Strategic Alliances: An Integrated Framework. Organization Studies 22(2) (2001) 251–283.
54. Hertzum, M.: The importance of trust in software engineers' assessment and choice of information sources. Information and Organization, January, 12(1) (2002) 1–18
55. Elangovan, A.R., Shapiro D.L.: Betrayal of trust in organizations. The Academy of Management Review 23(3), July (1998) 547–566

Leveraging Feedback on Processes in SOA Projects

Daniel Lübke and Kurt Schneider

Faculty of Electrical Engineering and Computer Science,
Software Engineering Group, University Hannover
{daniel.luebke, kurt.schneider}@inf.uni-hannover.de

Abstract. The development of large, business-critical software systems often requires several improvement cycles. There are many users and stakeholders involved, as well as a variety of large and complex business processes. However, such an iterative or evolutionary development process can be costly and time-consuming, when problems are reported slowly and changes take time. We propose a technical approach to generate user interfaces for SOA systems and to weave an experience forum service into the system. By tightly integrating the experience exchange mechanisms with the system itself, we benefit from SOA being so closely related to business processes. We use lessons learned in building experience bases: Generating both user interfaces and experience forum components provides opportunities to index and relate feedback automatically. This has been a key to effective experience reuse. Improved feedback and more effective communication can make SOA-based development of large software systems faster and less costly.

1 Introduction

Information systems are designed to support a large number of users in process-oriented applications. Due to the process-oriented nature, Information Systems have to be flexibly designed and need extensive customization to optimally match the processes of a company. Therefore, these projects are highly resource-intensive and carry high risks.

But Information Systems not only need to match the processes, they need to support the users fulfilling their tasks within the processes. This means e.g. that the users need to be guided through their tasks and get assistance if functionality is non-trivial. Many factors, like screen design, flexibility and functionality of the business processes, and online assistance, like help systems, become very important in this regard.

However, designing these elements correctly is problematic due to the large and, thus, inhomogeneous user base and the complexity formalized business processes tend to have. Normally, the formal process is different from the lived one. Therefore, communication becomes an essential success factor, especially under the above-mentioned circumstances. This is the only way software and business process-related problems can be easily found and fed back to the development organization, which can fix the problems in one of the next iterations. Furthermore, user acceptance of the final product will depend on involving them into the project.

R. Messnarz (Ed.): EuroSPI 2006, LNCS 4257, pp. 195–206, 2006.
© Springer-Verlag Berlin Heidelberg 2006

2 Service Oriented Architecture

Service Oriented Architecture (SOA) is an architectural style used for building and combining large Information Systems. SOA aims to better support process-oriented applications than traditional design methods by aligning the software directly with the business process. The software system is, therefore, composed of fine-grained and loosely-coupled software components, so-called services. Services are normally remotely accessible. Each service offers functionality in a business sense, e.g. "add customer", which directly relates to business opportunities or business functions.

These services are grouped by so-called compositions into running processes. The composition describes a workflow which calls services as appropriate and resembles the corporation's business processes [1]. A particular composition corresponds to a business process. It is more formalized and enriched by technical information.

Since SOA projects try to directly support a company's processes the resulting software and compositions are highly company specific. Because of this, SOA projects are normally customization or custom software development projects, like the one described in [2].

The best known technology to realize SOAs is Web services. Web services are software components accessible by the SOAP protocol [3] standardized by the W3C. The Business Process Execution Language (BPEL) [4] is used to compose Web services to running processes. These BPEL compositions are accessible via SOAP as well, so that client applications or integration middleware are able to call them like a normal Web service. All larger software manufacturers are offering Web service interfaces to their Information Systems. For example, SAP embraces Web services in their ERP software and the Netweaver Platform[1]. Development solutions and frameworks are as well widely available for the Java and .Net platforms to offer service interfaces by easily creating Web services on top of existing or newly-developed applications.

3 Experience Feedback in Software Development

Development of complex software systems is a knowledge-intensive endeavor. Developers do not only need technical skills, but also domain knowledge, user interface design capabilities, and so forth. Whenever many roles and stakeholders are involved, large projects will rarely meet all customer requirements at the first attempt. There is usually a lengthy period of building, using, and improving the system.

With SOA, such a complex system is structured in a number of independently developed services that need to cooperate as an integrated system. There is an abundance of aspects that developers need to consider when they create SOA systems or services:

- *Usefulness*: Functionality of the services and options to choose from.
- *Usability*: Interface of an orchestrated (i.e., integrated) SOA system and how well it supports tasks in their respective work contexts.

---

[1] http://www.sap.com/solutions/netweaver/

- *Process*: The order of actions performed by the system or required by users following a business processes.

Developers typically lack domain knowledge; they do not know what customers and users may want. At the same time, customers and users do not know what could reasonably be expected from such a system. Fischer has called this the "symmetry of ignorance" [5]. Due to the wicked nature of the problem, and the symmetry of ignorance, several iterations and improvement steps will be needed to produce a satisfactory SOA system [6].

Experience-based process improvement was established with a similar problem in mind: Providing an ideal software process is a wicked problem, too [7]. It faces similar challenges as SOA system development: several roles and stakeholders need to reconcile their views of the product and the underlying process, and no stakeholder has a good understanding of the other positions: a multi-faceted symmetry of ignorance. Therefore, one should envisage an evolutionary improvement phase for both SPI and SOA.

The core driver of evolution in both settings is experience: We define

experience $=_{Def}$ an observation in a real situation,
    accompanied by an emotion
    leading to a (more general) conclusion.

In the case of experience-based process improvement, Basili's experience factory and experience base concepts have initiated several other approaches [8]. At DaimlerChrysler, for example, a large-scale experience-based SPI project (SEC) was carried out in the 1990ies [9]. Its intention was to reuse experience from actually doing something ("observation" in software development) as a driving force for improvement. In [10], a number of findings on realistic and unrealistic assumptions about experience exploitation were reported. These findings have several concrete implications for the construction of a computer-based experience exchange mechanism (often called "experience base"). Those implications were described in [11]. Experience was found to be a fragile material that can be a catalyst for processes, but need to be handled with care:

- Effort to write to an experience base must be strictly minimized in order to lower the input threshold.
- Reported experiences must be compared and engineered, since raw experiences will rarely be reused.
- Spreading experiences and best practices (as derived by experience engineering) needs to be actively supported. For example, "putting anything on the web" is never sufficient for reuse.
- In fact, the entire cycle of identifying, collecting, engineering, and spreading experiences needs to be actively pushed. This is the task of an organization like the "experience factory".
- Search machines are mostly inadequate for experience bases. Writers refuse to attribute and describe their experiences sufficiently, and readers should be allowed more associative access to experiences relevant to their task at hand.

Indexing experiences and derived material (best practices) by the process steps in which they were encountered has shown to be an effective mean of organizing an experience base [12].

- The ability to support easy feedback and fast evolution is crucial for the success of experience-based evolution.

Since SOA shares several characteristics with SPI, it is rewarding to consider experience-based approaches to foster SOA evolution. By adopting the findings ("meta-experiences") from experience-based SPI, we take the above-mentioned lessons seriously. We propose to support SOA evolution by adding experience exploitation mechanisms. Their usefulness has been demonstrated in the (similar) realm of SPI [11].

4   Understanding Information Flows

Based on the above comparison of experience-based SPI and SOA evolution, the situation of feedback in SOA evolution can be analyzed in more depth. Figure 1 depicts a typical situation in the FLOW notation for information flows [13]. FLOW is a research project at the University of Hannover. FLOW addresses many aspects of information flow optimization in software projects, such as quality technique tailoring, flow catalyst techniques or tools [10]. In this paper, only the basic notational elements are used to illustrate how our approach can facilitate feedback in SOA projects.

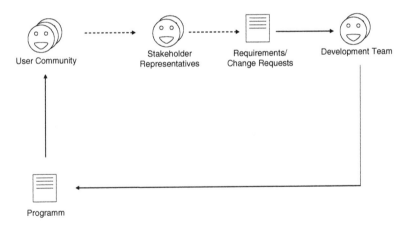

Fig. 1. Information Feedback Flows in SOA projects

Face symbols denote people or groups of people. Information coming from those sources is denoted by a dashed arrow, indicating the fragile nature of this flow. It can easily be interrupted, it is hard to repeat later (due to oblivion), but it can be fast when one person simply talks to another. In most process models, "talking" relationships are not denoted. As a consequence, those relationships depend on personal commitment – and often never occur.

As figure 1 shows, feedback from SOA users reaches the development team only after three problematic information transfer steps; the first flow requires people to take the initiative and engage in communication; stakeholder representatives need to remember this communication and invest effort in writing a change request. After some time, the developers will need to invest some more effort to read and understand the change request. There were three information flows: memorizing, writing, and reading transformation operations are required. If one fails or is omitted (e.g., in order to save effort), there is no flow reaching the development team. But even if it reaches the team, the transformations often cause misunderstandings. Each flow is not encouraged, but rather discouraged by personal effort, time invested, and unclear rewards.

There are variants to overcome the problem:

- On-site customers try to bridge the gap between the user community and developers. This works if and only if on-site customers can represent the entire community well enough. SOA systems are typically used by large and heterogeneous user groups. In addition, one on-site customer can hardly address all usability and business process, and system functionality issues at the same time. The spectrum is too wide, and a single person cannot do as much work and also report it.
- The Microsoft Report Mechanism (see figure 5a) invites users to report problems when and where they occur. This is definitely an interesting concept. In our personal environment, practically nobody ever reports a problem to Microsoft. We heard concerns about reporting outside the own company, when you do not exactly know what happens to the reports and what goes along with it. Those concerns can kill a good concept.

We conclude that we need to offer all real users (not just one representative) a chance to easily report experiences. They need to know who will see their contributions, and they should receive fast responses and see improvement they have initiated. For that purpose, we designed mechanisms to embed experience exchange with the tasks-at-hand, index them by their respective position in the business process, and facilitate fast feedback by automating orchestration, user interface generation, and experience administration.

5 Integrated Experience Forum

To improve the communication it is essential to short-circuit the end-users and the development team. Since all affected people are normally distributed through all company's locations, the communication needs to be technically supported. Normally, electronic media, like Intranets or email, are available at nearly all companies and could be used for accelerating and improving the communication. However, the separation of email clients and browsers from the actual Information System adds hindrance and reduces the likelihood of user feedback. Therefore, it is necessary to further reduce the effort necessary to provide feedback for improving the software and the business processes.

In order to shorten the feedback cycle we propose an *Experience Forum* similar to the Experience Base [8, 11]. The main difference between an Experience Forum and an Experience Base is the target group: While an Experience Base is used for sharing experiences within a development organization only, the Experience Forum is meant to extract experiences from the user community and share it among all users and the development organization. Consequently, the Experience Forum is a communication platform supposed to connect the user community and the development organization. Its integration into a project's communication structure can be seen in figure 2.

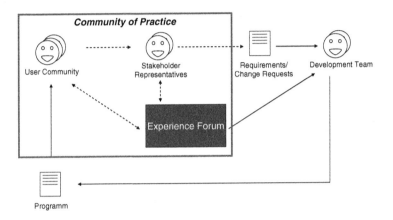

Fig. 2. Integration of the Experience Forum into the SOA project

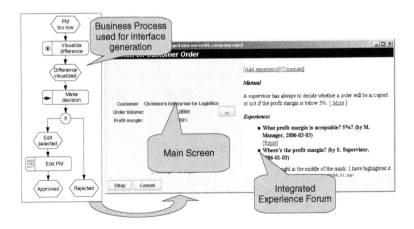

Fig. 3. Prototype screen of automatically generated user interfaces with Experience Forum

The Experience Forum is tightly integrated into the client application as can be seen in figure 3.In our prototype application it is implemented as a sidebar, showing context sensitive information about the current process step. Furthermore, the sidebar allows the user to add new experiences, to submit bug reports and suggestions, and to rate other users' experiences. The rating of experiences can be used to sort them. This is important if, as in our case the sidebar, the space available for displaying the experiences is limited. The rating assures that the best and most interesting experiences are displayed first and are therefore visible by default.

In many Experience Bases the user has to categorize his or her experiences. This is done by either filling in the context information in the experience description or by navigating in the Experience Base to the process step and submitting the experiences there. The advantage of integrating the Experience Forum into the process-supporting system is the availability of context information: The system uses the current process step for automatically indexing all information and experiences. All information is associated and linked to the current step. If the business process changes and the business function is moved, all information is moved as well.

This greatly reduces the effort needed for experience management, especially if it is combined with methods for automatically generating user interfaces from the same business processes [14]. In this scenario the whole client software is based on business process descriptions which it can use to display the user interface and retrieve all information and experience available for the current user.

Seeding of experience instruments is a critical success factor [11]. In case of the Experience Forum the initial seeding can be the user manual and the descriptions extracted from the business processes. This information is valuable to the user and can attract attention to the Experience Forum fostering user activity. This way the Experience Forum becomes the single source for exchanging and retrieving information and experiences about the Information System: User Documentation, experiences, feature requests and bug reports are all handled within the system and are directly accessible during the normal course of work.

All differences between Experience Bases and Experience Forums are illustrated in table 1.

6   Experience Forum Prototype

At our department a prototype Experience Forum has been developed. Our aim was to develop software which can easily be integrated into SOA-style applications. Since Web services are the most dominant implementation technology for SOA, we decided to offer the Experience Forum as Web services accessible by all applications. Therefore, all software can access the Experience Forum and integrate its functionality and profit from it.

As a foundation we used an existing Experience Base [15] which contained all functionality needed by the Experience Forum: The users can submit and retrieve experiences attached to a process description. While the process description originally resembled a development process, it is used for describing business processes in the Experience Forum. Experiences can be rated and commented on.

Table 1. Deriving concrete design recommendations for experience-based SOA

SPI/ Experience Base	SOA/ Experience Forum	Our conclusions for SOA
Minimize effort for writing and organizing SPI experiences	(same)	Offer experience editor integrated with the SOA product: "no single click away"
Fast experience engineering required	Experiences on different aspects need to be treated differently. Fast reactions in all cases!	Desired reactions include: - developers improve the system - peer users report better ways to use the system - process problems get resolved by the domain experts
Spread experience and reactions actively	Improve the system or respond to where the users work on similar tasks.	Embed experience display into all relevant SOA system tasks. Show answers to complaints, point to improvements made.
Experience factory for software process issues, with experience base	Community of users, blackboards (e.g. "wikis") for developers and domain experts	Different experience mechanisms are all mapped to the SOA user interface
Development process as index and search mechanism	Underlying business process for indexing and searching	All experience input, all complaints, and all kinds of experience output are indexed by already modeled process steps and displayed in their context. These process steps allow finer indexing than the development process phases.
Flexible experience base design (generating parts [15])	Low-threshold design for all changes	Generate user interface, add experience portion, and manage references automatically.
Focus group are a limited number of software developers	Focus group are a large group of normal users	The Experience Forum for supporting normal users must be very easy to use, and the experiences and information must be automatically indexed to manage a large user base, e.g. by attaching them automatically to the active process step.
Experience Base is normally available via the Intranet	Experience Forum is directly integrated into the Application	The direct integration into the application reduces the threshold of experience feedback by the users.
Experience Base is seeded with process guidelines and templates.	Experience Forum is seeded with user manuals.	The Experience Forum can utilize seeding contents which has to be produced by the project as well.

A wiki and a normal Forum are available for storing longer texts as well. The Experience Base is implemented as a J2EE application running on a JBoss application server.

The Web services were added on top the internal business logic layer of the Experience Base, which was implemented using Session Beans. Thus no changes to the old code base were needed.

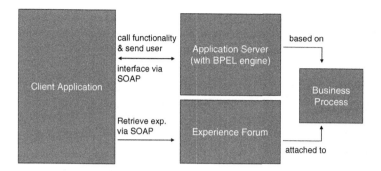

Fig. 4. Main Design of the Prototype System

The existing web interface was not changed and remained operational. However, newer systems can access the Experience Forum by calling the corresponding Web services. The number of systems accessing and supported by the Experience Forum is not limited: Therefore, one installation can be integrated into many Information Systems. Figure 4 shows the overall system architecture.

7 Discussion

The basic premise – getting user feedback for improving a software product – in itself is not new. The field of Requirements Engineering tries to get as much information about the software from the user, and agile methods – like Extreme Programming [16] – use very direct customer/user interaction by having an On-Site-Customer. However, all these approaches reach their limits when confronted with a large user base: One cannot interview all users of a system nor get feedback from them, and one On-Site-Customer cannot represent the whole user community.

Software companies and open source communities face the same problem: Their user base is probably distributed around the globe but feedback is necessary to further improve the product and find bugs. One way of getting feedback of occurred errors is the automatic collection of stack traces and error descriptions. If applications crash a stack trace is produced and the user is offered to send it to the developers. For example, Microsoft offers this functionality in Windows XP (see figure 5a) and the Mozilla Foundation uses the Talkback Agent to do the same for their Firefox browser (see figure 5b).

While such reports offer valuable information to the developers for fixing fatal bugs causing program crashes no feedback is given on all other aspects like usability or functional requirements

The KDE desktop environment has a crash assistant as well, offering the user to copy a stack trace to the clipboard in order to send it to the developers. Furthermore, each KDE application has a help menu entry for submitting bugs and wishes. This entry opens a web browser for adding the information to the Bugzilla[2] bug tracking system. While Bugzilla allows many kinds of feedback, like bug reports and feature

---

[2] http://bugs.kde.org/

requests, it is separated from the original application. The corresponding item in the help menu of KDE's applications is not prominent and direct access within the application to other users' experiences and comments is not possible.

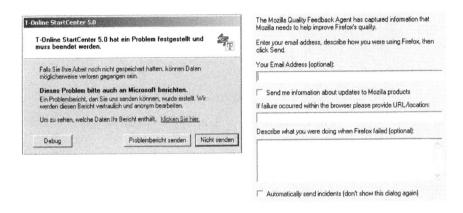

Fig. 5. (a) Windows Crash Report and (b) Mozilla Firefox Quality Feedback Agent

Many tax software packages like T@x developed by Buhl[3] are offering additional information in a side-pane. This information contains the relevant tax laws and other sections of the user's manual. However, the user cannot edit these texts and consequently no feedback can occur.

One problem common to all of these approaches is the communication of valuable information and experiences to an external party. One cannot know what is done with the stack trace or a memory dump possibly containing private data. Therefore, many people hesitate to submit their information to unknown or anonymous parties. If communicated in a right way to the users this can change with in-house projects, like most SOA projects are: Because information is only exchanged within the same organization and its trusted partners, information exchange can be less restricted.

Because users cannot only submit experiences but also can read everything, the Experience Forum also becomes a means of establishing a Community of Practice [17]: All users can share their experiences with each other. Because the Experience Forum is tightly integrated, the threshold is minimized for communication. People using the same functions and have access to them by means of the Information System are automatically able to communicate with each other and exchange ideas and experiences.

Furthermore, no additional security policies have to be maintained in separate discussion forums because the experiences can only be accessed using the Information System.

Besides these differences all approaches including our own share one challenge: The information gathered by the user feedback need to be fed into the development process. This is heavily dependent on the development methodologies used. For example, in XP the On-site customer would be responsible to read the feedback and form story cards out of them. These can be easily integrated into the Planning Game. In process-oriented projects someone needs to be responsible to collect the feedback

---

[3] http://onlineshop.buhl.de/buhl?art=207

and create the corresponding change requests. These change requests need to be approved by a change control board before they are passed to the development team.

The Experience Forum combines some existing approaches of user feedback and experience exchange. It combines the advantages of these mechanisms by providing information directly in the application and allows feedback to the developers as well as experience exchange in the user community possibly fostering a Community of Practice. Combined with the possibility to share information only in-house, the Experience Forums provides a very effective way of interacting with a large number of users.

However, an Experience Forum can only supplement Requirements Engineering practices. It is a mechanism for refining requirements and processes after the first production release. It cannot replace elicitation of initial requirements.

Furthermore, there are some risks associated, if the Experience Forum is not well embedded in the software project. For example, users submitting feedback expect that their feedback will lead to changes. If this does not happen, submitters will become unsatisfied and frustrated and will not provide further feedback – perhaps even in interviews, surveys etc. Also, it can be possible to collect too much feedback, which cannot be handled within the project's team. Although this scenario is unlikely as demonstrated by the user of Experience Bases, projects should plan how to handle such cases. For holding such many experiences and comments per process step, the Experience Forum needs to be extended: In such cases, search functionality and filtering need to be implemented.

8 Conclusions and Outlook

Large software projects trying to support business processes can benefit by using SOA as their design principle. SOA allows the direct support of business processes by arranging software components along business processes. Such projects promise to support business process more directly. For optimal support user feedback is necessary – which is not easy due to the large and inhomogeneous user base.

Our proposed solution is an Experience Forum. We build upon the experiences made with Experience Bases for improving the development process. Experience Forums allow information and experience exchange directly from within the application from the users to other users and the development project. By being available whenever the software system is used, Experience Forums are a light-weight solution for accessing and submitting information. By integrating the Experience Forum into the SOA landscape and by binding all information items to the business process, accessing these items is easy and the manual management can be minimized. Providing the Experience Forum functionality as yet another Web service, it is mechanism that can be used by any application.

Future work will address the following problems:

- Mechanisms of adopting elicited feedback at the developer side. As Experience Bases have shown, indexing feedback is crucial. We assume there is a potential for supporting reuse further by optimizing change and maintenance processes,
- After finishing our feasibility study and using the approach in University, we are now preparing to apply it in a large-scale Industrial environment.

Our current implementation demonstrates the feasibility of both generating user interfaces for SOA systems, and generating experience forum access along the way. Our experience in using experience exploitation mechanisms in Industry showed us how important it is to make feedback available at the developers' task at hand. Using system users' work context in the system as an index to locate their feedback and experiences offers a concrete and practical solution for many companies with large SOA systems.

References

1. Henkel, M., J. Zdarvkovic, and P. Johannesson. *Service-based Processes - Designfor Business and Technology.* in *ICSOC'04.* 2004. New York, USA: ACM.
2. Zimmermann, O., et al. *Second Generation Web Services-Oriented Architecture in Production in the Finance Industry.* in *OOPSLA'04.* 2004. Vancouver, Canada: ACM.
3. Mitra, N., *SOAP Version 1.2 Part 0: Primer*, 2003, http://www.w3.org/TR/soap12-part0/.
4. OASIS, *OASIS Web Services Business Process Execution Language (WSBPEL) TC*, 2006, http://www.oasis-open.org/committees/tc_home.php?wg_abbrev=wsbpel.
5. Fischer, G., *Social Creativity, Symmetry of Ignorance and Meta-Design.* Knowledge-Based Systems Journal, 2000 **13**(7-8): p. 527-537.
6. Rittel, W.J. and M.M. Webber, *Planning Problems are Wicked Problems*, in *Developments in Design Methodology*, N. Cross, Editor. 1984, John Wiley & Sons, 135-144: New York. p. 135-144.
7. Schneider, K. *Experience Based Process Improvement.* in *European Conference on Software Quality (ECSQ 2002.* 2002. Helsinki, Finland: Springer.
8. Basili, V., G. Caldiera, and D.H. Rombach, *The Experience Factory.* Encyclopedia of Software Engineering. 1994: John Wiley and Sons.
9. Houdek, F. and K. Schneider, *Software Experience Center. The Evolution of the Experience Factory Concept.*, in *International NASA-SEL Workshop.* 1999.
10. Schneider, K. *Realistic and Unrealistic Expectations about Experience Exploitation.* in *Conquest 2001.* 2001. Nürnberg, Germany: ASQF Erlangen.
11. Schneider, K. and T. Schwinn, *Maturing Experience Base Concepts at DaimlerChrysler.* Software Process Improvement and Practice, 2001. **6**: p. 85-96.
12. Schneider, K. and J.v. Hunnius. *Effective Experience Repositories for Software Engineering.* in *International Conference on Software Engineering.* 2003. Portland, Oregon.
13. Schneider, K. and D. Lübke. *Systematic Tailoring of Quality Techniques.* in *World Congress of Software Quality 2005.* 2005. Munich, Germany.
14. Lübke, D. and T. Lüecke. *Using Event-Driven Process Chains for Model-Driven Development of Business Applications.* in *Multikonferenz Wirtschaftsinformatik 2006, Workshop XML4BPM.* 2006. Passau, Germany.
15. Buchloh, T., *Erstellung eines Baukastens für Experience Bases (Creation of a Construction Kit for Experience Bases)*, in *Software Engineering Group.* 2005, University Hannover: Hannover.
16. Beck, K., *Extreme Programming Explained.* 2000: Addison-Wesley.
17. Wenger, E., *Communities of Practice - Learning, Meaning, and Identity.* 1998, Cambridge, England: Cambridge University Press.

Taba Workstation: Supporting Software Process Improvement Initiatives Based on Software Standards and Maturity Models

Analia Irigoyen Ferreiro Ferreira[1,2], Gleison Santos[1], Roberta Cerqueira[2],
Mariano Montoni[1], Ahilton Barreto[1], Ana Regina Rocha[1], Sávio Figueiredo[1],
Andrea Barreto[1], Reinaldo C. Silva Filho[1], Peter Lupo[1], and Cristina Cerdeiral[1]

[1] COPPE/UFRJ - Federal University of Rio de Janeiro
POBOX 68511 – ZIP 21945-970 – Rio de Janeiro, Brazil
{gleison, montoni, ahilton, darocha, figueiredo,
ansoares, cabral}@cos.ufrj.br
[2] BL Informática Ltda.
Av. Visconde do Rio Branco 305/8th floor - Niterói - RJ - ZIP 24020-002
{analia, roberta}@blnet.com

Abstract. International software standards and maturity models play an important role in Software Process Improvement initiatives defining best practices and providing knowledge to the definition of software processes. Nevertheless, the definition and deployment of software processes based on that standards and models is an expensive and knowledge intensive task. This paper describes an approach to the definition and deployment of software processes in small and medium size Brazilian companies supported by a Process-centered Software Engineering Environment named Taba Workstation. It also presents results related to a software process improvement initiative undertaken in a Brazilian organization that demonstrates the feasibility of the presented approach.

1 Introduction

Recent research efforts about quality in the software area demonstrate that a concentrated effort is imperative to improve software processes in software development companies [1]. The ability to objectively improve the organization's processes and products within time and cost constraints in addition to the improvement deployment itself is the differential that must be present in software organizations. Moreover, focus on customer's needs is very important to guarantee the success of improvement projects since the success of an organization is totally related to customer's satisfaction. The increase of productivity and quality are tangible benefits that can be quantified and equated to a common measure, usually dollars. On the other hand, intangible benefits such as better quality of work life, better organizational learning and communications are difficult to quantify and convert to a common measure. Nevertheless, it is believed that intangible benefits in some cases can represent the biggest payoff to an organization that invests on process improvement [15]. Hyde and Wilson [16]

R. Messnarz (Ed.): EuroSPI 2006, LNCS 4257, pp. 207–218, 2006.
© Springer-Verlag Berlin Heidelberg 2006

highlight the intangible benefits in software process improvement and suggest that the realization of intangible benefits is important and should be factored into decisions to undertake software improvement initiatives.

Mainly in Brazil, there is an urge to enhance software processes performance aiming to improve the software products quality and to increase Brazilian companies' competitiveness both in national and international markets. Since 1993, with the foundation of PBQP Software (Subcommittee of Software of the Brazilian Program for Software Quality and Productivity), Brazil invests on Software Quality improvement [2].

One important characteristic of a software process deployment initiative is the selection of an appropriate reference model to be used during the definition of the software processes and appraisal of the organization. International standards like ISO/IEC 12207 [3] and ISO/IEC 15504 [4], and software process quality models like CMMI (Capability Maturity Model Integration) [5] were developed aiming to define the requirements of an ideal organization, i.e., a reference model to be used in order to assess the maturity of the organization and its capability to develop software.

Based on these standards and models, Brazilian industry and research institutions have worked together during the last two years to define the Reference Model for Brazilian Software Process Improvement (MR-MPS.BR) [6, 7, 8]. Seven maturity levels were established in the MR-MPS.BR: Level G (Partially Managed), Level F (Managed), Level E (Partially Defined), Level D (Largely Defined), Level C (Defined), Level B (Quantitatively Managed) and Level A (Optimization). For each of these maturity levels, processes were assigned based on the ISO/IEC 12207 international standard and on the process areas of levels 2, 3, 4 and 5 of CMMI staged representation. The difference of MR-MPS levels graduation compared to CMMI staged representation aims to enable a more gradual and adequate software process deployment in small and medium size Brazilian companies. This model has been deployed in many companies in Brazil and official appraisals were already conducted.

This paper describes an approach to the definition and deployment of software processes in small and medium size Brazilian companies started in 2003. The use of Taba Workstation, a Process-centered Software Engineering Environment (PSEE) that supports software processes definition, deployment and enactment, is a key factor of this approach whose goal is to increase the capability of organizations through the adequate use of Software Engineering techniques in their software processes aiming to enhance the software products quality and, thus, increase organizational competitiveness. In order to evidence the benefits of this approach we describe its use in a Brazilian organization, named BL Informática. As results from its quality program, the company has obtained during this period the ISO 9001:2000 [9] certification, and has been evaluated on MPS.BR Level F. BL Informática will be evaluated on CMMI Level 3 process areas by an official SCAMPI appraisal scheduled to July 2006.

The next section describes the Taba Workstation. Section 3 presents how software processes deployment is carried out with the Taba Workstation use. In section 4, describes the software process improvement initiative at BL Informática. Section 5 presents the quantitative results of this initiative. Finally, section 6 presents some lessons learned, and point out future directions and conclusions.

2 Taba Workstation

Taba Workstation [17] is a Process-centered Software Engineering Environment (PSEE) composed of several integrated CASE tools to support software processes definition, deployment and enactment. Knowledge Management tools are also integrated into the environment to facilitate the organizational knowledge preservation and support activities execution. The Taba Workstation has been developed since 1990 in the context of an academic project and it is not commercialized. Nevertheless, it is granted to small and medium size Brazilian organizations with no costs. During the last years, the Taba Workstation evolved to comply with CMMI levels 2 and 3 processes areas and MPS.BR levels G, F, E, D and C processes.

2.1 Software Processes Definition Based on Software Standards and Maturity Models in the Taba Workstation

The Software Processes definition approach adopted in the Taba Workstation establishes phases and intermediary products using the ISO/IEC 12207 as a basis for the definition of standard software processes. Figure 1 depicts this approach.

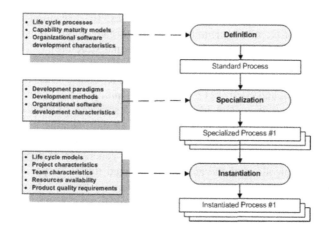

Fig. 1. Software processes definition approach in the Taba Workstation

The standard processes and the specialized processes are considered to be organizational level processes. The instantiated processes are project level processes. This approach guarantees the implementation of some practices of CMMI Level 3 process areas and MPS.BR Level E, for instance, the establishment of defined processes for each process area and tailoring criteria of these processes to each project.

During the Standard Process definition phase it is also considered the organizational software development characteristics related to the work environment, knowledge and experiences of the teams involved and the organizational software development experience and culture. From the Standard Process, different software processes can be specialized according to different kinds of software produced by the organization, (e.g., specialists and information systems) and to development paradigms adopted (e.g., object oriented or structured). At this point practices required by the maturity models are included in the organizational set of standard processes. The definition of the organizational standard process for a specific organization is done during the configuration of a specific PSEE for the organization. The configured environment for the organization contains not only the standard process and the specialized processes, but also specific knowledge related to software development and maintenance. By using this environment, software engineers are able to generate instantiated environments to each of the projects to be developed.

In order to be used in a specific project, the most adequate specialized process must be instantiated to satisfy the characteristics of the project (e.g., size and complexity of the product and relevant quality characteristics), development team characteristics etc. At this time, the life cycle model, methods and tools are selected. Once the software process for a specific project has been defined and a PSEE has been instantiated, the basic means for software process deployment and enactment are established. At this point, software engineers have access to several CASE tools designed to support the activities in the instantiated software process of the project.

2.2 Taba Workstation CASE Tools

The CASE tools integrated in the environments offer automated support to: (i) definition of the organizational set of standard processes; (ii) execution of pilot project aiming process improvement; (iii) tailoring of the organization standard processes for a specific project; (iv) definition of the organizational structure [12]; (v) acquisition, filtering, packaging and dissemination of organizational knowledge [13]; (vi) planning the organization of specific projects; (vii) time, costs, risks, human resources planning, monitoring and control [12, 14]; (viii) planning and execution of Configuration Management activities; (ix) identification of software product quality requirements; (x) documentation planning; (xi) supporting the planning and monitoring of corrective actions; (xii) supporting measurement and analysis activities based on the GQM method; (xiii) project monitoring through the generation of periodic reports and measures; (xiv) controlling of the activities executed during a specific project; (xv) requirements management; (xvi) supporting software technical solutions through the use of design rationale; (xv) supporting software verification and validation planning and execution; and (xvi) post mortem analysis.

3 Software Processes Deployment with the Taba Workstation

Since 2003 the Taba Workstation is been used by the Brazilian software industry. The first organizations that used it were part of the Qualisoft Project [10], an initiative of RioSoft (a non-governmental organization that integrates the Softex Program - Society for the Support of Brazilian Software Production and Exportation) and the Federal University of Rio de Janeiro. This ongoing project aims to form a pool of small and medium size organizations with similar characteristics in order to decrease the overall cost of processes deployment and increase the feasibility of their quality program. Since then, others organizations have used the **Taba Workstation** independently with good results.

Although the way software processes were deployed has evolved in order to cope with characteristics and goals of each organization or pool of organizations, the following basic activities are always conducted:

(i)   Understanding of the individual characteristics and main goals of the organizations;

(ii) Definition of software development and maintenance processes adequate to the organizational culture;

(iii) Training in Software Engineering methods and techniques and in the software processes defined;

(iv) Use of Taba Workstation [11] environments and CASE tools; and

(v)   Follow-up of the companies to support the deployment of the software processes through the execution of pilot projects.

In order to understand the individual characteristics and main goals of the organizations, interviews to high managers are carried out by the process specialists. Alternatively, the high manager or the person responsible for the software quality initiative in the organization is asked to fill out a form with questions related to the organizational culture, software process stages and quality management systems adopted, common software development practices, main problems in the current software development and maintenance processes, and organizational objectives related to software process improvement. The following steps comprise the definition of software development and maintenance standard processes adequate to the organization or the pool organizations and configuration of a specific PSEE to each organization, as explained in section 2.1. In parallel to the processes definition activity, training in Software Engineering methods and techniques are provided to the members of the organizations. This training comprises lectures on topics such as Software Engineering, Software Process, Knowledge Management, Software Products Quality, Project Management, Supplier Agreement, Risk Management, Configuration Management, Measurement and Analysis, Requirements Engineering, Peer-review, Tests, Technical Solution, Product Integration, Decision Analysis and Resolution. The training program is adapted according to the organizations processes objectives, for example, cover the process areas of CMMI Level 3 or MPS.BR Level G processes (Project Management and Requirements Management). After the software engineering theoretical training, project managers and software developers are trained in the standard software processes defined.

3.1 The Qualisoft Project Phases

The first phase of the Qualisoft Project started on August 2003 and addressed a pool of 10 organizations. The second phase started on January 2004 addressing a second pool of 9 organizations. The third phase started on January 2005 and addressed more 5 organizations. The next phase is about to start and will address at least 5 more organizations.

The processes defined to the first phase were based only on the international standard ISO/IEC 12207. For the second phase these processes were refined and adjusted to comply with the practices defined in CMMI Level 2 process areas and the processes of its equivalent MPS.BR Level F. For the third phase, two companies decided to have their processes adherent to the CMMI Level 3 processes areas and MPS.BR Level C processes. All the processes maintained compliance with the ISO/IEC 12207. The following steps focused on the deployment of the processes and the configuration of a PSEE to support the processes in the organizations. These steps were carried out individually considering the particularities of each organization. Initially, the standard processes were adapted to each company characteristics, such as types of software developed, documents produced and software development paradigms adopted. A PSEE was configured to each organization after the approval of the adaptations.

The next section presents the software processes improvement initiative at BL Informática which participates of the Qualisoft Project since its beginning.

4   Software Processes Improvement at BL Informática

BL Informática is a Brazilian organization founded in 1987 concerned with software development, maintenance, deployment and integration. The major objective in its quality policies is to focus on customers, team members and stockholders satisfaction through implementation of solutions in information technology developed with defined, controlled and continuously improved.

In order to demonstrate the feasibility of the approach presented, we discuss in this section the three phases of the software process improvement initiative at BL Informática started in 2003 aiming to improve its products development quality. The next section describes the quantitative results of this initiative.

4.1   First Phase: ISO 9001 Certification

BL Informática's quality program started in 2003 when the company decided to be ISO 9001:2000 certified until 2004. The definition of development and maintenance processes consistent with this standard was the first step to accomplish this goal. COPPE/UFRJ consulting was requested to support this activity since the company had no experience in software process definition. When the QualiSoft Project was created, BL Informática formalized the participation in its first phase.

To decrease the impact during the initial stages of its process deployment the company decided not to use the Taba Workstation. At first, the development process was executed without any management tool support during all the analysis phase of the pilot project. But difficulties to manage the project pointed out that a CASE tool was necessary to support the process utilization and, moreover, to support the planning, control and execution of the project. Due to this, Taba Workstation utilization was reconsidered and from this moment on the environment configured to the organization started to be used. In the beginning the environment was used only to control the flow of the software process activities. Eventually all Taba Workstation CASE tools started to be used to support each step of the process enactment. In parallel the process's adaptation to the organization culture proceeded maintaining its original characteristics.

Despite the pilot project had not satisfied the schedule its execution has been considered successful. The clients have followed the project closer and were aware of all artifacts produced and non-compliances detected and performed evaluations expected at the end of each activity.

After one year the process was considered stabilized. The deployment required more time and resources than estimated but produced better results than expected. The success factors as pointed out by team members were: (i) high level management support; (ii) trainings investments; (iii) the existence of a process group engaged with the results and confidence in future benefits; (iv) the use of **Taba Workstation** CASE tools and the internal CASE tools SGP (from the acronym in Portuguese for Process Management System) and SGD (from the acronym in Portuguese for Document Management System).

The main benefits achieved during this phase were: (i) decrease of rework; (ii) production of artifacts with better quality; (iii) better Software Engineering understanding due to team members' qualification; (iv) dissemination of "process culture" by the organization; (v) maintenance of the knowledge on software engineering inside the organization making the project team more independent. The main difficulties of this initial phase were related to cultural changes needed by project teams and clients in order to follow the processes.

4.2 Second Phase: MPS.BR Level F

Due to the great results accomplished, BL Informática decided to evolve its process improvement initiative during 2004. The organizational intended to have its processes evaluated as MPS.BR Level F compliant. A new version of software processes was defined and deployed according to Qualisoft Project's second phase schedule.

The main factors that have made this phase also a success were: (i) the constancy of internal and external ISO 9001:2000 auditing; (ii) the commitment of project teams; (iii) the knowledge about Project Management; (iv) high level management support; (v) the use of **Taba Workstation** CASE tools and the internal CASE tools and SFT (from the acronym in Portuguese for Workflow System).

The bigger accomplishment of this phase was the success of the Level F MPS-BR evaluation which became an important motivation factor to the company continues its quality program. The project teams' confidence regarding the organization maturity, the high management feeling of return of investment and the team motivation were crucial for the quality program consolidation in the organization.

This phase required more resources than planed but the benefits achieved were considered very important for the beginning of the next process improvement phase: the CMMI Level 3 evaluation.

4.3 Third Phase: CMMI Level 3

This phase had more impact in the organization than the previous ones. The structure of the quality team had to be changed and expanded in order to address the CMMI Level 3 process areas requirements. The deployment of a MPS-BR Level F based process requires more involvement of project managers; most team members perceive the results without significantly changing the way they execute theirs activities. As CMMI Level 3 focuses mainly in engineering activities most developers' activities are also affected. Besides, as the process group only had strong experience in project management techniques it was necessary more support to the definition and deployment of the new processes. The investments on training, consulting activities and action plans to risks mitigation were the largest compared to the other phases.

The most important success factors of this phase until the moment are: (i) high level management support and endorsement of critical risk mitigation actions (for example, new resources hiring, training and investment on tools so project schedules can be satisfied and clients satisfaction is not affected even if a new process version is used by the first time); (ii) external consulting support and knowledge transfer; (iii) improvement of communication mechanisms and systems to ease the information exchange, appraisals of improvement proposals, lessons learned dissemination and distribution of tasks; (iv) investment in external and internal trainings.

Among the main benefits of this ongoing phase we can highlight: (i) improvement of the knowledge the company has about its capacity and productivity (for example, know in how much time a requirement will be implemented); (ii) increase of lessons learned regarding the technologies used and requirements development; (iii) decrease of time spent on activities regarding testing and codification.

The most important lesson learned of this phase was the importance of the early understanding of how new activities of the software process (like CMMI Level 3 practices related to engineering areas) affect each team member. The earlier the changes are understood, the easier the process deployment.

5   Quantitative Analysis of Software Process Improvement Initiative at BL Informática

Even before the beginning of its software process improvement initiative BL Informática gathers quantitative data related to the execution of its software projects. Analyzing this data we could observe that the distribution of time spent on software development activities has significantly changed. In this section we present and discuss (i) the increase of the time expended during management activities, and (ii) the relation between the adoption of specific software quality activities and time expended on rework[1] along the project.

5.1   Project Management Activities Improvement

Table 1 and Figure 2 show the mean time spent during software projects at different phases of processes enactment in the organization. "Construction and Tests" category comprises activities like planning and execution of tests (e.g., unit tests or functional tests) and peer reviews and codification activities. "Analysis and Design" category comprises activities like requirements elicitation, use cases elaboration, architectural design, database design etc. "Management" category comprises all activities related to

---

[1] A rework activity is defined as any activity that comprises change or adjustment of artifacts produced on early project phases, e.g., changes to ill defined requirements during codification.

project planning and monitoring. "Others" comprises uncategorized activities (for example, general purpose meetings).

Table 1. Evolution of time expended in software development activities

	Construction and Tests	Analysis and Design	Management	Others
Before Process Adoption	19,1%	66,0%	11,5%	3,4%
1st Phase – ISO 9001 Process	34,9%	39,7%	14,9%	10,5%
2nd Phase – MPS.BR Level F	34,8%	50,5%	7,9%	6,8%
3rd Phase – CMMI Level 3	27,3%	51,8%	17,8%	3,1%

Before the process adoption the activities of project teams were not clearly defined so project managers sometimes had to perform analysis and construction tasks deviating themselves from the execution of management tasks. Besides that, a large amount of time was spent in rework during the construction and test of the software.

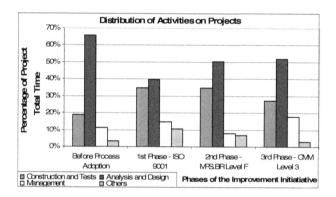

Fig. 2. Time division by the project activities

Due to the definition of project management activities in the first version of the process, manager had more time to plan and control its projects. Time spent by managers decreased due to the use of appropriate case tools after the deployment of the second version of the process. The effort to execute Analysis and Design activities increased and quality evaluations of the artifacts produced were executed continuously and not only during the construction phase. The evaluation of each artifact was done using a generic checklist which evolved in order to reflect the organization characteristics and its products. The third version of the process caused the increase of the time elapsed with the management activities because the manager were, for the first time, no longer responsible for analysis and design activities, only for project management activities.

5.2 Relation Between Software Quality and Rework

Table 2 and Figure 3 show the relation between quality related activities effort expended and rework during software projects.

Table 2. Relation between time expended in rework and software quality related activities

	Rework	Quality Activities
Before Process Adoption	44,0%	0,0%
1st Phase – ISO 9001 Process	26,7%	9,2%
2nd Phase – MPS.BR Level F	11,2%	3,0%
3rd Phase – CMMI Level 3	7,3%	10,8%

Quality activities were not conducted before the adoption of the first version of the process. Due to that 44% of total time of the projects was spent in rework activities. The adoption of quality assurance activities in the first version of the process caused the decrease of time expended in rework activities.

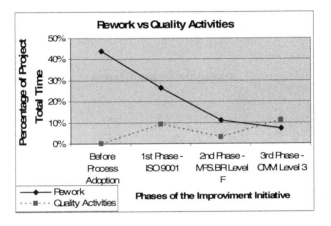

Fig. 3. Software Quality Activities and Rework Relation

Along the Qualisoft Project's second phase, time expended in rework has been continuously reduced due to more rigorous artifacts evaluation. Finding errors in early phases of the project caused the decrease of the number of evaluations of a specific artifact and thus the reduction of the time expend in evaluations. The time spent on quality activities increased after the adoption of the third version of the process due to the larger number of artifacts being evaluated and to the necessity of involvement of new roles in these evaluation activities. Besides, the checklists used to evaluate the new artifacts of the process were evolving in the organization, forcing more and longer evaluations.

6 Conclusions

This paper described an approach to the definition and deployment of software processes in small and medium size Brazilian companies with the support of **Taba Workstation**, a Process-centered Software Engineering Environment. By applying this approach to define and deploy software processes based on ISO/IEC 12207, CMMI and

MPS.BR, organizations can significantly increase both competitiveness and software products and services quality. The **Taba Workstation** is been used by the Brazilian software industry since 2003, and was identified during three official SCAMPI appraisals as one of the greatest organizational strengths to facilitate the success of software process deployment initiatives and to overcome the inherent difficulties. Moreover, it was also identified as an important organizational asset to guarantee the quality of software process and product quality in other three official MPS.BR appraisals.

The quantitative results of applying the presented approach in BL Informática are significant: it has obtained ISO 9001:2000 certification, has been evaluated MPS.BR Level F and is currently engaged in the CMMI Level 3 appraisal process. Furthermore, the processes and product's quality have improved and costs and conflicts decreased. As a direct effect of these achievements we can point out high management strong support to all software process improvement activities, great collaborators` satisfaction and significant decrease of people turnover.

Nevertheless, the **Taba Workstation** is continuously evolving. The next steps comprises the evaluation of the adequacy of its CASE tools that support CMMI Level 3 process areas, and definition and integration of other tools to support CMMI Level 4 and 5 process areas which will support organizations to achieve even higher levels of software development maturity.

Acknowledgement

Authors wish to thank Benito Diaz Paret, Riosoft coordinator, Márcio Pecegueiro Amaral, Qualisoft Project and Towards CMMI Level 3 coordinator in Riosoft, BL Informática board of directors and development team and TABA Project development team.

References

1. Fuggetta, A.: Software Process: A Roadmap, in Finkelstein, A. (ed.) The Future of Software Engineering, ACM Press, (2002)
2. Weber, K. C., Pinheiro, M.: Software Quality in Brazil, In.: Quality World Magazine, The Institute of Quality Assurance (IQA), London, UK, Vol. 21, Issue 1.1, Nov. (1995)
3. ISO/IEC 12207:2000 - Information technology – software process life cycle (2000)
4. ISO/IEC 15504 –1 Information Technology – Process Assessment, - Part 1: Concepts and Vocabulary (2003)
5. Chrissis, M. B., Konrad, M, Shrum, S.: CMMI: Guidelines for Process Integration and Product Improvement. Addison-Wesley (2003)
6. SOFTEX, MPS.BR – Melhoria de Processo do Software Brasileiro, Guia Geral (v. 1.1), http://www.softex.br/mpsbr/ (in portuguese), (2006)
7. Rocha, A. R., Montoni, M., Santos, S., Mafra, S., Figueiredo, S., Albuquerque, A., Mian, P.: Reference Model for Software Process Improvement: A Brazilian Experience. In.: Lecture Notes of Computer Science (LNCS), ISBN 3-540-30286-7, pp. 130-141, presented at the EuroSPI 2005, Budapest, Hungary (2005)
8. Weber, K.C., Araujo, E.R., Rocha, A.R., Machado, C., Scalet, D., Salviano, C.: Brazilian Software Process Reference Model and Assessment Method. In.: Computer and Information Sciences – ISCIS 2005, LNCS 3733, pp 403-411 (2005)

9. ISO 9001:2000 - Quality management systems - Requirements, (2000)
10. Santos, G., Montoni, M., Rocha, A. R., Figueiredo, S., Mafra, S., Albuquerque, A., Paret, B. D., Amaral, M.: Using a Software Development Environment with Knowledge Management to Support Deploying Software Processes in Small and Medium Size Companies, In.: 3rd Conf. Professional Knowledge Management Experiences and Visions, Kaiserslautern, Germany, April 10-13 (2005), 72-76
11. Montoni M., Santos G., Villela K., Rocha A. R., Travassos G. H., Figueiredo S., Mafra S., Albuquerque A., Mian P.: Enterprise-Oriented Software Development Environments to Support Software Products and Process Quality Improvement. In.: Lecture Notes of Computer Science (LNCS), ISBN 3-540-26200-8, pp. 370-384, presented at the 6th Int. Conference on Product Focused Software Process Improvement, Oulu, Finland, June (2005)
12. Santos, G., Villela, K., Schnaider, L., Rocha, A. R.. Travassos, G. H., Building ontology based tools for a software development environment, In: Workshop Learning Software Organization, Banff, Canada, 2004 (Lecture Notes in Computer Science, vol 3096, pp 19-30)
13. Montoni, M., Miranda, R., Rocha, A. R.. Travassos, G. H., Knowledge Acquisition and Communities of Practice: an Approach to Convert Individual Knowledge into Multi-Organizational Knowledge, In: Workshop Learning Software Organization, Banff, Canada, 2004. (Lecture Notes in Computer Science, vol 3096, pp 110-120)
14. Farias, L., Travassos, G. H., Rocha, A. R. C., Knowledge Management of Software Risks In: Journal of Universal Computer Science, vol 9 n 7 (2003), 670- 681
15. Krasner, H., The Payoff for SPI: what it is and how to get it. Software Process Newsletter, IEEE Computer Society 1:1-6 (1994)
16. Hyde, K., Wilson, D., Intangible Benefits of CMM-based Software Process Improvement, In: Software Process Improvement and Practice, vol 9 n 4 (2004), 217-228
17. Oliveira, K, Zlot, F., Rocha, A. R., Travassos, G., Galotta, C., Menezes, C. Domain Oriented Software Development Environment, Journal of Systems and Software, vol 72/2 (2004) pp 145-161

Author Index

Aho, Anne-Maria   62
Ahonen, Jarmo J.   62, 183
Anker, Tore Dybå Geir   5

Barreto, Ahilton   207
Barreto, Andrea   207
Börjesson, Anna   74
Borzovs, Juris   50

Cahill, Brent   111
Carrington, David   111
Cerdeiral, Cristina   207
Cerqueira, Roberta   207
Coleman, Gerry   28

Demirörs, Onur   88
Dingsøyr, Torgeir   5
Dybå, Tore   159

Ferreira, Analia Irigoyen Ferreiro   207
Figueiredo, Sávio   207
Filho, Reinaldo C. Silva   207

Hakonen, Harri   135
Hanssen, Geir Kjetil   5

Jäntti, Marko   40
Järvi, Antero   135
Juutilainen, Päivi   183

Kankaanpää, Irja   183
Kinnunen, Kari   40
Koskinen, Jussi   183
Koutsoukos, Georgios   147

Lübke, Daniel   195
Lupo, Peter   207

Mäkilä, Tuomas   135
Maoutsidis, Dimitri   171
Messnarz, R.   1
Moe, Nils Brede   159
Montoni, Mariano   207
Münch, Jürgen   123

Nygaard, Jens Olav   5

O'Connor, Rory   28

Richardson, I.   1
Rocha, Ana Regina   207
Runeson, P.   1

Santos, Gleison   207
Schneider, Kurt   195
Siakas, Errikos   171
Siakas, Kerstin V.   171
Sihvonen, Hanna-Miina   62
Sivula, Henna   183
Šmite, Darja   50
Soini, Jari   100
Song, Brian   111
Soto, Martín   123
Stålhane, Tor   16
Strooper, Paul   111

Tarhan, Ayça   88
Tenhunen, Vesa   100
Tilus, Tero   183
Tukiainen, Markku   100

Lecture Notes in Computer Science

For information about Vols. 1–4175

please contact your bookseller or Springer

Vol. 4270: H. Zha, Z. Pan, H. Thwaites, A.C. Addison, M. Forte (Eds.), Interactive Technologies and Sociotechnical Systems. XVI, 547 pages. 2006.

Vol. 4269: R. State, S. van der Meer, D. O'Sullivan, T. Pfeifer (Eds.), Large Scale Management of Distributed Systems. XIII, 282 pages. 2006.

Vol. 4267: A. Helmy, B. Jennings, L. Murphy, T. Pfeifer (Eds.), Autonomic Management of Mobile Multimedia Services. XIII, 257 pages. 2006.

Vol. 4265: N. Lavrač, L. Todorovski, K.P. Jantke (Eds.), Discovery Science. XIV, 384 pages. 2006. (Sublibrary LNAI).

Vol. 4264: J.L. Balcázar, P.M. Long, F. Stephan (Eds.), Algorithmic Learning Theory. XIII, 393 pages. 2006. (Sublibrary LNAI).

Vol. 4257: I. Richardson, P. Runeson, R. Messnarz (Eds.), Software Process Improvement. XI, 219 pages. 2006.

Vol. 4254: T. Grust, H. Höpfner, A. Illarramendi, S. Jablonski, M. Mesiti, S. Müller, P.-L. Patranjan, K.-U. Sattler, M. Spiliopoulou (Eds.), Current Trends in Database Technology – EDBT 2006. XXXI, 932 pages. 2006.

Vol. 4253: B. Gabrys, R.J. Howlett, L.C. Jain (Eds.), Knowledge-Based Intelligent Information and Engineering Systems, Part III. XXXII, 1301 pages. 2006. (Sublibrary LNAI).

Vol. 4252: B. Gabrys, R.J. Howlett, L.C. Jain (Eds.), Knowledge-Based Intelligent Information and Engineering Systems, Part II. XXXIII, 1335 pages. 2006. (Sublibrary LNAI).

Vol. 4251: B. Gabrys, R.J. Howlett, L.C. Jain (Eds.), Knowledge-Based Intelligent Information and Engineering Systems, Part I. LXVI, 1297 pages. 2006. (Sublibrary LNAI).

Vol. 4249: L. Goubin, M. Matsui (Eds.), Cryptographic Hardware and Embedded Systems - CHES 2006. XII, 462 pages. 2006.

Vol. 4248: S. Staab, V. Svátek (Eds.), Engineering Knowledge in the Age of the Semantic Web. XIV, 400 pages. 2006. (Sublibrary LNAI).

Vol. 4247: T.-D. Wang, X. Li, S.-H. Chen, X. Wang, H. Abbass, H. Iba, G. Chen, X. Yao (Eds.), Simulated Evolution and Learning. XXI, 940 pages. 2006.

Vol. 4245: A. Kuba, L.G. Nyúl, K. Palágyi (Eds.), Discrete Geometry for Computer Imagery. XIII, 688 pages. 2006.

Vol. 4243: T. Yakhno, E.J. Neuhold (Eds.), Advances in Information Systems. XIII, 420 pages. 2006.

Vol. 4241: R.R. Beichel, M. Sonka (Eds.), Computer Vision Approaches to Medical Image Analysis. XI, 262 pages. 2006.

Vol. 4239: H.Y. Youn, M. Kim, H. Morikawa (Eds.), Ubiquitous Computing Systems. XVI, 548 pages. 2006.

Vol. 4238: Y.-T. Kim, M. Takano (Eds.), Management of Convergence Networks and Services. XVIII, 605 pages. 2006.

Vol. 4236: L. Breveglieri, I. Koren, D. Naccache, J.-P. Seifert (Eds.), Fault Diagnosis and Tolerance in Cryptography. XIII, 253 pages. 2006.

Vol. 4234: I. King, J. Wang, L. Chan, D. Wang (Eds.), Neural Information Processing, Part III. XXII, 1227 pages. 2006.

Vol. 4233: I. King, J. Wang, L. Chan, D. Wang (Eds.), Neural Information Processing, Part II. XXII, 1203 pages. 2006.

Vol. 4232: I. King, J. Wang, L. Chan, D. Wang (Eds.), Neural Information Processing, Part I. XLVI, 1153 pages. 2006.

Vol. 4229: E. Najm, J.F. Pradat-Peyre, V.V. Donzeau-Gouge (Eds.), Formal Techniques for Networked and Distributed Systems - FORTE 2006. X, 486 pages. 2006.

Vol. 4228: D.E. Lightfoot, C.A. Szyperski (Eds.), Modular Programming Languages. X, 415 pages. 2006.

Vol. 4227: W. Nejdl, K. Tochtermann (Eds.), Innovative Approaches for Learning and Knowledge Sharing. XVII, 721 pages. 2006.

Vol. 4225: J.F. Martínez-Trinidad, J.A. Carrasco Ochoa, J. Kittler (Eds.), Progress in Pattern Recognition, Image Analysis and Applications. XIX, 995 pages. 2006.

Vol. 4224: E. Corchado, H. Yin, V. Botti, C. Fyfe (Eds.), Intelligent Data Engineering and Automated Learning – IDEAL 2006. XXVII, 1447 pages. 2006.

Vol. 4223: L. Wang, L. Jiao, G. Shi, X. Li, J. Liu (Eds.), Fuzzy Systems and Knowledge Discovery. XXVIII, 1335 pages. 2006. (Sublibrary LNAI).

Vol. 4222: L. Jiao, L. Wang, X. Gao, J. Liu, F. Wu (Eds.), Advances in Natural Computation, Part II. XLII, 998 pages. 2006.

Vol. 4221: L. Jiao, L. Wang, X. Gao, J. Liu, F. Wu (Eds.), Advances in Natural Computation, Part I. XLI, 992 pages. 2006.

Vol. 4219: D. Zamboni, C. Kruegel (Eds.), Recent Advances in Intrusion Detection. XII, 331 pages. 2006.

Vol. 4218: S. Graf, W. Zhang (Eds.), Automated Technology for Verification and Analysis. XIV, 540 pages. 2006.

Vol. 4217: P. Cuenca, L. Orozco-Barbosa (Eds.), Personal Wireless Communications. XV, 532 pages. 2006.

Vol. 4216: M.R. Berthold, R. Glen, I. Fischer (Eds.), Computational Life Sciences II. XIII, 269 pages. 2006. (Sublibrary LNBI).

Vol. 4215: D.W. Embley, A. Olivé, S. Ram (Eds.), Conceptual Modeling - ER 2006. XVI, 590 pages. 2006.

Vol. 4213: J. Fürnkranz, T. Scheffer, M. Spiliopoulou (Eds.), Knowledge Discovery in Databases: PKDD 2006. XXII, 660 pages. 2006. (Sublibrary LNAI).

Vol. 4212: J. Fürnkranz, T. Scheffer, M. Spiliopoulou (Eds.), Machine Learning: ECML 2006. XXIII, 851 pages. 2006. (Sublibrary LNAI).

Vol. 4211: P. Vogt, Y. Sugita, E. Tuci, C. Nehaniv (Eds.), Symbol Grounding and Beyond. VIII, 237 pages. 2006. (Sublibrary LNAI).

Vol. 4210: C. Priami (Ed.), Computational Methods in Systems Biology. X, 323 pages. 2006. (Sublibrary LNBI).

Vol. 4209: F. Crestani, P. Ferragina, M. Sanderson (Eds.), String Processing and Information Retrieval. XIV, 367 pages. 2006.

Vol. 4208: M. Gerndt, D. Kranzlmüller (Eds.), High Performance Computing and Communications. XXII, 938 pages. 2006.

Vol. 4207: Z. Ésik (Ed.), Computer Science Logic. XII, 627 pages. 2006.

Vol. 4206: P. Dourish, A. Friday (Eds.), UbiComp 2006: Ubiquitous Computing. XIX, 526 pages. 2006.

Vol. 4205: G. Bourque, N. El-Mabrouk (Eds.), Comparative Genomics. X, 231 pages. 2006. (Sublibrary LNBI).

Vol. 4204: F. Benhamou (Ed.), Principles and Practice of Constraint Programming - CP 2006. XVIII, 774 pages. 2006.

Vol. 4203: F. Esposito, Z.W. Raś, D. Malerba, G. Semeraro (Eds.), Foundations of Intelligent Systems. XVIII, 767 pages. 2006. (Sublibrary LNAI).

Vol. 4202: E. Asarin, P. Bouyer (Eds.), Formal Modeling and Analysis of Timed Systems. XI, 369 pages. 2006.

Vol. 4201: Y. Sakakibara, S. Kobayashi, K. Sato, T. Nishino, E. Tomita (Eds.), Grammatical Inference: Algorithms and Applications. XII, 359 pages. 2006. (Sublibrary LNAI).

Vol. 4200: I.F.C. Smith (Ed.), Intelligent Computing in Engineering and Architecture. XIII, 692 pages. 2006. (Sublibrary LNAI).

Vol. 4199: O. Nierstrasz, J. Whittle, D. Harel, G. Reggio (Eds.), Model Driven Engineering Languages and Systems. XVI, 798 pages. 2006.

Vol. 4198: O. Nasraoui, O. Zaiane, M. Spiliopoulou, B. Mobasher, B. Masand, P. Yu (Eds.), Advances in Web Minding and Web Usage Analysis. IX, 177 pages. 2006. (Sublibrary LNAI).

Vol. 4197: M. Raubal, H.J. Miller, A.U. Frank, M.F. Goodchild (Eds.), Geographic, Information Science. XIII, 419 pages. 2006.

Vol. 4196: K. Fischer, I.J. Timm, E. André, N. Zhong (Eds.), Multiagent System Technologies. X, 185 pages. 2006. (Sublibrary LNAI).

Vol. 4195: D. Gaiti, G. Pujolle, E. Al-Shaer, K. Calvert, S. Dobson, G. Leduc, O. Martikainen (Eds.), Autonomic Networking. IX, 316 pages. 2006.

Vol. 4194: V.G. Ganzha, E.W. Mayr, E.V. Vorozhtsov (Eds.), Computer Algebra in Scientific Computing. XI, 313 pages. 2006.

Vol. 4193: T.P. Runarsson, H.-G. Beyer, E. Burke, J.J. Merelo-Guervós, L.D. Whitley, X. Yao (Eds.), Parallel Problem Solving from Nature - PPSN IX. XIX, 1061 pages. 2006.

Vol. 4192: B. Mohr, J.L. Träff, J. Worringen, J. Dongarra (Eds.), Recent Advances in Parallel Virtual Machine and Message Passing Interface. XVI, 414 pages. 2006.

Vol. 4191: R. Larsen, M. Nielsen, J. Sporring (Eds.), Medical Image Computing and Computer-Assisted Intervention – MICCAI 2006, Part II. XXXVIII, 981 pages. 2006.

Vol. 4190: R. Larsen, M. Nielsen, J. Sporring (Eds.), Medical Image Computing and Computer-Assisted Intervention – MICCAI 2006, Part I. XXXVVIII, 949 pages. 2006.

Vol. 4189: D. Gollmann, J. Meier, A. Sabelfeld (Eds.), Computer Security – ESORICS 2006. XI, 548 pages. 2006.

Vol. 4188: P. Sojka, I. Kopeček, K. Pala (Eds.), Text, Speech and Dialogue. XV, 721 pages. 2006. (Sublibrary LNAI).

Vol. 4187: J.J. Alferes, J. Bailey, W. May, U. Schwertel (Eds.), Principles and Practice of Semantic Web Reasoning. XI, 277 pages. 2006.

Vol. 4186: C. Jesshope, C. Egan (Eds.), Advances in Computer Systems Architecture. XIV, 605 pages. 2006.

Vol. 4185: R. Mizoguchi, Z. Shi, F. Giunchiglia (Eds.), The Semantic Web – ASWC 2006. XX, 778 pages. 2006.

Vol. 4184: M. Bravetti, M. Núñez, G. Zavattaro (Eds.), Web Services and Formal Methods. X, 289 pages. 2006.

Vol. 4183: J. Euzenat, J. Domingue (Eds.), Artificial Intelligence: Methodology, Systems, and Applications. XIII, 291 pages. 2006. (Sublibrary LNAI).

Vol. 4182: H.T. Ng, M.-K. Leong, M.-Y. Kan, D. Ji (Eds.), Information Retrieval Technology. XVI, 684 pages. 2006.

Vol. 4180: M. Kohlhase, OMDoc – An Open Markup Format for Mathematical Documents [version 1.2]. XIX, 428 pages. 2006. (Sublibrary LNAI).

Vol. 4179: J. Blanc-Talon, W. Philips, D. Popescu, P. Scheunders (Eds.), Advanced Concepts for Intelligent Vision Systems. XXIV, 1224 pages. 2006.

Vol. 4178: A. Corradini, H. Ehrig, U. Montanari, L. Ribeiro, G. Rozenberg (Eds.), Graph Transformations. XII, 473 pages. 2006.

Vol. 4177: R. Marín, E. Onaindía, A. Bugarín, J. Santos (Eds.), Current Topics in Artificial Intelligence. XV, 482 pages. 2006. (Sublibrary LNAI).

Vol. 4176: S.K. Katsikas, J. Lopez, M. Backes, S. Gritzalis, B. Preneel (Eds.), Information Security. XIV, 548 pages. 2006.